365 Ways to Cook Chinese

Rosa Lo San Ross

A JOHN BOSWELL ASSOCIATES BOOK

HarperCollins*Publishers*

Dear Reader:

We welcome your recommendations for future 365 Ways books. Send your suggestions and a recipe, if you'd like, to Cookbook Editor, HarperCollins Publishers, 10 East 53rd Street, New York, NY 10022. If we choose your title suggestion or your recipe we will acknowledge you in the book and send you a free copy.

Thank you for your support.

Sincerely yours,
The Editor

365 WAYS TO COOK CHINESE. Copyright © 1994 by John Boswell Management, Inc. All rights reserved. Printed in the United States of America. No part of this book may be used or reproduced in any manner whatsoever without written permission except in the case of brief quotations embodied in critical articles and reviews. For information address HarperCollins Publishers, Inc., 10 East 53rd Street, New York, NY 10022.

HarperCollins books may be purchased for educational, business, or sales promotional use. For information, please write:
Special Markets Department, HarperCollins Publishers, Inc.
10 East 53rd Street, New York, NY 10022

FIRST EDITION

Series Editor: Susan Wyler
Design: Nigel Rollings
Index: Maro Riofrancos

Library of Congress Cataloging-in-Publication Data

Ross, Rosa.
    365 ways to cook Chinese / Rosa Ross. — 1st ed.
      p.   cm.
    "A John Boswell Associates book."
    Includes index.
    ISBN 0-06-016961-3
    1. Cookery, Chinese.   I. Title.   II. Title: Three hundred and sixty-five ways to cook Chinese.   III. Title: Three hundred sixty-five ways to cook Chinese.
TX724.5.C5R67   1994
641.5951—dc20   94-2452

94 95 96 97 98 DT/HC 10 9 8 7 6 5 4 3 2 1

Contents

Introduction to Chinese Cooking 1
Ingredients for a Wok Pantry 3
Special Equipment 8

1   Appetizers, Relishes, Pickles, and
Condiments   9

Cold Sesame Noodles, Shrimp Toasts, and Barbecued Spareribs are just a few of the starters and snacks you'll find in this chapter along with a selection of useful relishes and dips.

2   Soups and Stocks   27

To begin an Eastern or Western meal, nothing's more satisfying than a bowl of Hot and Sour Soup, Crab Corn Chowder, Watercress Soup with Bean Curd, or, of course, Won Ton Soup.

3   Chinese Fast Food   41

Stir-frying is a breeze with easy recipes like Diced Chicken with Cashews, Broccoli with Beef, Sliced Chicken with Asparagus, Sweet and Sour Pork, Pineapple Duck in Ginger Fruit Sauce, and Shrimp and Scallops with Peas.

4   Chinese Stews and Braises   71

Savory and slow cooking, these succulent dishes include Oyster-Flavored Drumsticks, Red-Braised Duck, Yang Chow Lion's Head, and Stewed Lamb with Garlic, Ginger, and Vegetables.

5   Especially Hot and Spicy   85

Chinese chile paste, hot oil, whole dried red chiles, and crushed hot flakes add the zip to over three dozen great spicy dishes, among them Shredded Cold Chicken with Hot Peanut Dressing, Hunan Braised Beef on a Bed of Spinach, Double-Cooked Szechuan Pork, and Shrimp in Spicy Black Bean Sauce.

6   The Chinese Way with Vegetables   107

Fresh Vegetable Buddha's Delight and Baked Vegetarian Bean Curd Pockets to Braised Chinese Mushrooms and Snow Peas with Water Chestnuts represent the delectable assortment of vegetable dishes that can star in a meatless meal or accompany almost any Asian or American menu.

7   **Banquet Dishes**   129

Special dishes for entertaining from elegant classics, such as Shark Fin Soup and Peking Duck, to authentic creations, such as Firepot Hong Kong Style and Salt-Baked Chicken.

8   **Great Ways with Noodles and Rice**   153

Explore the universal love of pasta with Chinese noodle dishes: Cold Noodles with Peanut Sauce and Cucumbers, Chicken Lo Mein, Rice Sticks with Singapore-Style Shrimp. Rice bowl offerings include Cantonese Roast Pork Rice, Fried Rice with Eggs and Scallions, and Chicken Rice Casserole.

9   **Chinese Light**   181

Steamed and poached recipes like Hoisin Chicken Strips with Cilantro, Pearl Meatballs, Flower Shrimp, and Steamed Black Sea Bass are rich in flavor and lower in fat.

10   **Little Packages, Big Packages**   193

Dim sum and wrapped foods include Minced Cornish Game Hen in Lettuce Leaves, Fried Won Tons, Potsticker Dumplings, Beggar's Chicken, Mu Shu Pork Packages, and Salmon-Cabbage Pillows.

11   **Main-Course Salads and Other Cold Dishes**   213

Cold dishes such as Lemon-Flavored Chicken and Bean Sprout Salad, Sesame Chicken Salad, Roast Duck with Tropical Fruit Salad, and Hoisin Beef Salad, range from the traditional to the contemporary.

12   **Chinese Sweets**   227

Simple desserts, such as Toffee Apples, Gingered Oranges, Sesame Puffs with Honey, Almond Cookies, and Lichee Sorbet, offer a delightful way to end any meal.

Index   237

Introduction to Chinese Cooking

To most of us, Chinese cooking hardly needs an introduction. The tantalizing, exotic flavors we enjoy in restaurants and take-out parlors make our mouths water. In this book I have included 365 recipes that will show you how to prepare delicious Chinese dishes so easily that you can enjoy this food at home—every day, if you wish. The ingredients are simple, but be assured neither taste nor authenticity has been sacrificed. From Cold Sesame Noodles, Fried Won Tons, and Hot and Sour Soup to Kung Pao Chicken, Stir-Fried Beef, and Mu Shu Pork Packages, you'll find all your favorites here.

Besides being satisfying and delectable, eating the Asian way is quick, healthy, and economical. If you follow my tips on how to stock a wok pantry, a quick trip to any supermarket is all the shopping necessary to cook and eat Chinese.

In China, food and culture are intrinsically bound. Attitudes toward cooking and eating have always been dominated by two factors: pleasure and health. Perhaps this is why Chinese food is still so popular all over the world today.

In its 5,000-year history Chinese cuisine has been governed by the *tsai/fan* principle. *Tsai* is the word that covers any cooked dish of meat, fish, and vegetable, and *fan* is the literal word for cooked rice, but includes any starch component of an everyday meal. No meal is complete unless it is built around these two elements, and the proper balance and harmony of *tsai* and *fan* are what contribute to a well-balanced, complete Chinese meal, which we feel ensures a healthy diet.

If you want to eat as the Chinese do, keep in mind the underlying *tsai/fan* principle, but also remember that an everyday menu is planned according to the number of people eating. There is a Cantonese saying: "A meal has as many tastes as number of diners." So dinner for four should have four tastes, or *tsai* dishes. When you are planning a menu in this way, it is also important to vary your cooking methods. A well-balanced Chinese menu would *not* consist of four or more stir-fried dishes, which would lack variety of cooking methods and would be too much last-minute work. A typical menu, therefore, might include a stir-fried dish, a soup, a braised vegetable, a steamed fish, and *fan*, or rice. At a family meal, all these dishes are placed in the middle of the table, and each diner picks from the communal dish with chopsticks. Soup is usually served at the middle or end of a meal, rather than as a first course. At a banquet or formal dinner, dishes are served sequentially, or one at a time.

Many of us, however, enjoy Chinese flavors, but prefer to fit them into a more typical American-style menu of soup first, then a main course with a vegetable, a rice or noodle dish, and dessert. Any of the recipes in this book would be just as delicious and satisfying when presented in this way. It is my hope that *365 Ways to Cook Chinese Food* offers so much variety and great taste that these dishes will become a part of your everyday repertoire.

To most people, Chinese cooking means stir-frying. I have included many recipes in this book for this common, everyday cooking method, with its quick, easy technique and resulting healthy fresh-tasting food. Stir-frying seems to have been embraced by everyone. We use the wok and stir-frying techniques even when we cook dishes that are totally un-Chinese. Using a wok to stir-fry meat, fish, poultry with an added complement of vegetables, served on a bowl of rice, yields a perfectly balanced meal. There is no easier way to produce a dinner in 10 minutes or less. In stir-frying the aim of cutting things small is to equalize and reduce cooking time. Make sure that everything is sliced the same size, even if not quite paper-thin, to ensure even cooking. The delicious tastes will still be there. After all, the cook is in charge, and in your kitchen that's you.

In addition to stir-frying, Chinese cooking utilizes several other lesser known methods. Here you will find a whole chapter devoted to recipes that use cooking methods such as braising, stewing, poaching, steaming, and roasting. These methods usually require a longer cooking time, but compensate for this with very little time needed to prepare the dishes. I urge you to try these recipes, especially the ones that allow for cooking ahead of time and reheating. Combining these do-ahead dishes with one or two stir-fried dishes will eliminate the hectic last-minute flurry of stir-frying all the dishes in a menu. This is what often flusters cooks when trying something new.

All the recipes in this book are easy and accessible, because all but a few of the ingredients required to produce authentic-tasting dishes are available in supermarkets across the country. Simplicity does not mean we have compromised taste. Believe me, the delicious dishes you cook from this book will bring you nothing but compliments and requests for more!

Some principles to remember: Chinese food is governed by the availability and use of fresh ingredients, as well as the use of preserved and dried ingredients; nutrition and health; and a harmonious balance of tastes, flavors, textures, fragrance, appearance, and color. The basis of fresh-tasting, good Chinese food is the use of three aromatic vegetables: fresh scallions, fresh ginger, fresh garlic—together or in any combination.

I have kept these recipes easy and simple. With 365 tried and tested recipes you could produce a different dinner every night of the year. Only a handful require a special trip to an Asian market, but be assured that they all taste delicious and authentic. So, as the Chinese say, "Good eating!"

INGREDIENTS FOR A WOK PANTRY

Here is a list of basics for a wok pantry. If you keep a stock of these items, you will find that shopping for Chinese cooking is a breeze. All you will need is the fresh items for a dish; for example, flank steak and a bunch of broccoli for Broccoli with Beef. Most of these ingredients are shelf stable, but I have given you hints on special storage where applicable. Explanatory notes have been included where necessary. The starred items are more unusual items used in only one or two specific recipes.

*AGAR-AGAR: Also called *kanten* in Japanese. A form of seaweed gelatin available in threads, powdered, and in squares. We use the thread form as a cold ingredient for texture. When used as a gel, it has the ability to set without refrigeration.

ASIAN SESAME OIL: Made from toasted sesame seeds. Used as an aromatic flavoring oil. Has a dark color and nutty flavor. Not to be confused with regular sesame oil sold in health food stores, which is light in color and does not have the same taste.

BAMBOO SHOOTS: Sold in cans—sliced or whole. Rinse in warm water before using. Can be stored in fresh salted water in a covered container in the refrigerator for up to 2 weeks. Change water every 2 or 3 days.

BEAN CURD: Fresh soybean product, high in vegetable protein. There are several varieties: firm, soft, and silken. Available in 1-pound blocks, covered with water, in sealed plastic containers; or in squares, about 3 x 3 inches. May be kept under water, refrigerated, about 3 days. Bean curd sours when it is not fresh.

*BEAN CURD, DRY: Another form of bean curd, available in sticks or sheets. Should be soaked in warm water until soft and pliable before use.

*BEAN CURD CHEESE: There are two varieties of this fermented bean curd. One is red in color (*nam yue*) and the other is ivory-colored (*fu yue*). Both may be served as pickles or used as an ingredient in cooking. Strong, cheesy flavor. Refrigerate after opening.

BEAN SAUCE: Also called yellow bean sauce, bean paste, and yellow bean paste. Preserved spiced soybean sauce, sold in jars or cans, ready to use as an ingredient. Refrigerate after opening.

BEAN THREADS: Also called cellophane noodles or glass noodles. Thin noodles made from mung bean flour. Soak in warm water until soft before using in soups and stir-fried dishes as an ingredient.

BLACK BEANS: Fermented and salted. Sold dried in packets or ready to use as a sauce in jars or cans. These dried fermented soybeans should be rinsed to remove excess salt, and slightly mashed.

CAYENNE: Ground hot red pepper powder. Used to spice dishes.

CHILE PASTE: Also called chile paste with garlic and Szechuan chile paste. Hot and spicy sauce sold in jars. May be used as an ingredient or as a hot sauce straight from jar. Refrigerate after opening.

CHILE PEPPERS: Fresh or dried. Dried chile peppers keep indefinitely in a sealed container and are useful to have on hand to add spice to dishes. The fresh will keep in the refrigerator for up to 10 days. Remove seeds and ribs if you prefer your food less spicy.

CHINESE FIVE-SPICE POWDER: Also called five fragrant spices. Equal quantities of finely ground cinnamon, cloves, fennel seed, star anise, and Szechuan peppercorns.

*CHINESE SAUSAGE (*lop cheung*): Air-dried pork sausage with sweetish anise flavor. Used as an ingredient or by itself. Steam to warm before serving. Store, tightly wrapped, in refrigerator.

CILANTRO: Fresh herb sometimes called Chinese parsley or fresh coriander. Store, wrapped, in refrigerator. Chop just before using to preserve flavor and aroma.

COCONUT MILK: Unsweetened, canned. Used as an ingredient in savory and sweet dishes. May be homemade by grating fresh coconut, placing in a cheesecloth bag, and pouring boiling water (2 cups, approximately) over coconut. Squeeze to extract all liquid.

DRIED CHINESE MUSHROOMS: Dried shiitake mushrooms. There are many grades and prices. For everyday use, buy least expensive variety. Soak in warm water and remove stems before using. Soaking water is often used as a flavoring ingredient in dish. A stronger mushroom flavor than fresh mushrooms. Meatier varieties are used in dishes calling for dried mushrooms as main ingredient.

DRY SHERRY: Good all-purpose wine for cooking. Chinese wine may be substituted.

*FISH SAUCE (*nuoc nam*): Salty, anchovylike sauce used in Southeast Asian cooking.

GINGER: Fresh tuber available in produce sections of many supermarkets. Seasonally available as new ginger, before skin has formed on ginger root. New ginger has a waxy appearance with pinkish tips. Can be stored in vegetable bin of refrigerator, or for longer storage, submerged in dry white wine or sherry in a covered glass container, refrigerated.

GLUTINOUS RICE: Also called sticky rice or sweet rice. A starchy short-grain rice used in savory dishes, stuffings, and sweets.

HOISIN SAUCE: A sweet, spicy sauce used as an ingredient or as a table sauce. Sometimes thinned with soy sauce. Available in cans or jars. Refrigerate after opening.

*JELLYFISH: Dry and salted. A texture food used in banquet cuisine. Must be soaked and rinsed before using.

*LEMONGRASS: Lemonlike, fragrant herb used in Southeast Asian dishes. Can be stored refrigerated or cut up and frozen. Also available dry, but lacks fresh flavor in this form.

OIL: Vegetable oil has been used in these recipes, unless otherwise specified. Peanut oil may be used for deep-frying. I do not recommend using peanut oil as an all-purpose oil, as its nutty flavor masks the tastes of subtler dishes. Oil used for deep-frying can be cooled, strained, and stored in covered container in a cool place to be reused. May be used several times before discarding.

OYSTER SAUCE: Bottled sauce made from oysters and soy sauce. Used as an ingredient. Refrigerate after opening.

PLUM SAUCE: Also duck sauce. Fruity spicy sauce, made from plums. Mostly used as a dipping sauce, but sometimes as an ingredient. Refrigerate after opening.

RICE FLOUR NOODLES: There are two varieties. Dried (*mei fun*), which comes as thin threads used in Chinese dishes, and a flat, linguine shape, preferred by Thais and other Southeast Asians. Dried rice noodles or sticks should be soaked before using. Fresh rice noodles, called *ho fun*, may be purchased in Asian markets. They are ready to eat.

*RICE PAPER: Dry wrapper for spring rolls made from rice flour and water. Must be soaked before use. May be eaten without cooking for soft wrappers or can be fried. Store tightly wrapped.

SCALLIONS: Use both white and green parts of scallion. Gives Chinese food its fresh, characteristic flavor.

SESAME PASTE, ASIAN: Made from toasted sesame seeds. Do not substitute tahini.

*SHARK FIN: A texture food used in banquet cuisine. Sold in various dried forms. Has no flavor of its own. Requires long soaking and preparation. Refer to recipe for Shark Fin Soup.

*SHRIMP PASTE: Made from salted, fermented shrimp. Comes in jars. Also dried and salted. Used sparingly as an ingredient.

SOY SAUCE: There are three kinds of soy sauce available:

Light or thin soy sauce is used in cooking when we wish the food to remain white, particularly in fish, seafood, and chicken dishes. Regular Kikkoman soy sauce, which is readily available in supermarkets, while slightly darker, is an acceptable substitute. Kikkoman Lite is a reduced-sodium soy sauce and should not be substituted unless low sodium is desired. Light soy sauce is also the soy most commonly used at table. In the following recipes, any one that calls simply for "soy sauce" means light soy sauce.

Dark soy sauce (also double dark or black) colors food dark. When it is used in cooking, the technique is often called "red cooking." In this book, we have specified dark soy sauce when this is the desired effect. The taste is slightly less salty and a little heavier. While it is not ideal, you may use thin or regular soy sauce if dark soy sauce is not available.

Mushroom soy sauce is a dark soy sauce flavored with dried Chinese mushrooms. Very desirable in dishes calling for a rich savory flavor.

STAR ANISE: One of the five spices. Has a strong licorice flavor and smell. Also used alone. The entire pod, with the seeds inside, is used.

SZECHUAN PEPPER OR PEPPERCORNS: One of the five spices. Also used alone. Very fragrant and aromatic, but not spicy. Sometimes toasted for more fragrance.

TANGERINE PEEL: Dried orange-flavored peel. Available in Chinese markets. Used as an ingredient.

*TAPIOCA FLOUR: Used in certain dumpling wrapper doughs.

TREE EARS OR TREE FUNGUS: Dried, mushroomlike fungi with little flavor. Prized for its texture. Must be soaked in warm water before using. Water is always discarded.

VINEGAR: We use cider or rice vinegar, of which there are three varieties: white and red, which are interchangeable, and black, which has its own distinctive flavor.

WATER CHESTNUTS: Available in cans or fresh. Canned water chestnuts should be rinsed. May be stored 1 or 2 days in salted water, covered, in the refrigerator. Fresh water chestnuts turn powdery as they age, so chose firm ones. They must be peeled before using, but have a wonderful sweet flavor. Store in a paper bag in vegetable bin of the refrigerator.

WHEAT FLOUR NOODLES (*mein*): Available fresh or dried. Fresh noodles may be frozen for longer storage. Any fresh or dried spaghetti-shaped pasta makes a good substitute.

*WHEAT STARCH: Powder made from rinsing a ball of dough to separate starch from gluten. Required for specific dumpling wrappers.

WON TON SKINS: Wrappers made from wheat flour and/or eggs and water. May be stored frozen or refrigerated.

SPECIAL EQUIPMENT

As with all cooking equipment, there are choices galore. There is, however, not too much you will require in the way of special equipment. Here are a few basic items that will make Chinese cooking a pleasure:

WOK: If you are buying only one wok, buy a 14-inch round wok made of carbon steel. A classic wok has two metal handles, but many of us are more comfortable with a single skillet-type handle. If you are cooking on an electric burner, be sure that the wok's bottom has a flat area about 5 inches in diameter. A new wok should be washed with soap and water to remove any grease. Then it should be tempered by rubbing well with vegetable oil and placing over medium-high heat. Heat for about 1 hour. You can reoil it once or twice during this time, but be careful not to burn your fingers. Once a wok is tempered, do not wash with detergent. Use very hot water and a stiff brush or plastic scrubby. Dry thoroughly before storing to prevent any rust.

WOK COVER: This should be aluminum or stainless steel.

CHINESE CLEAVER: These require a little getting used to, but a 3-inch wide blade, made of carbon steel, is easy to keep sharp and can be used to transfer chopped items to plate or wok in one motion. Any good sharp knife you are comfortable using will do the job.

SPATULA: A special long-handled spatula with slight lips at the edges is useful for stir-frying.

STRAINER: A wire strainer or "spider" is the perfect utensil for draining fried or poached items.

LADLE: A Chinese ladle measures out just enough to fill a rice bowl.

WIRE RACK: A 9-inch round wire rack that sits inside the wok can be used for wok smoking and steaming.

BAMBOO STEAMER BASKETS WITH LID: The perfect utensil for steaming. A 10-inch round basket set, usually with two tiers and a lid, is a good all-purpose choice. They come in different sizes. The bamboo lid absorbs condensation, and the baskets are very attractive. Some foods can be served directly from the baskets. Key to making your bamboo steamers last is to be sure they are completely air-dried before stacking to prevent mildew.

Chapter 1

Appetizers, Relishes, Pickles, and Condiments

Appetizers start a meal, so we begin our book with a selection of appetizer recipes. Traditionally, one or more appetizers are served at the start of a Chinese meal. They are so popular that I often prepare a selection, such as Vegetable Pear Rolls, Shrimp Balls, Chicken Satay, and Barbecued Spareribs, to pass as hors d'oeuvres at Western-style cocktail parties.

In everyday cooking, white rice or sometimes plain soupy noodles are the staple foods. Tangy relishes and pickles make nice side dishes with these bland foods, but they can also be used to begin a meal. I always add one or two to my assorted appetizer plates. Included are some simple pickles that can be eaten almost as they are being made.

In this chapter, you will also find recipes for flavored oils, condiments, dipping sauces, and dressings. These are easy to make and are considered basics in Chinese cooking. Use them to add perfume to your finished dishes, or as dips. Incidentally, they also make great gifts, packaged in pretty bottles.

1 COLD SESAME NOODLES

Prep: 15 minutes   Cook: 8 minutes   Chill: 1 hour   Serves: 6

For perfect sesame noodles, do not dress noodles more than 30 minutes in advance, or they will absorb too much dressing.

1 pound fresh wheat flour noodles or dried thin spaghetti	2 tablespoons cider vinegar
	1 tablespoon sugar
	¼ to ½ teaspoon cayenne
¼ cup Asian sesame oil	1 teaspoon salt
¼ cup soy sauce	3 garlic cloves, minced
2 tablespoons sesame paste	

1. Fill a 10-quart pot with water, bring to a boil, and cook noodles until firm but cooked through, about 8 minutes. Drain and immediately rinse under cold running water until noodles are completely cold. Drain well. Toss in 2 tablespoons sesame oil and 2 tablespoons soy sauce. Cover and chill about 1 hour.

2. In a small bowl, whisk together sesame paste and 3 tablespoons warm water until smooth. Add remaining 2 tablespoons sesame oil, remaining 2 tablespoons soy sauce, vinegar, sugar, cayenne, salt, and minced garlic.

3. Just before serving toss cold noodles with sesame dressing.

2 CHINESE EGGPLANT SALAD

Prep: 15 minutes   Cook: 16 minutes   Chill: 30 minutes   Serves: 6

Chinese serve this eggplant dish as an appetizer, but I like it so much that I often serve it as a vegetable dish. It improves if prepared up to 3 days in advance.

4 Japanese eggplants or 1 large eggplant	1 small dried hot red pepper, crushed
1 tablespoon vegetable oil	1 tablespoon soy sauce
2 scallions, minced	2 teaspoons sugar
1 teaspoon minced fresh ginger	½ teaspoon black pepper
	1 tablespoon Asian sesame oil
1 garlic clove, minced	

1. Cut eggplant into 2-inch cubes. Heat vegetable oil in a wok. Add scallions, ginger, garlic, and hot red pepper and stir-fry until aromatic, about 2 seconds. Add eggplant and cook, tossing frequently, 1 minute.

2. Add soy sauce, sugar, black pepper, and ¼ cup water. Bring to a simmer, cover, and cook until eggplant is tender, about 15 minutes. Remove from heat and drizzle on sesame oil. Let cool, then cover and refrigerate until cold, about 30 minutes.

3   SAVORY STUFFED MUSHROOMS
Prep: 20 minutes   Cook: 13 to 14 minutes   Serves: 4 to 6

16 large dried Chinese
   mushrooms, 2 inches in
   diameter
¼ pound ground pork
¼ pound shrimp, shelled and
   deveined
2 slices of fresh ginger plus
   1 teaspoon minced

1 egg, beaten
2 tablespoons plus 1 teaspoon
   cornstarch
2 teaspoons vegetable oil
2 tablespoons dry sherry
2 tablespoons soy sauce
2 teaspoons sugar
2 teaspoons Asian sesame oil

1. In a medium bowl, soak mushrooms in 2 cups warm water until soft, about 15 minutes. Drain, reserving ½ cup liquid. Remove and discard mushroom stems.

2. In a food processor, combine pork, shrimp, 1 teaspoon minced ginger, egg, and 2 tablespoons of cornstarch. Pulse to grind until mixture is smooth. Fill mushroom caps with pork and shrimp mixture.

3. In a large skillet, heat vegetable oil over medium heat. Add ginger slices and cook until brown, about 2 minutes. Remove with a slotted spoon and discard. Add sherry, soy sauce, sugar, and reserved mushroom soaking water. Bring to a boil, reduce heat, and add mushrooms, stuffed sides up. Simmer until filling is cooked, about 10 minutes.

4. In a small bowl, blend remaining 1 teaspoon cornstarch with 2 tablespoons cold water until smooth. With a slotted spoon, remove stuffed mushrooms to a platter. Stir cornstarch into sauce, bring to a boil, and cook, stirring, until thickened and smooth, 1 to 2 minutes. Pour sauce over mushrooms. Drizzle with sesame oil and serve.

4   CHICKEN LIVERS WITH OYSTER SAUCE
Prep: 5 minutes   Cook: 6 minutes   Serves: 4

These livers may be served whole in the traditional way, or chopped and spread on toast points as an East/West appetizer.

½ pound chicken livers
2 tablespoons vegetable oil
3 tablespoons minced shallots

1 tablespoon oyster sauce
2 tablespoons port
2 tablespoons Cognac

1. Clean chicken livers and trim off any fat. Separate into lobes, if livers are large. Heat oil in a wok. Add shallots and cook over medium-high heat until soft, about 1 minute. Add livers and stir-fry until cooked but still pink inside, about 3 minutes. Add oyster sauce and port, stirring to blend well.

2. Add Cognac and carefully ignite with a match. Cook until flames die out. (You may skip this step and just let the Cognac simmer for 2 minutes to cook off the alcohol.)

5   SHRIMP BALLS

Prep: 20 minutes   Cook: 15 minutes plus 3 minutes per batch
Makes: about 40

This recipe doubles easily. To save last-minute work when you are entertaining, these can be made up to a day ahead and reheated in a 350°F oven for 10 to 15 minutes.

½ pound thin-sliced firm-textured white bread	1 teaspoon soy sauce
1 scallion	1 teaspoon Asian sesame oil
1 (7-ounce) can water chestnuts	2 teaspoons cornstarch
	1 egg white
1 pound shrimp, shelled and deveined	½ teaspoon salt
	⅛ teaspoon pepper
	½ cup vegetable oil

1. Preheat oven to 200°F. Trim crusts off bread and discard. Cut bread slices into ¼-inch cubes. Spread on a cookie sheet and dry in oven 15 minutes. Crumble coarsely.

2. In a food processor, mince scallion and water chestnuts. Add shrimp and pulse once or twice to chop coarsely. Add soy sauce, sesame oil, cornstarch, egg white, salt, and pepper. Pulse to blend well. Remove to a bowl.

3. Wet hands in cold water and form shrimp mixture into balls no larger than 1 inch in diameter. Roll in bread crumbs to coat.

4. In a large skillet, heat vegetable oil over medium heat. Add shrimp balls in batches without crowding and cook, turning often, until lightly browned and cooked through in center, about 3 minutes per batch. Remove with a strainer or slotted spoon and drain on paper towels. Serve hot.

6   SHRIMP TOASTS

Prep: 15 minutes   Cook: 3 to 5 minutes per batch
Makes: 36

Shrimp toasts can be deep-fried in advance and reheated in a 350°F oven. They are quite good even when frozen and rewarmed in the oven.

1 baguette loaf of French bread	2 tablespoons cornstarch
	½ teaspoon salt
1 pound medium shrimp, shelled and deveined	¼ teaspoon pepper
	1 tablespoon sesame seeds
1 scallion	2 cups vegetable oil
1 egg	

1. Preheat oven to 250°F. Cut baguette into 36 slices about ½ inch thick. Set bread slices in a single layer on a cookie sheet and dry in oven 10 minutes. Do not allow bread to brown.

2. In a food processor, combine shrimp and scallion. Pulse until coarsely chopped. Add egg, cornstarch, salt, and pepper and pulse until well blended. Mixture should not be too finely chopped.

3. Spread shrimp mixture on baguette rounds, mounding slightly. Sprinkle a few sesame seeds on top and press gently so they adhere.

4. In a wok, heat oil to 375° or until a cube of bread browns in 1 minute. Add shrimp toasts, shrimp side down, to oil in batches without crowding. Deep-fry until golden, 2 to 3 minutes. Turn over and fry until bread becomes crisp and golden, 1 to 2 minutes. Drain well on paper towels. Repeat with remaining toasts. Serve hot.

---

7   CHICKEN SATAY

Prep: 20 minutes   Chill: 2 hours   Cook: 15 to 17 minutes
Makes: 24

Even though it is Malaysian in origin, this dish is much loved by Hong Kong Chinese. It fits well into our summer lifestyle of outdoor grilling. You'll need small bamboo skewers for this recipe.

1½ **pounds skinless, boneless**
    chicken breasts
2 **medium onions**
6 **garlic cloves**
2 **tablespoons soy sauce**
¼ **cup lime juice**
1 **teaspoon black pepper**

½ **cup crunchy peanut butter**
1 **cup unsweetened coconut**
    milk
1 **tablespoon brown sugar**
3 **small dried hot red peppers**
1 **teaspoon anchovy paste**

1. Soak 24 bamboo skewers about 6 inches long in a bowl of cold water at least 20 minutes. Cut chicken breasts into 24 thin strips.

2. In a food processor, mince onions and garlic. Remove half of this mixture to a small bowl and reserve. Add soy sauce and 3 tablespoons lime juice to food processor. Combine well and coat chicken strips. Cover and refrigerate 2 hours.

3. Return reserved onion and garlic mixture to food processor. Add remaining 1 tablespoon lime juice, black pepper, peanut butter, coconut milk, brown sugar, dried hot red peppers, and anchovy paste. Process until smooth.

4. Transfer mixture to a nonstick saucepan and cook over low heat 10 minutes. Some oil will separate out of the sauce. Gently blot off excess oil with paper towels, if desired. Remove sauce to a small bowl for serving.

5. Prepare a medium-hot fire in a barbecue grill or preheat broiler. Thread chicken strips onto wet bamboo skewers. Grill or broil until chicken is cooked through, about 5 to 7 minutes. Serve satay on their skewers with sauce on the side for dipping.

8   STEAMED SPARERIBS

Prep: 10 minutes   Chill: 30 minutes   Cook: 45 minutes   Serves: 8

2 pounds baby back
   spareribs, cut in thirds
   lengthwise
2 tablespoons soy sauce
1 tablespoon dry sherry
2 teaspoons minced scallion
½ teaspoon minced fresh
   ginger

1 tablespoon fermented black
   beans, rinsed and mashed
1 tablespoon vegetable oil
½ cup cornstarch
½ teaspoon Chinese five-spice
   powder
¼ teaspoon salt

1. Separate ribs into single pieces.

2. In a large bowl, mix together soy sauce, sherry, scallion, ginger, and black beans. Add ribs and toss to coat well. Cover and refrigerate 30 minutes.

3. Coat a 9-inch heatproof plate with oil. In a shallow bowl, mix cornstarch, five-spice powder, and salt. Toss ribs in seasoned cornstarch to coat and remove to oiled plate. Place in a bamboo steamer. Pour any remaining marinade over ribs. Cover and steam about 45 minutes, until ribs are tender.

9   BARBECUED SPARERIBS

Prep: 10 minutes   Chill: 6 hours   Cook: 20 to 30 minutes   Serves: 6

If the ribs are not already cut in half, ask your butcher to do this for you.

1 rack baby back ribs (about
   1 pound), cut in half
   crosswise
½ cup hoisin sauce
¼ cup soy sauce
2 teaspoons Asian sesame oil

1 teaspoon Chinese five-spice
   powder
¼ cup dark brown sugar
2 teaspoons salt
1 teaspoon pepper

1. Trim any excess fat from ribs.

2. In a dish large enough to hold ribs, mix together hoisin sauce, soy sauce, sesame oil, Chinese five-spice powder, brown sugar, salt, and pepper. Add ribs and rub to coat all over with marinade. Cover and refrigerate at least 6 hours. Remove from refrigerator about 1 hour before cooking.

3. Preheat oven to 450°F. Cook ribs on a rack 25 to 30 minutes, until meat is tender and there is no trace of pink near bone. Or grill ribs on a covered outdoor grill over ashy coals 20 to 25 minutes, turning every 3 minutes to cook evenly.

10   SOY-BRAISED CHICKEN WINGS
Prep: 5 minutes   Cook: 20 minutes   Serves: 8

1 tablespoon vegetable oil	2 pounds chicken wings
2 scallions, minced	2 tablespoons dry sherry
1 teaspoon minced fresh	½ cup mushroom soy sauce
ginger	½ teaspoon sugar

1. Heat oil in a wok. Add scallions and ginger, and stir-fry over high heat 30 seconds until aromatic. Add chicken wings, dry sherry, mushroom soy, sugar, and 1 cup water.

2. Bring to a simmer, cover, and reduce heat to medium. Cook until chicken is tender but not falling apart, about 20 minutes. Serve at room temperature.

11   SKEWERED PORK CUBES WITH FRESH PINEAPPLE
Prep: 10 minutes   Chill: 6 hours   Cook: 12 minutes
Makes: about 36

This nontraditional appetizer is quick and easy. I usually serve the skewers on a flat leaf-lined basket, using the top of the pineapple as a garnish.

3 pounds boneless pork butt	2 garlic cloves, minced
¼ cup fish sauce *(nuoc nam)*	2 teaspoons Tabasco sauce
1 tablespoon soy sauce	3 tablespoons vegetable oil
1 tablespoon lime juice	1 fresh pineapple, peeled,
¼ cup brown sugar	cored, and cut into 1-inch
½ cup minced cilantro leaves	cubes

1. Trim all excess fat from pork and cut meat into 1-inch cubes. In a medium bowl, mix together fish sauce, soy sauce, lime juice, 2 tablespoons brown sugar, cilantro, garlic, and Tabasco sauce. Add pork cubes and toss to coat. Cover and refrigerate for 6 hours or overnight.

2. Remove pork from marinade; reserve marinade. Divide meat cubes into 3 batches. In a wok, heat 1 tablespoon oil. Add 1 batch of meat and stir-fry over high heat, tossing frequently, 3 minutes. Remove to a plate, repeat twice with remaining oil and remaining 2 batches of pork.

3. When all the meat is cooked, return pork to wok, pour reserved marinade over meat, and sprinkle on remaining 2 tablespoons brown sugar. Cook, tossing, until pork cubes are nicely browned and coated with sauce, about 3 minutes. Remove from heat.

4. To serve, place a piece of pork and a piece of pineapple on long toothpicks or small skewers. These may be eaten hot or at room temperature.

12   PLUM-FLAVORED PORK TENDERLOIN

Prep: 15 minutes   Chill: 3 hours   Cook: 30 to 35 minutes
Serves: 4 to 6

For honored guests, starting a meal with an appetizer platter of sliced meat is a sign of respect. This dish with a sauce made from fresh plums is not only delicious but very pretty and, of course, the red color denotes good luck.

4 ripe red plums, about ¾ pound	2 teaspoons minced fresh ginger
2 tablespoons hoisin sauce	2 tablespoons orange juice
2 tablespoons soy sauce	1 tablespoon lemon juice
1 teaspoon pepper	4 pork tenderloins (about ¾ pound each)
1 tablespoon Asian sesame oil	

1. Cut plums into quarters and remove seeds. In a small saucepan, cook plums with 2 tablespoons cold water until soft and mushy, about 15 minutes. Let cool. Add hoisin sauce, soy sauce, pepper, sesame oil, ginger, orange juice, lemon juice, and ¼ cup water. Stir to blend marinade well.

2. Trim pork tenderloins, if necessary. Place in a roasting pan and coat with marinade. Cover pan with plastic wrap and refrigerate 3 hours.

3. Preheat oven to 400°F. Roast pork in marinade, uncovered, until pork is white throughout, 30 to 35 minutes. Remove meat to a carving board, slice, and arrange on a platter. Spoon pan juices over meat. Serve warm or at room temperature.

13   SUGARED WALNUTS

Prep: 5 minutes   Cook: 5 minutes   Makes: 2 cups

Sugared walnuts are great with drinks. Traditionally, these nuts are prepared in a complicated technique that requires making a sugar syrup, coating the nuts, and deep-frying them, a step that tends to put one off, as the oil bubbles up quite violently. This very simple recipe makes walnuts that are just as good.

2 tablespoons vegetable oil	¼ cup sugar
2 cups shelled walnuts	

1. Heat oil in a wok over medium heat. Add walnuts and cook, tossing constantly, until they are lightly toasted, about 1 minute. Be careful not to let nuts burn.

2. Sprinkle sugar over nuts and continue tossing over medium heat until sugar is caramelized and nuts are evenly coated. With a slotted spoon, remove to an oiled cookie sheet and separate nuts. Discard excess caramel in wok. Let nuts cool and dry before serving.

3. Store dry nuts in an airtight container up to 1 week.

14   TEA EGGS
Prep: 5 minutes   Cook: 65 minutes   Makes: 12

Tea eggs have a beautiful marbled look, which I like to enhance by coating them with sesame oil. They are served as an appetizer or side course, either hot or cold. They are fun to make and keep several days in the refrigerator.

12 eggs	**½ teaspoon salt**
⅓ cup dark soy sauce	**1 star anise**
2 teaspoons lapsang souchong tea leaves or 4 tea bags	**2 teaspoons Asian sesame oil**

1. In a large saucepan, cover eggs with cold water. Bring just to a boil, reduce heat, and simmer 15 minutes. Drain eggs and plunge into a bowl of cold water. Let cool 10 minutes. Remove eggs from water and roll, pressing gently to crack eggshells lightly until they are covered with fine cracks.

2. In saucepan, combine soy sauce, tea leaves, salt, and star anise. Bring to a simmer, add eggs, and return to a boil. Reduce heat to low and simmer eggs 50 minutes. Remove from heat and let eggs cool in liquid.

3. To serve, shell eggs, which will have a marbled appearance. Coat eggs with sesame oil and serve cold or at room temperature.

15   VEGETABLE PEAR ROLLS
Prep: 30 minutes   Cook: none   Makes: 36

While these rolls are not classically Chinese, they are Eastern in style and are so delectable that I had to include this recipe.

1 lemon	**36 rice paper sheets (about 6 inches round)**
2 ripe firm pears	**Fresh mint sprigs**
2 carrots	**Peanut Hoisin Dip (page 21)**
3 celery ribs	
4 scallions	

1. Fill a medium bowl with cold water and squeeze juice from lemon into water. Peel pears and cut in half. Scoop out cores. Cut each pear into 36 wedges about ¼ inch thick. Place pear wedges in acidulated water. Peel carrots and cut into 36 sticks about the same size as pear pieces. Do the same with celery ribs. Cut scallions into similar size pieces. Arrange vegetable sticks in separate piles on a plate.

2. Fill a large bowl with tepid water. Dip 1 rice sheet briefly in water and lay on a flat work surface. Place 1 piece each of pear, carrot, celery, and scallion and a sprig of mint on rice sheet, a little off center. Roll in sides and then roll up as for a spring roll. Repeat until you have formed 36 rolls. Rolls should be kept between sheets of damp paper towels. They can be made 1 day ahead, wrapped well, and refrigerated. Serve cold with Peanut Hoisin Dip.

16   SPRING ROLLS
Prep: 30 minutes   Chill: 30 minutes   Cook: 15 minutes
Makes: 10

1 boneless loin pork chop, about ½ pound	½ cup bean sprouts
2 cups plus 1 tablespoon vegetable oil	1 small carrot, finely shredded
1 scallion, minced	1 teaspoon soy sauce
¼ cup sliced bamboo shoots, shredded	½ teaspoon pepper
½ cup finely shredded Chinese (Napa) cabbage	1 teaspoon cornstarch
	½ teaspoon salt
	10 spring roll or egg roll wrappers
	Soy Vinegar Dip (recipe follows)

1. With a cleaver or large knife, cut pork into fine shreds and then coarsely chop. Or coarsely chop in a food processor. Heat 1½ teaspoons of oil in a wok. Add pork and stir-fry over high heat until no longer pink, about 5 minutes. Remove to a bowl.

2. Heat another ½ tablespoon oil in wok. Add minced scallion, bamboo shoots, cabbage, bean sprouts, and carrot. Stir-fry until just wilted, about 2 minutes. Add soy sauce, pepper, and cooked pork. Blend cornstarch with ¼ cup cold water. Add to wok and cook until thickened, stirring to blend well. Season with salt. Remove filling to a bowl, let cool slightly, then refrigerate 30 minutes.

3. Separate wrappers and lay on a flat work surface. Place 1 heaping teaspoon of filling at one corner and spread across wrapper to form a thick sausage. Fold up one corner of wrapper, roll over again, fold in sides, and roll up to form a spring roll. Seal with cold water and set on a wax paper-lined cookie sheet. Repeat with remaining wrappers.

4. Heat 2 cups of oil in a wok to 375°F, or until a cube of bread browns in 1 minute. Deep-fry spring rolls 2 or 3 at a time until crisp and golden. Remove with a strainer and drain on paper towels. Serve warm by themselves or with Soy Vinegar Dip.

17   SOY VINEGAR DIP
Prep: 5 minutes   Cook: none   Makes: about ¾ cup

This is a classic dip for dumplings. You can vary it by using cider vinegar and a few drops of sesame oil.

½ cup soy sauce	2 tablespoons finely shredded fresh ginger
¼ cup rice vinegar	Pinch of sugar

In a small bowl, mix together soy sauce, vinegar, shredded ginger, and sugar. Stir to dissolve sugar. Refrigerate any leftover dip.

18   SWEET-SPICY CABBAGE RELISH

Prep: 10 minutes   Cook: none   Chill: 1 hour   Serves: 6 to 8

This tasty cabbage is traditionally served in small portions as part of a mixed appetizer plate.

2 cups finely shredded Chinese (Napa) cabbage	1 teaspoon crushed hot red pepper
½ cup cilantro leaves	2 teaspoons sugar
2 tablespoons soy sauce	2 teaspoons minced fresh ginger
¼ cup rice vinegar	1 garlic clove, minced
2 tablespoons Asian sesame oil	1 scallion, minced

1. In a medium bowl, toss cabbage with cilantro leaves.

2. In a small bowl, combine soy sauce, vinegar, sesame oil, hot pepper, sugar, ginger, garlic, and scallion. Stir to dissolve sugar. Pour over cabbage and toss to mix well.

3. Cover and refrigerate until chilled, at least 1 hour or up to a day, before serving.

19   CUCUMBER PICKLE

Prep: 10 minutes   Cook: 2 to 3 minutes   Chill: overnight
Makes: 2 cups

2 seedless English hothouse cucumbers, peeled	2 cups rice vinegar
1 small white onion, sliced	2 tablespoons sugar
1 small dried hot red pepper	½ teaspoon salt

1. Slice cucumbers as thinly as possible. Place in a bowl. Add onion to cucumbers and toss to mix lightly. Transfer to a sterile 1-pint glass jar with lid. Add hot red pepper.

2. In a small nonreactive saucepan, cook vinegar, sugar, and salt over medium heat, stirring, until all sugar has dissolved, 2 to 3 minutes. Pour hot syrup over cucumbers, making sure that vegetables are completely covered. Cover with lid and refrigerate overnight or longer.

20   DAIKON AND CARROT PICKLE

Prep: 10 minutes   Cook: 2 to 3 minutes   Chill: overnight
Makes: 2½ cups

2   cups sliced daikon
½   cup thinly sliced carrot
1   teaspoon coriander seeds

3   cups rice vinegar
1   teaspoon sugar
½   teaspoon salt

1. In a bowl, toss daikon and carrot together to mix. Place in a glass container and add coriander seeds.

2. In a small nonreactive saucepan, heat vinegar with sugar and salt, stirring until sugar dissolves, 2 to 3 minutes. Pour over daikon mixture. Cover and refrigerate overnight or longer before serving. This pickle keeps well for at least 3 days.

21   LOTUS ROOT PICKLE

Prep: 10 minutes   Cook: 2 to 3 minutes   Chill: 1 week
Makes: about 1 cup

Fresh lotus root is seasonally available in oriental markets. It is prized for its health-giving properties and is served in many different ways. Chefs like to use it as a garnish, as the slices have a natural lacy pattern that is very pretty. Refrigerated, these pickles keep for months.

¼   pound fresh lotus root,
     peeled
1   cup rice vinegar

2   teaspoons sugar
⅛   teaspoon salt

1. Slice lotus root as thinly as possible. Place in a sterile glass canning jar.

2. In a small nonreactive saucepan, combine vinegar, sugar, and salt. Cook over medium heat, stirring, until all sugar is dissolved, 2 to 3 minutes. Pour hot vinegar over lotus slices, making sure that all pieces are covered with liquid. Cover with a lid and refrigerate. Pickles should be kept at least 1 week before serving.

22 AGAR-AGAR AND DAIKON SALAD
Prep: 10 minutes   Cook: none   Chill: 1 hour   Serves: 4

This salad is traditionally served as part of an appetizer plate.

2 ounces agar-agar in threads
1 cup finely shredded daikon
3 tablespoons rice vinegar
2 tablespoons safflower oil

2 teaspoons Asian sesame oil
1 tablespoon sugar
1 teaspoon salt

1. Soak agar-agar threads in a medium bowl of very cold water until soft, about 10 minutes. Drain agar-agar and cut into 2-inch pieces. In a serving bowl, toss agar-agar with shredded daikon.

2. In a small bowl, mix vinegar, safflower oil, sesame oil, sugar, and salt. Whisk to blend well. Pour dressing over agar-agar and daikon and toss. Cover and refrigerate 1 hour before serving.

23 MARINATED COLD TOFU
Prep: 5 minutes   Cook: none   Chill: 30 minutes   Serves: 4

1 pound firm tofu
1 scallion, minced
1 teaspoon minced fresh
    ginger

½ teaspoon minced garlic
1 tablespoon soy sauce
1 teaspoon lemon juice
2 teaspoons Asian sesame oil

1. Drain tofu thoroughly and cut into 1-inch cubes. Place in a glass dish.

2. In a small bowl, combine scallion, ginger, garlic, soy sauce, lemon juice, and sesame oil. Whisk to blend well. Pour over tofu cubes, cover, and refrigerate 30 minutes before serving.

24 PEANUT HOISIN DIP
Prep: 5 minutes   Cook: none   Makes: 1 cup

1 scallion
½ cup crunchy peanut butter
2 tablespoons hoisin sauce
1 tablespoon soy sauce

1 tablespoon Asian sesame oil
2 tablespoons lemon juice
½ to 1 teaspoon Tabasco sauce,
    to taste

In a food processor, coarsely chop scallion. Add peanut butter, hoisin sauce, soy sauce, sesame oil, lemon juice, and Tabasco. Process until smooth. This sauce keeps well, covered and refrigerated, for 2 weeks.

25 EGG CREPES
Prep: 2 minutes   Cook: 6 minutes   Makes: 6

These thin sheets of egg are used in several different ways. They can be rolled up and cut into ribbons for soup, fried rice, and the like, or they can be used as crepelike wrappers filled with different fillings to make "packages."

4 eggs   **1 to 2 tablespoons oil**

1. In a medium bowl, beat eggs until yellow and white are well blended.

2. In a 7- to 8-inch skillet, heat 1 tablespoon oil. Pour in about 3 tablespoons beaten egg, or just enough to form a thin crepe. Cook over moderate heat until just set. Egg sheet should not be browned. Repeat until all egg is used up, oiling skillet as needed.

Egg Ribbons: Prepare crepes as directed above. Roll each one up into a cigar shape and cut crosswise into ¼-inch ribbons.

26 HERBED TOFU DIP
Prep: 5 minutes   Cook: none   Makes: 2 cups

The fresh flavors and low calories make this dip ideal to serve with crudités, shrimp chips, or potato chips.

1 pound soft tofu
1 scallion, minced
1 teaspoon minced fresh ginger
½ teaspoon minced fresh thyme or ¼ teaspoon dried

½ teaspoon minced fresh mint or ¼ teaspoon dried
2 teaspoons salt
1 teaspoon freshly ground pepper
2 teaspoons Asian sesame oil

1. In a food processor or blender, process tofu until creamy smooth. Add scallion, ginger, thyme, mint, salt, and pepper. Blend well.

2. Remove dip to a serving bowl and stir in sesame oil.

FLAVORED OILS

In Chinese cooking, flavored oils have two uses. They are often served at table and used as dips as soy sauce is, and they are also used in cooking as a "perfume" when they are added to enhance the aromatic properties of a dish. Of course, the most common flavored oil we have is sesame oil. I often use the oils in this chapter as a base for salad dressings, where I find the subtle aromas they add to salads provides an intriguing extra dimension.

27 CHILE OIL
Prep: 10 minutes   Cook: 2 minutes   Stand: 24 hours   Makes: 2 cups

Because chile oil goes rancid very easily, it is best to make your own. This version is particularly pungent. Since you will probably not use this up very quickly, remember to keep it refrigerated.

12 **small dried hot red peppers**
1 **teaspoon cayenne**

1 **teaspoon paprika**
2 **cups safflower or canola oil**

1. In a spice grinder or blender, crush dried red peppers. Place in a 1-pint heatproof glass jar with lid. Add cayenne and paprika.

2. Heat oil over medium heat until it just begins to smoke, about 2 minutes. Pour over red pepper mix. Let stand until cool. Cover and leave at room temperature 24 hours. If you wish a clear oil, strain out red peppers. Oil should be kept refrigerated.

28 CHILE, BLACK BEAN, AND GARLIC OIL
Prep: 10 minutes   Cook: 2 minutes   Stand: 24 hours   Makes: 2 cups

8 **small dried hot red peppers**
1 **tablespoon fermented black beans**

3 **garlic cloves**
2 **cups safflower or canola oil**

1. In a spice grinder or blender, grind dried red peppers, black beans, and garlic to a coarse paste.

2. Heat oil until just beginning to smoke, about 2 minutes. Pour over red pepper mix. Let cool, then pour into a clean glass jar with a lid. Let stand at room temperature overnight. Oil is now ready to use or can be refrigerated for up to 2 weeks. For longer storage, strain oil and keep refrigerated.

29 GINGER OIL

Prep: 5 minutes   Cook: 2 minutes   Stand: 24 hours   Makes: 2 cups

¼ cup finely minced fresh
  ginger

2 cups safflower or canola oil

1. Place minced ginger in a 1-pint heatproof glass jar with a lid.

2. Heat oil until just beginning to smoke, about 2 minutes, Pour over ginger and let stand at room temperature 24 hours. Strain off ginger. Oil is now ready to use. Cover and refrigerate for up to 3 months.

30 SCALLION OIL

Prep: 5 minutes   Cook: 2 minutes   Stand: 30 minutes
Makes: 1 cup

1 scallion, minced
1 teaspoon salt

1 cup safflower or canola oil

1. Place minced scallions and salt in a clean ½-pint heatproof glass jar with a lid.

2. Heat oil until just beginning to smoke, about 2 minutes. Pour over scallion and salt mix. Let stand 30 minutes. Oil is now ready to use, or it can be covered and refrigerated overnight. If you wish to keep oil longer, strain off scallions after 24 hours.

31 FRESH GINGER DRESSING

Prep: 5 minutes   Cook: none   Makes: ½ cup

Here is a refreshing dressing for green salads, Eastern or Western style.

1 tablespoon tarragon vinegar
3 tablespoons extra-virgin
    olive oil
½ teaspoon salt

½ teaspoon freshly ground
    pepper
2 teaspoons minced fresh
    ginger

In a small bowl, whisk together vinegar, oil, salt, and pepper until well blended. Add ginger and whisk to mix.

32 MUSTARD SESAME VINAIGRETTE

Prep: 5 minutes   Cook: none   Makes: ⅓ cup

2 tablespoons grainy mustard
2 teaspoons rice vinegar
¼ teaspoon sugar
¼ teaspoon salt

¼ teaspoon freshly ground
   pepper
2 tablespoons vegetable oil
1 tablespoon Asian sesame oil

In a small bowl, whisk together mustard, vinegar, sugar, salt, and pepper. Slowly whisk in vegetable oil and sesame oil until well blended.

33 SESAME VINAIGRETTE

Prep: 5 minutes   Cook: none   Makes: 1 cup

½ cup safflower oil
2 tablespoons olive oil
2 teaspoons Asian sesame oil
2 tablespoons rice vinegar
1 tablespoon soy sauce

1 garlic clove, minced
½ teaspoon pepper
¼ teaspoon sugar
Pinch of salt

In a small bowl, combine safflower oil, olive oil, sesame oil, vinegar, soy sauce, garlic, black pepper, sugar, and salt. Whisk briskly until well blended. Or place all ingredients in a covered jar and shake well.

34 WILD PEPPER MIX

Prep: 5 minutes   Cook: 3 minutes   Makes: 1 cup

This pepper mix is often served as a dip for crisp poultry as well as poached chicken. I find it works wonderfully as a spicy salt for flavoring grilled chicken or seafood.

½ cup Szechuan peppercorns   ½ cup coarse (kosher) salt

1. In a dry wok, roast Szechuan peppercorns and salt over medium heat, tossing constantly, until salt is aromatic and slightly browned, about 3 minutes.

2. Pour into a spice grinder or blender and grind together. Store in an airtight jar.

Chapter 2

Soups and Stocks

No book on Chinese cooking would be complete without a chapter on soups. All Chinese, but particularly Cantonese, love clear broths with something floating in them, either pieces of squash as in Silk Squash Soup, or leafy greens, as in Watercress Soup Chinese Style. Of course, you'll find an easy recipe for Won Ton Soup and Egg Flower (Egg Drop) Soup here. And so that all your soups taste as good as possible, I have included three recipes for stock: classic Chinese Chicken Stock, Vegetable Stock, and a Rich Meat Stock. These are the bases for great-tasting soups.

In addition to clear broths, there are several recipes for thick soups, which are not only hearty but healthful, since they are not thickened with cream. Served with crusty garlic bread, Crab Corn Chowder could be a meal in itself. Chicken in Coconut Broth and Shrimp in Lemongrass Broth borrow flavors from Southeast Asia.

If you serve these soups as a first course in a Western-style meal, the suggested number of servings will be quite adequate, but if served in small Chinese soup bowls, each recipe will give you generous portions.

35 CHINESE CHICKEN STOCK

Prep: 10 minutes   Cook: 4 hours 10 minutes   Makes: 6 cups

1 (3- to 4-pound) chicken or chicken parts	1 whole scallion
	1 slice of fresh ginger

1. Remove liver from chicken and discard. Rinse well.

2. Place chicken in a stockpot and add cold water to cover. Bring to a boil, reduce heat to medium-low, and simmer 10 minutes, skimming scum that rises to top.

3. Add whole scallion and ginger and continue to simmer 4 hours. If stock reduces during this time to expose chicken parts, top off with more cold water.

4. Strain stock and discard chicken parts and vegetables. Degrease and chill rapidly, preferably over ice.

5. Stock can be refrigerated for up to 3 days, or frozen. For convenience, stock can be reduced to a more concentrated form by rapid boiling before storage.

36   VEGETABLE STOCK
Prep: 15 minutes   Cook: 2 hours   Makes: 8 cups

1 medium onion
4 carrots
1 celery rib

1 head of romaine lettuce
1 scallion
1 slice of fresh ginger

1. Peel onion and carrots. Clean and rinse all vegetables.

2. Place onion, carrots, celery, lettuce, scallion, and ginger in a stockpot and cover with 10 cups cold water. Bring to a boil, reduce heat, and simmer gently 2 hours. Strain; discard vegetables.

3. Stock can be refrigerated 5 days or frozen up to 2 months.

37   RICH MEAT STOCK
Prep: 10 minutes   Cook: 4 hours 25 minutes to 6 hours 35 minutes
Makes: 10 cups

6 dried Chinese mushrooms
2 tablespoons vegetable oil
2 pounds pork bones
1 pound pork loin

4 pounds chicken parts
1 ham hock, about ½ pound
4 scallions
6 slices of fresh ginger

1. In a small bowl, soak dried Chinese mushrooms in 1 cup warm water for 10 minutes.

2. In a large stockpot, heat oil. Add pork bones and cook over heat, stirring occasionally, until browned, about 10 minutes. Add pork loin, chicken, and ham hock. Cook, stirring, until meat is browned, 5 to 10 minutes. Add scallions, ginger, mushrooms with their soaking water, and enough cold water to cover meat and bones.

3. Bring stock to a boil, reduce to a simmer, and cook, skimming off scum that rises to surface, for 10 to 15 minutes. Continue to cook stock for 4 to 6 hours, topping off with more cold water if stock reduces too much and meat parts are exposed.

4. Strain stock and discard all meat and vegetables. Degrease stock and reduce if desired for convenient storage. Stock can be kept refrigerated up to 3 days or frozen for up to 3 months.

38   BEAN CURD SOUP
Prep: 10 minutes   Cook: 2 minutes   Serves: 4

1 pound soft bean curd
6 dried Chinese mushrooms
3 cups Chinese Chicken Stock
     (page 27) or reduced-
     sodium canned broth
1 carrot, peeled and finely
     shredded

1 scallion, finely shredded
2 teaspoons soy sauce
½ teaspoon pepper
¼ cup lightly packed cilantro
     leaves

1. Cut bean curd into ½-inch slices and cut into cubes. Soak mushrooms in warm water until soft, about 10 minutes. Drain, reserving liquid. Remove stems and discard. Cut caps into thin shreds.

2. In a saucepan, bring stock to a boil. Add carrot, scallion, soy sauce, mushrooms, reserved mushroom liquid, and pepper. Simmer 2 minutes. Add bean curd and cilantro leaves. Remove from heat and serve.

39   BEEF BALL SOUP
Prep: 20 minutes   Cook: 15 minutes   Serves: 4 to 6

¼ pound lean ground beef
2 water chestnuts
1 tablespoon plus ¼ teaspoon
     minced fresh ginger
½ teaspoon soy sauce
¼ teaspoon black pepper
½ teaspoon Asian sesame oil

1 teaspoon cornstarch
3 cups Rich Meat Stock (page
     28)
   Salt and pepper
1 bunch of watercress (about
     ¼ pound), tough stems
     removed

1. In a food processor, combine ground beef, water chestnuts, ¼ teaspoon minced ginger, soy sauce, black pepper, sesame oil, and cornstarch. Process until mixture is very smooth and well blended. Form into small meatballs about ½ inch in diameter.

2. In a medium saucepan, combine stock with remaining 1 tablespoon minced ginger. Simmer 5 minutes. Strain and discard ginger.

3. Return stock to pan and bring to a boil. Season with salt and pepper to taste. Add meatballs and simmer 10 minutes. Add watercress, stir to wilt, and serve.

40   CHINESE CABBAGE SOUP
Prep: 15 minutes   Cook: 30 minutes   Serves: 6

3 tablespoons vegetable oil
1 medium onion, thinly sliced
1 teaspoon minced fresh
   ginger
6 cups finely shredded
   Chinese (Napa) cabbage
   (1 small head)

2 teaspoons soy sauce
2 teaspoons salt
1 teaspoon sugar
½ teaspoon pepper
2 tablespoons cornstarch
2 teaspoons Asian sesame oil

1. In a large saucepan, heat oil. Add onion and ginger and stir-fry over medium heat until soft, about 3 minutes. Add Chinese cabbage and stir-fry until softened, about 5 minutes. Stir constantly so cabbage does not burn. Add 6 cups water and bring to a simmer.

2. Add soy sauce, salt, sugar, and pepper. Simmer 20 minutes.

3. In a small bowl, mix cornstarch with ½ cup cold water until smooth and blended; stir into soup. Bring to a boil, stirring, until soup thickens, 1 to 2 minutes. Remove from heat, sprinkle on sesame oil, and serve.

41   CHICKEN IN COCONUT BROTH
Prep: 25 minutes   Cook: 20 minutes   Serves: 4 to 6

1 pound skinless, boneless
   chicken breast
1 cup unsweetened coconut
   milk
2 cups Chinese Chicken Stock
   (page 27) or reduced-
   sodium canned broth

1 stalk of lemongrass or a
   2 x ½-inch piece of lemon
   zest
Salt
1 dried hot red pepper,
   crushed (optional)
6 basil leaves, shredded
1 cup cooked white rice

1. Slice chicken breast into thin strips.

2. In a medium saucepan, combine coconut milk and chicken broth. Bring to a boil. Add lemongrass or lemon zest and simmer 10 minutes. Add chicken strips and simmer, stirring, 5 minutes. Season with salt and hot red pepper. Sprinkle slivered basil leaves on top. Simmer 5 minutes.

3. To serve, divide rice among individual serving bowls and top with soup.

42 CHICKEN CORN SOUP
Prep: 20 minutes   Cook: 12 minutes   Serves: 4

½ pound skinless, boneless
   chicken breast
2 cups corn kernels, fresh or
   frozen
1 tablespoon vegetable oil
3 scallions, minced
2 teaspoons minced fresh
   ginger

3 cups Chinese Chicken Stock
   (page 27) or reduced-
   sodium canned broth
1 tablespoon dry sherry
1 teaspoon sugar
   Salt and pepper
2 tablespoons cornstarch

1. Trim any fat or gristle from chicken and cut meat into fine shreds.
Coarsely chop corn in a blender or food processor.

2. In a large saucepan, heat oil over medium heat. Add scallions and ginger
and cook a few seconds until aromatic. Add chicken stock and chopped
corn. Bring to a boil. Add shredded chicken and immediately stir to separate
chicken shreds. Simmer until chicken is cooked, about 1 minute. Add
sherry, sugar, and salt and pepper to taste. Bring to a boil, reduce heat, and
simmer 10 minutes.

3. In a small bowl, mix cornstarch with ¼ cup cold water; stir into soup.
Bring soup to a boil, stirring until thickened. The soup should be translucent
but not too thick. Serve at once.

43 VELVET CORN SOUP
Prep: 15 minutes   Cook: 20 minutes   Serves: 4

2 cups corn kernels, fresh or
   frozen
1 tablespoon vegetable oil
4 scallions, minced
1 teaspoon minced fresh
   ginger
1 tablespoon dry sherry

3 cups Chinese Chicken Stock
   (page 27) or reduced-
   sodium canned broth
1 teaspoon sugar
2 tablespoons cornstarch
2 egg whites, lightly beaten
   Salt and pepper

1. In a food processor, using pulsing motion, coarsely chop corn kernels.

2. In a large saucepan, heat oil over medium heat. Add scallions and ginger
and cook a few seconds until aromatic. Add sherry, chicken stock, sugar,
and chopped corn. Bring to a simmer and cook 15 minutes.

3. In a small bowl, mix cornstarch with ¼ cup cold water; stir into soup.
Bring soup to a boil, stirring, until thickened. Remove soup from heat and
swirl in beaten egg whites with a fork. Add salt and pepper to taste. Serve at
once.

44　CRAB CORN CHOWDER
Prep: 25 minutes　Cook: 20 minutes　Serves: 8

This hearty Chinese chowder tastes light and delicious, but is filling enough for a Sunday night supper when served with a few dumplings, or even just crusty bread.

4　cups corn kernels, fresh or frozen	6　cups Chinese Chicken Stock (page 27) or reduced-sodium canned broth
1　pound cooked crabmeat	
1　tablespoon vegetable oil	2　tablespoons dry sherry
4　scallions, minced	2　teaspoons sugar
1　tablespoon minced fresh ginger	Salt and pepper
	¼　cup cornstarch
	4　egg whites, lightly beaten

1. In a food processor, using the pulsing motion, coarsely chop corn kernels. Carefully pick through crabmeat to remove bits of shell.

2. In a saucepan, heat oil and sauté minced scallions and ginger until aromatic. Add broth, sherry, sugar, and salt and pepper to taste. Add corn kernels and simmer 15 minutes. Add crabmeat and stir well to blend.

3. In a small bowl, whisk cornstarch with ½ cup cold water. Add to soup and bring to a boil, stirring, until soup thickens.

4. Remove from heat and swirl in lightly beaten egg whites with a fork. Adjust seasonings, if necessary, and serve.

45　CLEAR SOUP WITH FISH FILLETS AND SPINACH
Prep: 15 minutes　Cook: 13 minutes　Serves: 6

2　teaspoons vegetable oil	1　teaspoon soy sauce
1　slice of fresh ginger	¼　teaspoon pepper
3　cups Chinese Chicken Stock (page 27) or reduced-sodium canned broth	½　pound flounder fillets, cut into 2-inch pieces
2　teaspoons dry sherry	½　pound fresh spinach, washed and drained

1. In a large saucepan, heat oil until just smoking. Add ginger slice and cook 1 minute. Discard ginger.

2. Add stock, sherry, soy sauce, and pepper. Bring to a boil. Reduce heat to simmer and cook 10 minutes.

3. Add fish fillets and simmer until fish turns white and opaque, about 2 minutes. Add spinach and stir to wilt. Serve at once.

46   EGG FLOWER SOUP

Prep: 10 minutes   Cook: 2 to 3 minutes   Serves: 4 to 6

This is a prettier name for the familiar egg drop soup.

3 cups Chinese Chicken Stock
   (page 27) or reduced-
   sodium canned broth
1 teaspoon soy sauce
¼ teaspoon pepper
¼ teaspoon minced fresh
   ginger

1 tablespoon cornstarch
   Salt
4 eggs, beaten
1 scallion, minced
2 teaspoons Asian sesame oil

1. In a medium saucepan, bring chicken stock to a simmer. Add soy sauce, pepper, and minced ginger. Whisk cornstarch with ½ cup cold water until smooth. Add to soup. Bring to a boil and cook, stirring, until thickened, 1 to 2 minutes. Season with salt to taste.

2. Reduce heat so that soup is simmering. Gradually drop beaten egg into simmering soup, ¼ cup at a time. Egg should form clusters, or "flowers," as it hits hot soup.

3. Stir in minced scallions, sprinkle with sesame oil, and serve.

47   COLD MELON SOUP

Prep: 15 minutes   Cook: 45 minutes   Chill: 3 hours   Serves: 8

When I was a girl in Hong Kong, honeydews were considered a great luxury and quite a treat. This soup, while not traditional, would be very popular there.

1 carrot, peeled and halved
1 celery rib, halved
1 bay leaf
1 sprig of fresh thyme or
   1 teaspoon dried thyme
   leaves
¼ cup finely slivered fresh
   ginger

1 honeydew melon (about
   4 pounds)
   Salt
1½ tablespoons lime juice
   Lime slices

1. In a large saucepan, bring 6 cups water to a boil. Add carrot, celery, bay leaf, and thyme. Cover, reduce heat to low, and simmer 30 minutes.

2. Strain broth and return to pot. Add slivered ginger and simmer 15 minutes.

3. Meanwhile, quarter melon, remove seeds, and peel. Cut into chunks. In a food processor, in batches, process melon with about 1 cup of ginger broth to a smooth puree. Stir puree into remaining broth. Season with salt to taste. Refrigerate, covered, 3 hours, or overnight.

4. Just before serving, stir in lime juice. Serve garnished with lime slices.

48   HOT AND SOUR SEAFOOD SOUP
Prep: 20 minutes   Cook: 10 to 12 minutes   Serves: 6

2 dried Chinese black
   mushrooms
½ pound flounder fillets
3 cups Vegetable Stock (page
   28)
3 tablespoons cider vinegar
2 teaspoons soy sauce
½ teaspoon cayenne

¼ pound medium shrimp,
   shelled and deveined
¼ cup sliced bamboo shoots,
   finely shredded
4 water chestnuts, coarsely
   chopped
2 tablespoons cornstarch
   Salt and black pepper

1. Soak mushrooms in warm water for 10 minutes, or until soft. Drain, reserving liquid. Remove and discard stems. Cut caps into fine shreds. Cut fish into 1-inch-wide pieces.

2. In a saucepan or wok, combine broth with reserved mushroom soaking liquid. Bring to a boil. Add vinegar, soy sauce, and cayenne. Add shrimp, bamboo shoots, water chestnuts, and mushrooms. Return to a boil and simmer 5 minutes.

3. In a small bowl, whisk cornstarch with ½ cup cold water, add to soup, and return to a boil. Cook, stirring, until soup thickens, 3 to 5 minutes. Add fish and cook until fish turns white and opaque, about 2 minutes. Season with salt and pepper to taste. Serve hot.

49   SHRIMP IN LEMONGRASS BROTH
Prep: 15 minutes   Cook: 15 minutes   Serves: 4

3 cups Vegetable Stock (page
   28)
2 stalks lemongrass, cut into
   2-inch pieces
2 ounces bean threads
3 tablespoons cider vinegar
2 teaspoons soy sauce

1 fresh chile pepper, seeded
   and minced
½ pound medium shrimp,
   shelled and deveined
1 scallion, minced
   Salt and pepper
1 tablespoon slivered mint
   leaves

1. In a medium saucepan, bring stock and lemongrass to a boil. Cover and simmer 10 minutes. Meanwhile, in a small bowl, soak bean threads in warm water until soft, about 10 minutes. Drain.

2. Add vinegar, soy sauce, and chile to broth and bring to a boil. Add shrimp, reduce heat to medium, and cook until shrimp turn pink, about 3 minutes.

3. Add bean threads and scallion. Season with salt and pepper to taste. Top with slivered mint leaves to serve.

50 HOT AND SOUR SOUP

Prep: 15 minutes   Cook: 9 to 10 minutes   Serves: 6

1 small boneless pork chop
  (about 2 ounces)
2 dried Chinese mushrooms
3 cups Chinese Chicken Stock
  (page 27) or reduced-
  sodium canned broth
3 tablespoons cider vinegar
2 teaspoons soy sauce
½ teaspoon cayenne
¼ cup sliced bamboo shoots,
  cut into shreds

2 water chestnuts, coarsely
  chopped
½ pound firm bean curd, cut
  into ½-inch dice
2 tablespoons cornstarch
1 egg, lightly beaten
½ teaspoon freshly ground
  black pepper
Salt

1. Trim pork and cut into thin shreds. Soak mushrooms in ½ cup warm water until soft, about 10 minutes. Drain, reserving liquid. Stem mushrooms and cut caps into shreds, discarding stems.

2. In a large saucepan or wok, bring chicken stock and mushroom soaking water to a boil. Add vinegar, soy sauce, and cayenne. Simmer 5 minutes. Add pork strips and stir immediately to separate. Simmer until pork is cooked through, about 2 minutes. Add bamboo shoots, water chestnuts, and mushroom strips. Simmer 2 minutes longer, then add bean curd cubes.

3. Return soup to a simmer. Blend cornstarch with ½ cup cold water and add to soup. Bring to a boil, stirring, until thickened. Remove from heat and stir in beaten egg with a fork. Add black pepper and salt to taste.

51 SHRIMP AND WATERCRESS SOUP

Prep: 20 minutes   Cook: 5 to 6 minutes   Serves: 4

3 cups Chinese Chicken Stock
  (page 27) or reduced-
  sodium canned broth
2 teaspoons soy sauce
¼ teaspoon pepper
½ pound medium shrimp,
  shelled and deveined

2 bunches of watercress
  (about ½ pound), tough
  stems removed
Salt
2 teaspoons Asian sesame oil

1. In a large saucepan, combine chicken broth, soy sauce, and pepper. Bring to a boil, reduce heat to medium, and simmer 2 minutes. Add shrimp and cook until shrimp curl and turn pink, about 3 minutes.

2. Add watercress and stir to wilt. Season with salt to taste. Sprinkle on sesame oil and serve.

52   WATERCRESS SOUP CHINESE STYLE
Prep: 10 minutes   Cook: 10 to 11 minutes   Serves: 4

2 bunches of watercress
   (about ½ pound)
3 cups Chinese Chicken Stock
   (page 27) or reduced-
   sodium canned broth

2 teaspoons dry sherry
1 teaspoon soy sauce
¼ teaspoon pepper
2 teaspoons Asian sesame oil

1. Rinse watercress well. Pick off and discard tough stems. Break watercress into sprigs.

2. In a large saucepan, bring broth to boil. Add sherry, soy sauce, and pepper. Simmer 10 minutes.

3. Add watercress and stir to wilt. Drizzle sesame oil over soup and serve at once.

53   WINTER MELON SOUP
Prep: 20 minutes   Cook: 20 minutes   Serves: 6

4 dried Chinese mushrooms
1 pound winter melon
½ pound boneless, skinless
   chicken breast
¼ pound lean pork
2 ounces Smithfield, country,
   or Black Forest ham
4 water chestnuts

4 cups Chinese Chicken Stock
   (page 27) or reduced-
   sodium canned broth
1 piece of dried tangerine or
   orange peel, 2 x 1 inch
   Salt and pepper
2 eggs, beaten

1. In a small bowl, soak dried mushrooms in ½ cup warm water for 10 minutes. Drain, reserving liquid; stem mushrooms and cut caps into thin strips, discarding stems.

2. Peel winter melon and trim away seeds and stringy part. Cut melon into 2-inch cubes. Cut chicken breast, pork, and ham into thin strips. Slice water chestnuts in half horizontally and cut into thin strips.

3. In a large saucepan, bring chicken stock to a simmer. Add winter melon and tangerine peel. Simmer 10 minutes. Add chicken breast, pork, and ham, stirring to separate pieces. Add mushrooms with their soaking liquid and water chestnuts. Simmer 10 minutes longer. Season with salt and pepper to taste. Remove from heat. Immediately add beaten eggs and stir into threads. Serve at once.

54   SPICY SOUR SHRIMP SOUP

Prep: 20 minutes   Cook: 19 minutes   Serves: 6

4 ounces medium shrimp
1 stalk of lemongrass
2 ounces rice stick noodles
3 cups Vegetable Stock (page 28) or canned broth
2 teaspoons soy sauce
3 tablespoons cider vinegar

½ to 1 teaspoon cayenne
4 water chestnuts, coarsely chopped
3 scallions, cut into 2-inch lengths
Salt and freshly ground pepper

1. Shell and devein shrimp, reserving shells. Remove coarse outer leaves from lemongrass, crush stem, and cut into 2-inch pieces. In a bowl, soak rice sticks in warm water until soft, about 10 minutes; drain.

2. In a medium saucepan, combine stock with shrimp shells and lemongrass. Bring to a boil, reduce heat, and simmer 15 minutes. Strain and return stock to saucepan.

3. Add soy sauce, vinegar, and cayenne. Bring to a boil and add shrimp. Cook over medium heat just until shrimp turn pink, about 3 minutes.

4. Add rice sticks, water chestnuts, and scallions. Stir to blend. Season with salt and pepper to taste. Simmer 1 minute and serve.

55   SILK SQUASH SOUP

Prep: 10 minutes   Cook: 10 minutes   Serves: 4

This intriguing dark green squash, which has ridges along its length, is the common squash from which loofahs are made when the squash is dried. Silk squash is a prettier name.

1 silk squash
2 ounces bean threads
1 small boneless pork chop (about 2 ounces)
1 tablespoon soy sauce
1 tablespoon dry sherry
2 teaspoons cornstarch

1 tablespoon vegetable oil
1 slice of fresh ginger
2 cups Chinese Chicken Stock (page 27) or reduced-sodium canned broth
Salt and pepper

1. Peel silk squash and cut crosswise on a diagonal into 1-inch-thick slices. Soak bean threads in warm water and let stand 5 minutes; drain. Trim fat from pork and cut meat into thin shreds. In a small bowl, toss pork with soy sauce, sherry, and cornstarch.

2. In a wok, heat oil. Add ginger and stir-fry until it browns. Remove and discard. Add pork shreds to wok and stir-fry over high heat until meat loses its pink color, about 2 minutes. Add squash and stir-fry 1 minute.

3. Add chicken broth and bean threads. Bring to a boil and simmer 5 minutes. Season with salt and pepper to taste and serve.

56   ZUCCHINI GLASS NOODLE SOUP
Prep: 10 minutes   Cook: 10 minutes   Serves: 4

When bean threads are soaked and cooked, they become transparent and look like fragile glass. As Chinese like to give fanciful names to their dishes, I often refer to bean threads as glass noodles; thus, the name for this soup.

4 small zucchini
2 ounces bean threads (glass noodles)
4 cups Rich Meat Stock (page 28)

2 teaspoons soy sauce
¼ teaspoon pepper
Salt
1 scallion, minced

1. Slice zucchini crosswise on a diagonal into ¼-inch oval slices. Soak glass noodles in a bowl of warm water until soft, about 10 minutes.

2. In a medium saucepan, bring stock to a boil. Season with soy sauce and pepper. Add zucchini slices and simmer 5 minutes.

3. Drain glass noodles, cut into 4-inch lengths, add to soup, and simmer 5 minutes. Season with salt to taste. Sprinkle with minced scallion and serve.

57   WATERCRESS SOUP WITH BEAN CURD
Prep: 10 minutes   Cook: 3 to 4 minutes   Serves: 3 to 4

1 bunch of watercress (about ¼ pound)
1 (14½-ounce) can reduced-sodium chicken broth
1 teaspoon soy sauce

¼ teaspoon pepper
1 pound bean curd, cut into ¼-inch dice
2 teaspoons Asian sesame oil

1. Wash and drain watercress. Remove and discard tough stems.

2. In a medium saucepan, bring chicken broth to a simmer over medium heat. Add soy sauce and pepper and cook 2 minutes.

3. Add bean curd cubes and cook until heated through, 1 to 2 minutes. Add watercress and stir to wilt. Sprinkle with sesame oil and serve.

58 WON TON SOUP

Prep: 30 minutes   Cook: 2 to 3 minutes   Serves: 6

No chapter on Chinese soups would be complete without this recipe for Won Ton Soup. This is probably the first soup everyone had when being introduced to Chinese food, and it is still a favorite with many of us.

6 water chestnuts	24 won ton skins
¼ pound minced lean pork	1 egg, beaten with
1 teaspoon minced fresh	1 tablespoon water
ginger	3 cups Chinese Chicken Stock
1 teaspoon salt	(page 27) or reduced-
¾ teaspoon pepper	sodium canned broth
2 teaspoons cornstarch	2 teaspoons soy sauce
1 tablespoon Asian sesame oil	1 scallion, minced

1. In a food processor, mince water chestnuts coarsely. Add minced pork, ginger, salt, ½ teaspoon pepper, cornstarch, and 1 teaspoon sesame oil. Pulse until well blended.

2. Lay out won ton skins. Spoon approximately ½ teaspoon filling on center of each won ton skin. Brush edges lightly with beaten egg wash and fold corners over to form a triangle, enclosing filling. Press to seal well. Dab egg wash on one corner and stick to opposite corner to form a little hat-shaped won ton. Continue until all won tons are made. Place on a floured cookie sheet and cover with a clean kitchen towel.

3. In a large saucepan, bring stock to a simmer. Season with soy sauce and remaining ¼ teaspoon pepper.

4. In a large pot, bring 10 cups of water to a boil. Add won tons and cook until they rise to surface, 2 to 3 minutes. With a slotted spoon, transfer won tons to simmering soup.

5. Add remaining 2 teaspoons sesame oil and minced scallion to soup just before serving. Spoon 4 won tons into each of 6 individual bowls and ladle hot broth over won tons.

Chapter 3

Chinese Fast Food

This is it—what everyone thinks of as Chinese food—quick, fast, easy, stir-fried dishes. These simple recipes make stir-frying relaxed. Best of all, you will find that they show you how to produce authentic-tasting dishes even when you do all your shopping at the supermarket because, while I love to cook, I hate to shop. To me there is nothing more dismaying than having to go to three stores to find one or two ingredients. So in this whole chapter, I have included only five ingredients you may have to buy at an Asian market.

I have included recipes for many family favorites, such as Beef with Oyster Sauce, Ginger Beef, Chicken with Ham and Snow Peas, Kung Pao Chicken, Sweet and Sour Pork, and Clams with Black Bean Sauce.

After you try a few simpler recipes such as Ground Beef and Peas, Broccoli with Beef, Chicken with Celery and Bean Sprouts, Honeyed Ham Steak, or Stir-Fried Beef, you will be delighted at how easy it is to impress your friends and family with restaurant-style dishes like Crabmeat in a Cloud, Lobster with Scallions and Ginger, Lichee Chicken Balls, Everyday Velvet Chicken, Steak Kew, and Deep-Fried Shrimp in Shells. The diners, of course, will be delighted at how delicious it all tastes.

59 CHICKEN, BROCCOLI, AND WATER CHESTNUTS IN OYSTER SAUCE

Prep: 15 minutes   Cook: 10 to 12 minutes   Serves: 6

1 skinless, boneless chicken
   breast (10 to 12 ounces)
1 tablespoon cornstarch
2 teaspoons dry sherry
½ teaspoon salt
¼ teaspoon pepper
½ pound broccoli
3 tablespoons vegetable oil

1 garlic clove, minced
1 slice of fresh ginger, minced
¼ cup water chestnuts
2 tablespoons soy sauce
2 tablespoons oyster sauce
¼ cup chicken broth
1 teaspoon sugar

1. Cut chicken breast crosswise into thin slices about ¼ inch thick. In a bowl, toss chicken with cornstarch, sherry, salt, and pepper to coat evenly. Let stand 10 to 15 minutes.

2. Meanwhile, cut broccoli florets from stems. Peel and cut stems into 2-inch pieces about ½ inch thick. In a large saucepan of boiling salted water, cook broccoli stems and florets until broccoli is a bright green and crisp-tender, about 3 minutes. Drain and rinse under cold running water; drain well.

3. In a wok, heat oil over high heat until just smoking. Add garlic and ginger and stir-fry until aromatic, about 30 seconds. Add chicken and stir-fry until chicken becomes white and opaque, 3 to 5 minutes. Add water chestnuts, broccoli, soy sauce, oyster sauce, chicken broth, and sugar. Stir-fry until vegetables are tender and heated through, about 3 minutes. Serve.

60 CHICKEN CUBES IN YELLOW BEAN SAUCE

Prep: 10 minutes   Cook: 5 to 6 minutes   Serves: 4

1 pound skinless, boneless
   chicken breast
1 egg white
2 teaspoons cornstarch
2 teaspoons vegetable oil
2 tablespoons minced fresh
   ginger

¼ cup chicken broth
2 tablespoons yellow bean
   sauce
2 teaspoons sugar
1 tablespoon dry sherry

1. Cut chicken breast into 1-inch cubes. In a bowl, toss chicken cubes with egg white, cornstarch, and 2 tablespoons cold water until evenly coated. Let stand 5 to 10 minutes.

2. In a wok, heat oil over high heat just to smoking. Add ginger and stir-fry until aromatic, about 10 seconds. Add chicken cubes and stir-fry until chicken turns white, about 5 minutes.

3. Add chicken broth, bean sauce, sugar, and sherry. Bring to a boil, stirring to coat chicken pieces with sauce. Serve immediately.

61 CHICKEN WITH CELERY AND BEAN SPROUTS

Prep: 15 minutes   Cook: 9½ minutes   Serves: 4

1 whole skinless, boneless chicken breast (10 to 12 ounces)
1 tablespoon cornstarch
1 tablespoon plus 1 teaspoon soy sauce
3 tablespoons vegetable oil

2 teaspoons minced fresh ginger
2 celery ribs, diced
1 tablespoon dry white wine
½ cup chicken broth
2 cups bean sprouts
Salt and pepper

1. Cut chicken into slices about 2 x 1 x ¼-inch. In a medium bowl, toss chicken with cornstarch, 1 teaspoon soy sauce, and 1 tablespoon oil to coat evenly.

2. In a wok, heat remaining 2 tablespoons oil over high heat to smoking. Add ginger and stir-fry until aromatic, 30 seconds. Add celery and stir-fry 1 minute. Add chicken and stir-fry until chicken is white and opaque, about 5 minutes.

3. Add remaining 1 tablespoon soy sauce, wine, and chicken broth. Bring to a boil, reduce heat, and simmer 2 minutes. Add bean sprouts, stir to mix, and cook just until bean sprouts wilt, about 1 minute. Season with salt and pepper to taste and serve.

62 HOISIN DICED CHICKEN

Prep: 10 minutes   Cook: 7½ to 8½ minutes   Serves: 4

1 whole skinless, boneless chicken breast (10 to 12 ounces)
1 tablespoon cornstarch
1 tablespoon dry sherry
1 teaspoon salt
¼ teaspoon pepper
3 tablespoons vegetable oil

2 teaspoons minced fresh ginger
2 garlic cloves, peeled and minced
1 scallion, minced
2 tablespoons hoisin sauce
1 tablespoon soy sauce
¼ cup chicken broth
2 teaspoons Asian sesame oil

1. Cut chicken into 1-inch cubes. In a bowl, toss chicken with cornstarch, sherry, salt, pepper, and 1 tablespoon vegetable oil to coat evenly.

2. In a wok, heat remaining 2 tablespoons vegetable oil over high heat. Add ginger, garlic, and scallion and stir-fry until aromatic, about 30 seconds. Add chicken and cook, tossing, until chicken is white throughout, about 5 minutes.

3. Add hoisin sauce, soy sauce, and chicken broth, bring to a boil, and cook until slightly thickened, 2 to 3 minutes. Drizzle with sesame oil and serve.

63   SLICED CHICKEN WITH ASPARAGUS
Prep: 10 minutes   Cook: 8 minutes   Serves: 4

Although asparagus is not a Chinese vegetable, its fresh crunchy texture is a perfect foil for stir-fried chicken.

½ **pound fresh asparagus**
½ **pound skinless, boneless**
  chicken breast
2 **teaspoons cornstarch**
1 **tablespoon soy sauce**
½ **teaspoon lemon zest**
1 **tablespoon vegetable oil**

1 **tablespoon minced fresh**
  ginger
1 **scallion, minced**
2 **tablespoons dry sherry**
½ **teaspoon pepper**
½ **teaspoon sugar**
2 **teaspoons Asian sesame oil**

1. Trim tough ends off asparagus. Cut spears at an angle into 1½-inch pieces. Cut chicken breast crosswise on an angle into ¼-inch-thick slices. In a small bowl, toss chicken with cornstarch, soy sauce, and lemon zest.

2. In a wok, heat oil 10 seconds over medium heat. Add asparagus and stir-fry to coat with oil. Add 2 tablespoons water, reduce heat to low, cover, and cook until asparagus is just tender, about 2 minutes. With a slotted spoon remove to a plate.

3. Return wok to high heat. Add ginger and scallion and stir-fry until aromatic, about 10 seconds. Add chicken and stir-fry until white and opaque throughout, about 5 minutes. Add sherry, pepper, sugar, and asparagus. Stir-fry about 30 seconds to heat through. Remove from heat, drizzle with sesame oil, and serve.

64   DICED CHICKEN WITH CASHEWS
Prep: 15 minutes   Cook: 9 minutes   Serves: 4

1 **whole skinless, boneless**
  chicken breast (8 to 10
  ounces)
1 **tablespoon cornstarch**
1 **teaspoon soy sauce**
1 **tablespoon dry white wine**
½ **teaspoon salt**

¼ **teaspoon pepper**
3 **tablespoons vegetable oil**
½ **cup cashew nuts or**
  blanched whole almonds
½ **cup chicken broth**
2 **scallions, minced**
1 **teaspoon Asian sesame oil**

1. Cut chicken into 1-inch cubes. In a medium bowl, toss chicken with cornstarch, soy sauce, wine, salt, and pepper to coat evenly.

2. In a wok, heat vegetable oil over high heat. Add nuts and stir-fry until lightly browned, about 1 minute; be careful not to burn nuts. With a slotted spoon, remove nuts to paper towels and drain.

3. Return wok to high heat, add chicken, and stir-fry until chicken is white throughout, about 5 minutes. Add broth, bring to a boil, and cook 3 minutes. Add scallions and stir to blend. Remove from heat, stir in nuts, and drizzle with sesame oil.

65   CHICKEN WITH HAM AND SNOW PEAS
Prep: 15 minutes   Cook: 8 minutes   Serves: 4 to 6

1 pound skinless, boneless
    chicken breast
2 teaspoons soy sauce
2 teaspoons cornstarch
¼ pound snow peas
2 tablespoons vegetable oil
1 teaspoon minced fresh
    ginger

¼ pound baked ham steak, cut
    into thin strips
½ teaspoon salt
¼ teaspoon pepper
¼ cup chicken broth

1. Cut chicken into 1-inch pieces. In a small bowl, combine chicken pieces with soy sauce and cornstarch. Toss to mix well.

2. In a small saucepan, bring 2 cups of salted water to a boil. Add snow peas and cook until they turn bright green, about 2 seconds. Drain and rinse under cold running water to cool.

3. In a wok, heat oil on high heat until just smoking. Add ginger and stir-fry until aromatic, about 10 seconds. Add chicken and stir-fry until chicken turns white and opaque, about 5 minutes.

4. Add ham, snow peas, salt, pepper, and chicken broth. Simmer 3 minutes. Remove to a platter and serve.

66   SHREDDED CHICKEN WITH TREE EARS AND MUSHROOMS
Prep: 20 minutes   Cook: 8 to 10 minutes   Serves: 4

1 tablespoon dried tree ears
4 dried Chinese mushrooms
1 whole skinless, boneless
    chicken breast (8 to 10
    ounces)
1 tablespoon cornstarch
1 teaspoon soy sauce

½ teaspoon salt
¼ teaspoon pepper
2 teaspoons dry sherry
3 slices of fresh ginger,
    slivered
2 tablespoons vegetable oil
2 scallions, minced

1. In separate small bowls, soak tree ears and mushrooms in warm water until soft, about 15 minutes. Drain tree ears, discard water, and rinse in cold water. Coarsely chop. Drain mushrooms, reserving ½ cup soaking water. Remove and discard stems. Cut caps into thin shreds.

2. Cut chicken into thin shreds. In a medium bowl, toss chicken, cornstarch, soy sauce, salt, pepper, sherry, and ginger.

3. In a wok, heat oil over high heat until smoking. Add chicken and stir-fry until white, 3 to 5 minutes. Add tree ears and mushrooms and stir-fry 2 minutes. Add reserved mushroom water, bring to a boil, and simmer 3 minutes. Stir in scallions and serve.

67   LICHEE CHICKEN BALLS
Prep: 20 minutes   Cook: 10 to 13 minutes   Serves: 4

1 pound skinless, boneless
   chicken breast
1 teaspoon minced fresh
   ginger
2 teaspoons soy sauce
2 tablespoons cornstarch
¼ teaspoon white pepper
½ cup chicken broth

⅓ cup lichee juice (reserved
   from canned lichees)
¼ cup plum sauce
1 cup vegetable oil
2 scallions, cut into 2-inch
   lengths
6 water chestnuts
1 cup canned lichees

1. In a food processor, finely mince chicken. Add ginger, soy sauce, 1 table-spoon cornstarch, and pepper. Pulse until well combined. Wet hands with cold water and form pureed chicken into 1-inch balls.

2. In a bowl, combine chicken broth, lichee juice, plum sauce, and remaining 1 tablespoon cornstarch. Whisk sauce to mix well.

3. In a wok, heat oil over medium heat until just smoking. Add chicken balls and cook, tossing often, until light golden outside and cooked through, 7 to 10 minutes. Remove and drain on paper towels.

4. Discard all but 2 teaspoons of oil from wok. Return to heat and stir-fry scallions until softened, about 10 seconds. Add water chestnuts and lichees and toss to blend. Add reserved lichee juice sauce. Add chicken balls and bring to a simmer. Cook, stirring, until thickened, about 2 minutes.

68   KUNG PAO CHICKEN
Prep: 20 minutes   Stand: 30 minutes   Cook: 9 minutes   Serves: 4

1 pound skinless, boneless
   chicken breast
1 egg
3 tablespoons plus
   2 teaspoons cornstarch
2½ teaspoons salt
2 cups vegetable oil
3 tablespoons rice vinegar
1 tablespoon dry sherry
2 teaspoons sugar

1 green bell pepper, diced
2 scallions, minced
3 slices of fresh ginger,
   minced
2 garlic cloves, minced
2 small dried hot red peppers,
   crumbled
½ cup dry-roasted peanuts
1 tablespoon Asian sesame oil

1. Cut chicken into 1-inch cubes. In a bowl, toss chicken with egg, 3 table-spoons cornstarch, and 1 teaspoon salt to coat evenly. Let stand 30 minutes.

2. In a wok, heat vegetable oil to 375°F, or until a bread cube browns in 1 minute. Add chicken cubes and deep-fry until golden, about 5 minutes. Remove with a skimmer or slotted spoon and drain on paper towels.

3. Pour off oil from wok, leaving about 2 tablespoons. In a small bowl, whisk together vinegar, 3 tablespoons water, sherry, sugar, remaining 1½ teaspoons salt, and 2 teaspoons cornstarch. Set sauce aside.

4. Reheat oil over high heat until just smoking. Add green pepper and stir-fry 30 seconds. Add scallions, ginger, garlic, and hot red peppers. Stir-fry until aromatic, about 10 seconds, being careful not to burn vegetables.

5. Add sauce to wok. Bring to a boil, stirring until thickened, about 1 minute. Add chicken cubes and toss to mix well. Cook until chicken cubes are heated through, about 3 minutes. Add peanuts and mix well. Remove from heat and drizzle sesame oil over finished dish. Toss to blend. Serve.

---

69 EVERYDAY VELVET CHICKEN
Prep: 15 minutes   Chill: 20 minutes   Cook: 14 minutes   Serves: 6

Classically, velvet chicken is a dish in which the texture of the chicken is broken down by scraping and pounding the raw chicken meat until it is a paste. This chicken paste is then bound together with a mixture of egg whites and sometimes starch. The "remade" chicken has a new and interesting light texture prized by Chinese gourmets. Velvet chicken, however, is so delicious that it is worth enjoying even in this timesaving everyday version.

2 **pounds skinless, boneless chicken breasts**	1 **tablespoon dry sherry**
2 **egg whites**	1 **teaspoon soy sauce**
1 **tablespoon plus 2 teaspoons cornstarch**	½ **teaspoon pepper**
1¼ **teaspoons salt**	3 **tablespoons vegetable oil**
¼ **cup chicken broth**	1 **tablespoon minced fresh ginger**
	3 **scallions, minced**

1. Slice chicken breasts very thinly crosswise, then cut into thin strips about 1½ inches long. In a medium bowl, toss chicken strips with egg whites, 1 tablespoon of cornstarch, and ½ teaspoon salt until well mixed. Cover and refrigerate at least 20 minutes.

2. Bring a medium saucepan of water to a simmer. In ½-cup batches, poach chicken until white and opaque, about 3 minutes per batch. With a slotted spoon, transfer poached chicken pieces to a plate.

3. In a small bowl, combine remaining 2 teaspoons cornstarch, chicken broth, sherry, soy sauce, remaining ¾ teaspoon salt, and pepper. Set sauce aside.

4. Heat oil in a wok over high heat. Add ginger and then add chicken pieces. Toss to mix. Pour in reserved sauce and stir-fry 2 minutes, or until sauce boils and thickens. Add chopped scallions and toss to blend. Remove from heat and serve.

70   SHREDDED CHICKEN WITH PEA SPROUTS
Prep: 15 minutes   Cook: 5 to 7 minutes   Serves: 2

Unusual greens available seasonally in Chinese markets, pea sprouts are the tender green leaves from snow pea plants. If you cannot find them, just use green peas; even frozen ones will work well.

½ pound tender pea sprouts
½ pound skinless, boneless
    chicken breast
1 egg white
1 tablespoon cornstarch
6 tablespoons vegetable oil
1 slice of fresh ginger

1 scallion, cut in half
2 tablespoons dry sherry
2 tablespoons chicken broth
    or water
2 teaspoons soy sauce
    Salt and pepper

1. Trim pea sprouts of any tough stems. Shred chicken into matchstick-size pieces. In a bowl, combine chicken with egg white and cornstarch.

2. In a wok, heat oil over high heat until just smoking. Add ginger and scallion and cook until brown, about 2 minutes; discard. Add chicken and stir-fry until chicken turns white, 3 to 5 minutes. Add pea sprouts, sherry, chicken broth, and soy sauce. Toss to wilt sprouts and blend. Season with salt and pepper to taste and serve.

71   BROCCOLI WITH BEEF
Prep: 15 minutes   Cook: 9 to 10 minutes   Serves: 4

1 pound broccoli
¼ pound beef flank
1 tablespoon soy sauce
1 teaspoon cornstarch
½ teaspoon pepper
3 tablespoons vegetable oil

1 teaspoon minced fresh
    ginger
1 teaspoon sugar
¼ teaspoon salt
2 teaspoons brandy

1. Cut florets from broccoli stems and set aside. Peel stems and cut into 2 x ½-inch sticks. Bring a large saucepan of salted water to a boil. Add broccoli sticks and florets and cook until they turn a bright green color, about 2 minutes. Drain and rinse under cold running water; drain well.

2. Slice beef into strips about ¼ inch thick. In a small bowl, toss beef strips with soy sauce, cornstarch, and pepper.

3. In a wok, heat 2 tablespoons oil over high heat until just smoking. Add beef and stir-fry to desired doneness, about 2 minutes. Remove to a plate. Add 2 tablespoons water to marinade bowl.

4. Add remaining 1 tablespoon oil to wok; return to heat. Add ginger and stir-fry 2 seconds. Add broccoli, sugar, salt, brandy, and water in marinade bowl. Cover and steam 3 minutes, until broccoli is tender and water has evaporated. Return meat to wok. Toss with broccoli to heat through and serve.

72   BEEF WITH OYSTER SAUCE
Prep: 15 minutes   Cook: 11 to 14 minutes   Serves: 4

1 pound flank steak
2 tablespoons dark soy sauce
1 tablespoon plus 1 teaspoon
    cornstarch
1 tablespoon dry sherry
2 tablespoons vegetable oil

1 tablespoon minced fresh
    ginger
1 scallion, minced
2 tablespoons oyster sauce
1 teaspoon sugar
½ teaspoon pepper

1. Cut flank steak in half lengthwise, and cut into ¼-inch-thick slices. In a bowl, toss meat with soy sauce, 2 teaspoons cornstarch, and sherry until evenly coated. Let stand 10 minutes.

2. In a wok, heat oil over high heat until just smoking. Add ginger and scallion and stir-fry until aromatic, about 10 seconds. Add beef in 3 or 4 batches and stir-fry until browned outside but still pink inside, about 3 minutes per batch.

3. In a small bowl, dissolve remaining 2 teaspoons cornstarch in ⅓ cup cold water. Return meat to wok. Add oyster sauce, sugar, pepper, and cornstarch mixture. Bring to a boil, stirring, until sauce thickens, about 2 minutes. Remove from heat and serve.

73   BEEF WITH GREEN PEPPERS
Prep: 15 minutes   Cook: 10 minutes   Serves: 4

1 pound flank steak
1 tablespoon minced fresh
    ginger
1 tablespoon dark soy sauce
1 tablespoon cornstarch
1 tablespoon dry sherry
1 teaspoon salt

½ teaspoon freshly ground
    black pepper
2 tablespoons vegetable oil
1 garlic clove, crushed
1 tablespoon minced scallion
1 green bell pepper, diced
2 teaspoons Asian sesame oil

1. Cut flank steak lengthwise into 2-inch-wide strips, then cut crosswise into thin slices about ¼ inch thick. In a medium bowl, toss meat with ginger, soy sauce, 2 teaspoons cornstarch, sherry, salt, and pepper. Let stand 10 minutes.

2. In a wok, heat oil over high heat until smoking. Add garlic and stir-fry 5 seconds, then discard. Add scallion and stir-fry 5 seconds, then add beef in 2 batches and stir-fry until lightly browned but still pink in center, about 3 minutes per batch. Return all beef to wok.

3. Add green pepper and stir-fry until just tender, about 3 minutes. In a small bowl, dissolve remaining 1 teaspoon cornstarch in ¼ cup cold water and add to wok. Bring to a simmer and cook, stirring, until thickened, about 1 minute.

4. Remove from heat. Drizzle with sesame oil and serve.

74   BEEF WITH ARROWHEAD TUBERS

Prep: 20 minutes   Cook: 5 minutes   Serves: 4 to 6

Arrowhead tubers, called *tse goo*, are much loved by the Cantonese. They look like round pale brown water chestnuts and have a starchy, crunchy, slightly sweet taste. Arrowhead tubers can be braised by themselves or used in soups, steamed dishes, or stir-fries. This is a very simple home-style stir-fry that is quick and easy. Try these tubers if you see them in Chinatown.

¾ **pound flank steak, cut into 2 x ¼-inch strips**
2 **tablespoons soy sauce**
1 **tablespoon dry sherry**
1 **tablespoon cornstarch**
½ **teaspoon pepper**
2 **tablespoons vegetable oil**

1 **teaspoon minced fresh ginger**
1 **scallion, minced**
1 **garlic clove, minced**
½ **pound arrowhead tubers, peeled and thinly sliced**
¼ **cup chicken broth**

1. In a small bowl, toss beef strips with soy sauce, sherry, cornstarch, and pepper.

2. In a wok, heat oil until just smoking. Add ginger, scallion, and garlic. Stir-fry over high heat until aromatic, about 30 seconds. Add meat and arrowhead tubers and stir-fry until beef loses its pink color, about 3 minutes.

3. Add broth and stir-fry 1 minute, tossing to mix well. Remove from heat and serve.

---

75   SLICED BEEF WITH TOMATO AND ONION

Prep: 10 minutes   Cook: 6 to 7 minutes   Serves: 2

This American-style dish is popular in Chinese homes. I like to make it in summer when tomatoes are sun-ripe and full of flavor.

½ **pound filet mignon**
2 **teaspoons cornstarch**
1 **tablespoon soy sauce**
2 **small ripe tomatoes**
2 **tablespoons vegetable oil**

1 **scallion, minced**
1 **teaspoon minced fresh ginger**
1 **small onion, sliced**
2 **teaspoons Asian sesame oil**

1. Cut beef into 2 x 1 x ¼-inch slices. In a small bowl, toss meat with cornstarch and soy sauce to coat evenly. Cut tomatoes into 6 wedges each.

2. In a wok, heat vegetable oil over high heat until smoking. Add scallion and ginger and stir-fry until aromatic, about 30 seconds. Add onion and stir-fry until onion is soft, about 2 minutes. Add beef and stir-fry until meat is just browned, about 3 minutes.

3. Add tomatoes and 1 tablespoon water; toss to mix and heat through, 30 to 60 seconds. Remove from heat. Add sesame oil, stir to blend, and serve.

76   GINGER BEEF

Prep: 15 minutes   Cook: 10 to 14 minutes   Serves: 4

This dish is best made with new young pink ginger, which is available in late spring or early fall. If using regular ginger, rinse quickly with cold water for a less sharp taste.

1 **pound flank steak**	½ **cup shredded fresh ginger,**
2 **tablespoons dark soy sauce**	**preferably new young**
1 **tablespoon dry sherry**	**ginger**
1 **tablespoon plus 1 teaspoon**	2 **tablespoons minced scallion**
cornstarch	2 **teaspoons Asian sesame oil**
2 **to 4 tablespoons vegetable**	
oil	

1. Cut flank steak lengthwise into 2-inch-wide strips. Cut strips crosswise into very thin slices.

2. In a medium bowl, mix together soy sauce, sherry, and 2 teaspoons cornstarch. Add sliced steak and toss to coat. Let stand 10 minutes.

3. Combine remaining 2 teaspoons cornstarch with ¼ cup cold water, stirring to mix well.

4. In a wok, heat 2 tablespoons vegetable oil over high heat until just smoking. Add one-fourth of steak and stir-fry over high heat until meat is browned outside but still pink inside, 2 to 3 minutes. Repeat with remaining steak in 3 more batches, adding more oil if meat begins to stick. When all meat is cooked, return to wok, add shredded ginger, and stir-fry 2 minutes. Add cornstarch mixture and bring to a boil, stirring until thickened.

5. Remove from heat. Add minced scallion and sesame oil. Toss to blend and serve.

77 STEAK KEW
Prep: 15 minutes   Stand: 15 minutes   Cook: 3 to 5 minutes
Serves: 4

Here is a great recipe for lovers of rare beef—filet mignon with mushrooms, Chinese style.

1 pound filet mignon	¼ pound snow peas
2 garlic cloves, minced	2 tablespoons oyster sauce
2 teaspoons minced fresh ginger	1 tablespoon soy sauce
2 scallions, minced	1 teaspoon sugar
6 dried Chinese mushrooms	1 tablespoon cornstarch
	2 tablespoons vegetable oil

1. Cut steak into 1½-inch cubes. Toss with minced garlic, ginger, and scallions. Let stand 15 minutes.

2. Meanwhile, soak black mushrooms in ⅓ cup warm water until soft, about 10 minutes. Drain, reserving water for sauce. Remove and discard stems.

3. Bring a medium saucepan of salted water to a boil. Add snow peas and cook until bright green, about 2 *seconds*. Drain and rinse under cold running water.

4. In a small bowl, combine oyster sauce, soy sauce, sugar, cornstarch, and reserved water from mushrooms. Blend thoroughly. Set sauce aside.

5. In a wok, heat oil over high heat until smoking. Add beef cubes and stir-fry until lightly browned outside but still rare inside, 2 to 3 minutes. Add mushrooms, snow peas, and sauce mixture. Return to a boil and cook, tossing to mix well, until sauce thickens, 1 to 2 minutes. Remove from heat and serve.

78 BEEF WITH BLACK BEAN SAUCE
Prep: 15 minutes   Cook: 4 minutes   Serves: 4

1 pound flank steak	2 garlic cloves, peeled and minced
2 tablespoons dark soy sauce	2 tablespoons vegetable oil
1 tablespoon plus 1 teaspoon cornstarch	2 tablespoons minced scallions
1 tablespoon dry sherry	1 tablespoon minced fresh ginger
2 tablespoons fermented black beans	2 teaspoons Asian sesame oil

1. Cut flank steak lengthwise into 2-inch-wide strips, then slice crosswise thinly, no thicker than ¼ inch.

2. In a bowl, mix soy sauce, 2 teaspoons cornstarch, and sherry. Add meat and mix well. Let stand 10 minutes.

3. Rinse black beans of excess salt. In a small bowl, mash black beans slightly. Add garlic and 1 tablespoon vegetable oil. In another small bowl, dissolve remaining 2 teaspoons cornstarch in ¼ cup cold water.

4. In a wok, heat remaining 1 tablespoon vegetable oil over high heat until just smoking. Add scallions and ginger and stir-fry until aromatic, 5 to 10 seconds. Add black bean and garlic mixture and stir-fry 10 seconds. Add meat and stir-fry until meat is cooked but still slightly pink in center, about 3 minutes.

5. Add cornstarch mixture to wok. Bring to a boil and cook until thickened, stirring constantly to blend.

6. Remove from heat. Drizzle with sesame oil. Stir to blend and serve.

---

79   ORANGE BEEF

Prep: 15 minutes   Cook: 14 minutes   Serves: 4

This beef dish is unusual in that the meat is cooked until it is well done and chewy. If you must have your beef pink, just cook the meat a shorter time.

1 **pound filet mignon**	1 **tablespoon slivered orange**
2 **tablespoons dark soy sauce**	**zest**
1 **tablespoon cornstarch**	2 **tablespoons dry sherry**
¼ **teaspoon pepper**	½ **cup orange juice**
¼ **cup plus 2 tablespoons**	1 **tablespoon hoisin sauce**
vegetable oil	2 **teaspoons Asian sesame oil**
4 **slices of fresh ginger,**	
slivered	

1. Slice beef and cut into thin strips about 2 x ¼ inch. In a medium bowl, toss meat with 1 tablespoon soy sauce, cornstarch, and pepper. Divide meat into 2 batches.

2. In a wok or large skillet, heat 3 tablespoons vegetable oil over high heat until just smoking. Add one batch of meat, spread out in a single layer, and cook until meat is browned, about 5 minutes. With a slotted spoon, remove beef to a plate. Add remaining oil and cook second batch of meat. Remove to a plate. Drain off all but 2 tablespoons oil from wok.

3. Return wok to heat. Add ginger and orange zest and stir-fry 1 minute. Add sherry, orange juice, remaining 1 tablespoon soy sauce, and hoisin sauce. Cook over medium-high heat to reduce slightly, about 3 minutes. Return meat to wok and toss to coat with sauce. Remove from heat. Add sesame oil, stir to blend, and serve.

80   HOISIN BEEF CUBES
Prep: 20 minutes   Cook: 6 to 7 minutes   Serves: 4

1 **pound filet mignon**	¼ **cup water chestnuts**
1 **tablespoon cornstarch**	¼ **cup diced red bell pepper**
2 **tablespoons vegetable oil**	3 **tablespoons hoisin sauce**
3 **garlic cloves, minced**	2 **tablespoons soy sauce**
1 **tablespoon minced fresh**	2 **teaspoons Asian sesame oil**
ginger	1 **scallion, minced**

1. Cut meat into 1-inch cubes. Toss with cornstarch to coat.

2. In a wok, heat vegetable oil over high heat until just smoking. Add garlic and ginger and stir-fry until aromatic, about 10 seconds. Add meat and stir-fry until lightly browned, about 3 minutes.

3. Add water chestnuts, red pepper, hoisin sauce, soy sauce, and ¼ cup water. Stir-fry, tossing to blend, 3 minutes.

4. Remove from heat, add sesame oil, and stir to blend. Sprinkle with minced scallion before serving.

81   GROUND BEEF AND PEAS
Prep: 5 minutes   Cook: 11 to 15 minutes   Serves: 2

I like to prepare this quick and easy dish on days when I have nothing special in the house. Kids love it served with white rice.

1 **pound ground beef**	1 **medium onion, minced**
2 **tablespoons dark soy sauce**	1 **(10-ounce) package frozen**
½ **teaspoon pepper**	**peas, thawed**
2 **tablespoons vegetable oil**	**Salt**

1. In a small bowl, combine beef with soy sauce and pepper. Mix to blend well.

2. In a large skillet, heat oil over medium-high heat. Add onion and cook until golden, 3 to 5 minutes.

3. Add beef and cook, stirring to break up lumps, until meat loses its pink color, 3 to 5 minutes. Stir in peas and 2 tablespoons water. Cook until heated through, about 5 minutes. Season with salt to taste.

82 STIR-FRIED BEEF

Prep: 15 minutes   Cook: 7 to 10 minutes   Serves: 4

1 pound flank steak
2 tablespoons dark soy
  sauce
1 tablespoon cornstarch
1 tablespoon dry sherry
3 tablespoons vegetable oil

¼ cup chicken broth
2 teaspoons Asian sesame oil
1 tablespoon minced fresh
  ginger
2 tablespoons minced
  scallions

1. Cut flank steak lengthwise into 3 strips. Cut strips crosswise thinly into ¼-inch-thick slices.

2. In a medium bowl, combine sliced steak with soy sauce, cornstarch, and sherry. Toss to mix well.

3. In a wok, heat 1 tablespoon vegetable oil over high heat until just smoking. Add one-third of beef and stir-fry until browned but still pink inside, 2 to 3 minutes. Repeat with remaining meat in 2 more batches until all meat is cooked, adding oil as needed.

4. Return all meat to wok; add broth and sesame oil. Bring to a boil and toss to blend. The meat should just be coated lightly.

5. Turn off heat. Add ginger and scallions, stir to mix, and serve.

83 LIVER WITH GARLIC CHIVES

Prep: 5 minutes   Cook: 6 minutes   Serves: 4

The pungent flavor of garlic chives balances the liver perfectly. This is a wonderfully tasty dish, even for people who think they hate liver.

1 pound calves' liver, thinly
  sliced about ¼ inch thick
4 ounces garlic chives
3 tablespoons vegetable oil

1 small onion, thinly sliced
2 tablespoons soy sauce
½ teaspoon sugar
½ teaspoon pepper

1. Cut liver into 2 x 1-inch pieces. Cut garlic chives into 2-inch lengths.

2. In a wok, heat oil over high heat until smoking. Add onion and cook, stirring, until wilted, about 3 minutes. Add liver and stir-fry, tossing constantly, until liver is browned outside and just pink in center, about 2 minutes. Add garlic chives, soy sauce, sugar, and pepper. Stir-fry 30 seconds to wilt chives. Serve at once.

84 PINEAPPLE DUCK IN GINGER FRUIT SAUCE

Prep: 20 minutes   Cook: 9½ minutes   Serves: 4

You can order skinless, boneless duck breasts from some butchers and from specialty food shops. If you remove the breast from a whole duck yourself, cut up the remainder of the bird to use in another recipe, such as Red-Braised Duck on page 76.

1 skinless, boneless duck breast (about 1½ pounds)	1 cup fresh pineapple chunks
2 tablespoons soy sauce	½ red bell pepper, cut into 1-inch squares
1 tablespoon cornstarch	¼ cup dry sherry
½ teaspoon pepper	¼ cup unsweetened pineapple juice
½ cup candied ginger	1 tablespoon cider vinegar
3 tablespoons vegetable oil	2 teaspoons Asian sesame oil
2 tablespoons minced fresh ginger	

1. Cut duck into thin strips about 2 x 1 x ¼ inch. In a medium bowl, toss duck strips with soy sauce, cornstarch, and pepper to coat evenly. Soak candied ginger in ½ cup warm water until soft, about 10 minutes. Drain, reserving soaking water. Cut candied ginger into thin shreds.

2. In a wok, heat vegetable oil over high heat until just smoking. Add minced fresh ginger and stir-fry until aromatic, about 30 seconds. Add duck and stir-fry until tender and cooked through, about 5 minutes.

3. Add pineapple, red pepper, and candied ginger shreds. Stir-fry 1 minute. Add sherry, pineapple juice, reserved ginger water, vinegar, and sesame oil. Bring to a boil and cook, stirring, until slightly thickened, about 3 minutes. Serve.

85 PORK CUBES IN SWEET SAUCE
Prep: 5 minutes   Cook: 8 to 9 minutes   Serves: 4

1 pound well-trimmed
   boneless pork loin or
   tenderloin
1 tablespoon cornstarch
½ teaspoon salt
¼ cup vegetable oil
2 tablespoons minced fresh
   ginger

2 scallions, minced
2 tablespoons soy sauce
¼ cup hoisin sauce
1 tablespoon yellow bean
   sauce
2 tablespoons dry sherry
1 tablespoon sugar

1. Cut pork into ½-inch cubes. In a medium bowl, toss meat with cornstarch and salt to coat evenly.

2. In a wok, heat oil over high heat until smoking. Add pork cubes and stir-fry until lightly browned outside with no trace of pink in center, about 5 minutes. Remove to a plate. Drain excess oil from wok, but do not wipe clean.

3. Return wok to heat. Add ginger and scallions and stir-fry until fragrant, about 30 seconds. Add soy sauce, hoisin sauce, bean sauce, sherry, sugar, and ¼ cup water. Bring to a boil, reduce heat, add pork cubes, and simmer until heated through, 2 to 3 minutes.

86 FIVE FRAGRANT SPICE PORK WITH ASPARAGUS
Prep: 10 minutes   Stand: 10 minutes   Cook: 6 to 7 minutes
Serves: 4

½ pound lean pork
2 tablespoons dark soy sauce
1 tablespoon dry sherry
1 teaspoon sugar
½ teaspoon salt

½ teaspoon Chinese five-spice
   powder
1 teaspoon cornstarch
1 cup 2-inch lengths
   asparagus
3 tablespoons vegetable oil

1. Cut pork into 2 x 1-inch strips. In a medium bowl, toss pork strips with soy sauce, sherry, sugar, salt, five-spice powder, and cornstarch until evenly coated. Let stand 10 minutes.

2. Bring a medium saucepan of salted water to a boil over high heat. Add asparagus and cook until just tender, 2 to 3 minutes. Drain and rinse under cold running water; drain well.

3. In a wok, heat oil over high heat until smoking. Add pork and stir-fry until just done, about 3 minutes. Add blanched asparagus and 2 tablespoons water. Continue to stir-fry until dish is heated through, about 1 minute.

87   SWEET AND SOUR PORK
Prep: 15 minutes   Cook: 11 minutes   Serves: 6

2 pounds well-trimmed pork
     butt (shoulder), cut into
     1-inch cubes
1 egg
2 tablespoons cornstarch
1 teaspoon salt
¼ teaspoon black pepper
2 cups vegetable oil

1 slice of fresh ginger
¼ cup diced green bell pepper
¼ cup diced red bell pepper
2 tablespoons soy sauce
¼ cup sugar
¼ cup cider vinegar
1 tablespoon ketchup

1. In a bowl, combine pork with egg, 1 tablespoon cornstarch, salt, and black pepper. Toss to coat evenly.

2. In a wok, heat oil to 350°F. Add pork cubes and cook until crisp and golden, about 7 minutes. Remove with a slotted spoon and drain on paper towels.

3. Pour off and discard all but 1½ tablespoons oil from wok. Return wok to high heat. Add ginger and stir-fry until aromatic, about 2 seconds; discard. Add green and red peppers and stir-fry 1 minute to wilt.

4. In a small bowl, combine soy sauce, sugar, vinegar, ketchup, remaining 1 tablespoon cornstarch, and ⅓ cup cold water. Add to wok. Bring to a boil and cook, stirring, until sauce thickens, about 2 minutes.

5. Return pork to wok and heat through, about 1 minute. Mound on serving platter and serve.

88   BEAN CURD WITH GROUND PORK
Prep: 15 minutes   Cook: 6 minutes   Serves: 4

½ pound ground pork
1 tablespoon dry white wine
1 tablespoon plus 1 teaspoon
     cornstarch
1 teaspoon salt
½ teaspoon pepper
1 pound firm bean curd

2 tablespoons vegetable oil
1 scallion, minced
¼ teaspoon crushed Szechuan
     pepper
2 teaspoons soy sauce
¼ teaspoon sugar
2 teaspoons Asian sesame oil

1. In a small bowl, mix ground pork with wine, 1 teaspoon cornstarch, salt, and pepper. Let stand 10 minutes. Cut bean curd into ½-inch cubes. In another bowl, mix remaining 1 tablespoon cornstarch with ¼ cup cold water.

2. In a wok, heat vegetable oil until just smoking. Add pork, scallion, and Szechuan pepper and stir-fry until pork loses its pink color, about 5 minutes. Add soy sauce, sugar, and diced bean curd. Whisk cornstarch and water mixture to blend and add to wok. Stir gently. Bring to a boil and cook until sauce thickens, about 1 minute. Drizzle with sesame oil. Serve hot.

89 PORK AND EGGPLANT WITH BLACK BEAN SAUCE

Prep: 15 minutes   Cook: 18½ minutes   Serves: 4

½ pound ground pork
1 tablespoon plus 2 teaspoons
  soy sauce
1 teaspoon cornstarch
½ pound Japanese eggplant
1 tablespoon fermented black
  beans
2 tablespoons vegetable oil

1 teaspoon minced fresh
  ginger
2 garlic cloves, minced
1 scallion, minced
½ cup chicken broth
1 teaspoon sugar
  Salt and pepper

1. In a small bowl, toss pork with 2 teaspoons soy sauce and cornstarch to mix well. Cut unpeeled eggplant crosswise on a diagonal into ½-inch-thick slices. Rinse black beans of excess salt and mash slightly.

2. In a wok, heat oil over high heat. Add ginger, garlic, scallion, and black beans and stir-fry 30 seconds. Add pork and stir-fry until meat loses its pink color, about 3 minutes.

3. Add eggplant and stir to mix. Add remaining 1 tablespoon soy sauce, chicken broth, and sugar. Bring to a boil, reduce heat, cover, and simmer until eggplant is tender, about 15 minutes. Season with salt and pepper to taste and serve.

90 PORK WITH JICAMA

Prep: 15 minutes   Cook: 3 to 5 minutes   Serves: 4

The crunchy texture of jicama is what makes it so popular in Chinese cooking.

1 boneless pork chop
  (about ½ pound)
2 teaspoons cornstarch
1 teaspoon dry sherry
1 teaspoon salt
½ teaspoon pepper
2 tablespoons vegetable oil
1 scallion, minced

1 teaspoon minced fresh
  ginger
2 cups matchstick-size pieces
  jicama
2 tablespoons soy sauce
¼ cup chicken broth
½ teaspoon sugar
1 teaspoon Asian sesame oil

1. Cut pork into matchstick-size pieces. In a small bowl, toss pork with cornstarch, sherry, salt, and pepper to coat evenly.

2. In a wok, heat vegetable oil over high heat. Add scallion and ginger and stir-fry 5 seconds. Add pork and cook until meat is no longer pink, 3 to 5 minutes.

3. Add jicama, soy sauce, chicken broth, and sugar. Stir-fry until jicama is warmed through, stirring to mix well. Remove from heat, stir in sesame oil, and serve.

91 SLICED PORK WITH GREEN BEANS
Prep: 10 minutes   Cook: 8½ minutes   Serves: 4

½ pound green beans
1 pound boneless pork chops
1 tablespoon cornstarch
½ teaspoon salt
2 tablespoons vegetable oil
1 teaspoon minced fresh
   ginger

2 garlic cloves, minced
2 tablespoons soy sauce
2 teaspoons yellow bean
   sauce
2 tablespoons dry sherry
1 teaspoon sugar

1. In a large saucepan of boiling salted water, cook green beans until crisp-tender, about 3 minutes. Drain and rinse under cold running water; drain well.

2. Slice pork into strips about 1½ x ½ x ¼ inch thick. In a bowl, toss pork with cornstarch and salt to coat evenly.

3. In a wok, heat oil over high heat until smoking. Add ginger and garlic. Stir-fry 30 seconds. Add pork strips and cook until pork loses its pink color, about 3 minutes.

4. Add soy sauce, bean sauce, sherry, sugar, and 2 tablespoons water. Cook, stirring, until almost dry, about 2 minutes. Add string beans, toss to mix well and heat through, and serve.

92 SHREDDED PORK, BAMBOO SHOOTS, AND GREEN PEPPER IN BLACK BEAN SAUCE
Prep: 20 minutes   Cook: 6 minutes   Serves: 4

1 pound boneless pork loin
1 tablespoon cornstarch
1 tablespoon dry white wine
¼ teaspoon pepper
1 tablespoon fermented black
   beans
2 garlic cloves, minced
3 tablespoons vegetable oil
3 slices of fresh ginger,
   minced

¼ cup sliced bamboo shoots,
   finely shredded
¼ cup finely shredded green
   bell pepper
2 tablespoons soy sauce
2 tablespoons Chinese black
   vinegar or cider vinegar
2 tablespoons dry sherry
2 teaspoons sugar
   Salt

1. Slice pork and cut into matchstick-size shreds. In a bowl, toss pork with cornstarch, wine, and pepper. Rinse black beans and mash lightly. Mix with minced garlic.

2. In a wok, heat 1 tablespoon oil over high heat until just smoking. Add pork and stir-fry until cooked, about 3 minutes. Remove to a plate.

3. Return wok to heat, add remaining oil and ginger, and stir-fry 30 seconds. Add black bean mixture and stir-fry until aromatic, about 30 seconds. Add bamboo shoots and green pepper and stir-fry 1 minute. Add soy sauce, vinegar, sherry, and sugar. Cook 30 seconds. Return meat to wok and toss to heat through. Season to taste with salt and serve.

---

93   HONEYED HAM STEAK
Prep: 5 minutes   Cook: 19 minutes   Serves: 4

Although this dish does not sound Chinese, it is quite popular in Hong Kong homes, as its flavor is reminiscent of the famous Yunnan honeyed ham. You can try doing this with a slice of country or Smithfield ham, but in that case, be sure to soak the ham to remove excess salt. Serve the ham thinly sliced on a bed of greens such as spinach, accompanied by white rice.

¼ cup chopped fresh ginger	1 tablespoon soy sauce
1 tablespoon honey	1 tablespoon dark brown
1 ham steak, about ½ inch	sugar
thick (¾ pound)	1 tablespoon dry sherry
2 teaspoons vegetable oil	

1. In a small saucepan, combine ginger with 1 cup water. Bring to a boil, reduce heat, and simmer until water has reduced by half and is infused with ginger, about 10 minutes. Strain and discard ginger. Mix ginger water with honey. Stir until dissolved.

2. Trim ham steak of excess fat. In a skillet, heat oil over medium-high heat. Add ham steak and cook about 2 minutes on each side to brown lightly.

3. Add soy sauce, ginger-honey water, brown sugar, and sherry. Bring to a boil, reduce heat, and simmer until liquid is reduced to a syrupy thickness so it will coat ham, about 5 minutes. Slice ham thinly before serving.

94 LAMB WITH SCALLIONS

Prep: 15 minutes   Stand: 20 minutes   Cook: 13½ minutes
Serves: 6

1½ pounds boneless leg of lamb, trimmed of fat	8 scallions
2 tablespoons soy sauce	4 slices of fresh ginger, shredded
1 tablespoon cornstarch	¼ cup dry sherry
3 garlic cloves, minced	Salt
¼ cup vegetable oil	

1. Thinly slice lamb, then cut into slivers. In a medium bowl, toss meat with soy sauce, cornstarch, garlic, and 1 tablespoon oil. Let stand 20 minutes. Cut scallions into thin shreds 2 inches long.

2. In a wok, heat remaining oil until just smoking. Add lamb in 2 batches and stir-fry over high heat until cooked, about 5 minutes per batch. Remove to a plate.

3. Return wok to medium heat. Add scallions and ginger and stir-fry 30 seconds. Return meat to wok, add sherry, and toss to blend. Cook until sherry evaporates, 3 minutes. Season with salt to taste and serve.

95 SHRIMP WITH BLACK BEAN SAUCE

Prep: 20 minutes   Cook: 4½ to 5½ minutes   Serves: 4

1 pound medium shrimp,
        shelled and deveined
	1 tablespoon minced fresh
	        ginger

1 egg white	¼ cup diced red bell pepper
3½ tablespoons vegetable oil	¼ cup diced green bell pepper
1 tablespoon fermented black beans	2 tablespoons soy sauce
2 teaspoons cornstarch	2 tablespoons dry white wine
3 garlic cloves, minced	1 scallion, minced

1. In a medium bowl, toss shrimp with egg white and ½ tablespoon oil. Rinse black beans with cold water to remove excess salt. Mash coarsely. Dissolve cornstarch in 2 tablespoons cold water.

2. In a wok, heat remaining 3 tablespoons oil over high heat until smoking. Add garlic and ginger, then add black beans, red pepper, and green pepper. Stir-fry until vegetables are slightly softened, about 30 seconds. Add shrimp and stir-fry until shrimp turn pink, about 3 minutes. Add soy sauce and wine.

3. Stir dissolved cornstarch and add to wok. Bring to a boil and cook, stirring, until thickened, 1 to 2 minutes. Remove from heat, sprinkle with scallion, and serve.

96   DEEP-FRIED SHRIMP IN SHELLS
Prep: 10 minutes   Cook: 4 to 6 minutes   Serves: 4

Traditionally, these crisp shrimp are popped whole into the mouth, shells and all. The deep-frying makes the shells crunchy enough to eat and, of course, the Chinese love the heads as well. Try them this way if shrimp with heads are available.

1 **pound medium shrimp with shells (and heads, if available)**	1 **teaspoon Wild Pepper Mix (page 25)**
3 **cups vegetable oil**	2 **cups shredded lettuce**

1. Rinse shrimp under cold running water. Drain and dry well with paper towels.

2. In a wok, heat oil to 375°F, or until a bread cube turns brown in 1 minute. Deep-fry shrimp until they just turn pink, 3 to 5 minutes. Remove and drain well on paper towels.

3. Pour off oil from wok, but do not clean wok. Return shrimp to wok and toss with wild pepper mix until well blended. Serve on bed of shredded lettuce.

97   RED GARLIC SHRIMP
Prep: 10 minutes   Cook: 4½ to 6½ minutes   Serves: 4

¼ **cup plus 2 tablespoons vegetable oil**	2 **tablespoons dry white wine**
1 **pound large shrimp, shelled and deveined**	1 **teaspoon sugar**
6 **garlic cloves, minced**	2 **tablespoons chicken broth or water**
1 **tablespoon tomato puree**	3 **scallions, minced**
1 **tablespoon soy sauce**	**Salt and pepper**

1. In a wok, heat oil over high heat until beginning to smoke. Add shrimp and stir-fry until shrimp turn pink and opaque throughout, 3 to 5 minutes. Remove to a plate.

2. Add garlic to wok and stir-fry, tossing constantly, until aromatic, about 30 seconds. Add tomato puree, soy sauce, wine, sugar, and chicken broth. Reduce heat to medium. Cook, stirring, 1 minute. Return shrimp to wok. Toss to mix well. Remove from heat, stir in scallions, season to taste with salt and pepper, and serve.

98   SHERRIED SHRIMP WITH SNOW PEAS AND WATER CHESTNUTS

Prep: 15 minutes   Cook: 5 minutes   Serves: 4

1 pound medium shrimp,
   shelled and deveined
2 tablespoons dry sherry
1 tablespoon soy sauce
1 teaspoon cornstarch
2 cups snow peas
   (about ¼ pound)

2 tablespoons vegetable oil
1 scallion, minced
½ cup water chestnuts
½ teaspoon sugar
½ teaspoon salt
¼ teaspoon pepper

1. In a small bowl, toss shrimp with sherry, soy sauce, and cornstarch to coat evenly. Bring a saucepan of salted water to a boil. Add snow peas and cook until bright green, about 5 seconds. Drain and rinse under cold running water; drain well.

2. In a wok, heat oil over high heat until just smoking. Add scallion and stir-fry until softened and fragrant, about 30 seconds. Add shrimp and stir-fry until shrimp turns pink, about 3 minutes.

3. Add any remaining marinade water from shrimp bowl, whole chestnuts, and snow peas. Sprinkle with sugar, salt, and pepper. Stir-fry 1 minute, tossing to mix, and serve.

99   VELVET SHRIMP WITH CASHEWS

Prep: 10 minutes   Stand: 30 minutes   Cook: 3 to 4 minutes
Serves: 4

1 pound medium shrimp,
   shelled and deveined
1 egg white
2 teaspoons cornstarch
2 tablespoons vegetable oil
1 teaspoon minced fresh
   ginger

1 scallion, minced
1 garlic clove, minced
2 tablespoons sherry
1 tablespoon soy sauce
½ teaspoon pepper
¼ cup chicken broth
½ cup dry-roasted cashews

1. In a small bowl, combine shrimp with egg white and cornstarch. Cover and let stand 30 minutes.

2. In a wok, heat oil over medium-high heat until just smoking. Add ginger, scallion, and garlic. Stir-fry until aromatic, about 10 seconds. Add shrimp and stir-fry until shrimp just turn pink, about 2 to 3 minutes. Add sherry, soy sauce, pepper, chicken broth, and cashews. Continue stir-frying 1 minute longer, tossing to blend well, and serve.

100 SHRIMP OMELET WITH CHINESE BROWN SAUCE

Prep: 25 minutes   Cook: 6 to 9 minutes   Serves: 6

1 pound medium shrimp,
   shelled and deveined
6 eggs
1 teaspoon salt
½ teaspoon pepper
3 tablespoons vegetable oil
1 teaspoon minced fresh
   ginger

2 scallions, minced
½ cup minced celery
½ cup diced red bell pepper
2 cups bean sprouts
   Chinese Brown Sauce
   (recipe follows)

1. Coarsely chop shrimp. In a medium bowl, beat eggs with salt and pepper.

2. In a wok, heat oil over high heat. Add minced ginger and scallions and stir-fry until aromatic, about 10 seconds. Add celery and red bell pepper and stir-fry 1 minute. Add shrimp and cook until shrimp turn pink, 2 to 3 minutes. Add bean sprouts and toss to blend well.

3. Reduce heat to medium. Add beaten eggs and cook until eggs are set and bottom of omelet is lightly browned, 3 to 5 minutes. Turn omelet over and brown other side, if desired. Remove to a serving platter. Pour brown sauce over omelet and serve.

101 CHINESE BROWN SAUCE

Prep: 5 minutes   Cook: 2 to 3 minutes   Makes: 1 cup

1 cup Chinese Chicken Stock
   (page 27) or reduced-
   sodium canned broth
1 teaspoon dark soy sauce

2 teaspoons dry sherry
1 tablespoon cornstarch
1 teaspoon Asian sesame oil

In a small saucepan, combine chicken stock, soy sauce, sherry, cornstarch, and sesame oil. Bring to a boil and cook, stirring until sauce thickens, about 2 to 3 minutes.

102   SHRIMP AND SCALLOPS WITH PEAS
Prep: 15 minutes   Cook: 6½ minutes   Serves: 4

½ **pound medium shrimp,**
    shelled and deveined
2 **egg whites**
3 **tablespoons vegetable oil**
½ **pound sea scallops**
1 **scallion, minced**
2 **tablespoons soy sauce**

2 **tablespoons dry sherry**
2 **tablespoons chicken broth**
    or water
1 **(10-ounce) package frozen**
    tiny peas, thawed
  Salt and pepper

1. In a small bowl, toss shrimp with 1 egg white and 1 teaspoon oil. In another small bowl, toss scallops with remaining egg white and 1 teaspoon oil.

2. In a wok, heat remaining oil over high heat. Add scallion and stir-fry 30 seconds. Add shrimp and stir-fry until shrimp just begin to turn pink, about 2 minutes. Add scallops and continue to stir-fry until scallops turn white and opaque, about 2 minutes longer.

3. Add soy sauce, sherry, chicken broth, and peas to wok. Cook, stirring, 2 minutes, tossing to mix and heat through. Season with salt and pepper to taste and serve.

103   CLAMS WITH BLACK BEAN SAUCE
Prep: 20 minutes   Cook: 7 to 10 minutes   Serves: 4

If you like, you may substitute mussels for the clams. They should be cleaned in the same way, but the mussels must also be bearded, and their shells scrubbed more thoroughly. Sometimes, about 2 ounces of ground pork is also added and stir-fried with the black beans and garlic, making this a true Cantonese-style sauce.

3 **dozen littleneck clams, in**
    shells
1 **tablespoon fermented black**
    beans

2 **garlic cloves, minced**
2 **tablespoons vegetable oil**
1 **teaspoon soy sauce**

1. Wash and scrub clams under cold water. Drain in a colander. Rinse black beans to remove excess salt. In a small bowl, mash black beans coarsely. Add minced garlic and mix well.

2. In a wok, heat oil until smoking, add black beans and garlic, and stir-fry until garlic is softened and fragrant, about 15 seconds. Add clams, soy sauce, and ¼ cup water. Toss to mix and coat clams, reduce heat to medium, cover wok, and cook until clams open, 7 to 10 minutes. Discard any unopened clams and serve at once.

104   CRABMEAT IN A CLOUD
Prep: 15 minutes   Cook: 4 minutes   Serves: 4 to 6

½ pound crabmeat
4 dried Chinese mushrooms
¼ cup sliced bamboo shoots, shredded
¼ cup bean sprouts
2 scallions, cut into 2-inch pieces

8 egg whites
Pinch of salt
2 tablespoons vegetable oil
1 slice of fresh ginger
2 teaspoons soy sauce
½ teaspoon white pepper

1. Pick over crabmeat to remove any cartilage or shell. Soak dried mushrooms in a bowl of warm water until soft, about 10 minutes. Drain and discard stems. Cut caps into thin strips. In a bowl, combine mushrooms, bamboo shoots, bean sprouts, and scallions.

2. In a large bowl, beat egg whites with salt until stiff.

3. In a wok, heat oil over medium heat until just smoking. Add ginger and stir-fry until lightly browned, about 2 minutes; discard. Add mushrooms, bamboo shoots, bean sprouts, and scallions to wok. Stir-fry 5 seconds. Add crabmeat and toss to mix and heat through. Flavor with soy sauce and pepper.

4. Add egg whites and cook, gently folding into crab mixture, leaving some mounds of egg white to form "clouds," 2 minutes. Remove from heat and serve.

105   CRABMEAT OMELET
Prep: 20 minutes   Cook: 6½ minutes   Serves: 2

Chinese omelets are flat and pancake-shaped, like an Italian frittata.

½ pound fresh crabmeat
4 dried Chinese mushrooms
⅓ cup water chestnuts
¼ cup sliced bamboo shoots
4 eggs
½ teaspoon salt

¼ teaspoon pepper
2 tablespoons vegetable oil
½ teaspoon minced fresh ginger
2 scallions, minced
½ cup bean sprouts

1. Pick over crabmeat to remove any cartilage or shell. Soak mushrooms in a bowl of warm water until soft, about 15 minutes. Remove stems and discard. Cut caps into thin strips. Coarsely chop water chestnuts and bamboo shoots. Beat eggs with salt and pepper.

2. In a wok, heat oil over high heat until just smoking. Add minced ginger and scallions and stir-fry until fragrant, about 10 seconds. Add crabmeat, mushrooms, water chestnuts, and bamboo shoots and stir-fry 3 minutes, tossing to blend well. Add bean sprouts and toss to mix.

3. Reduce heat to medium. Pour beaten eggs over crabmeat mixture and cook over moderate heat until omelet is set, about 3 minutes. Serve at once.

106   LOBSTER WITH SCALLIONS AND GINGER

Prep: 20 minutes   Cook: 10 minutes   Serves: 4

You'll probably want your fish market to cut up the lobster as described in step 1. If so, purchase it as shortly before cooking as possible.

2 live lobsters, 1½ to 2 pounds each
1 cup vegetable oil
8 scallions, cut into 2-inch pieces
½ cup shredded fresh ginger
3 tablespoons soy sauce
3 tablespoons dry sherry
½ cup chicken broth
1 tablespoon cornstarch dissolved in ¼ cup cold water
2 teaspoons Asian sesame oil

1. Kill lobsters by inserting knife between head and body and severing spinal cord. Remove head, tail, and claws and set aside. Remove and discard sac near eyes and cut off and discard feelers. Section lobster parts into 2-inch chunks, leaving head intact.

2. In a wok, heat vegetable oil over high heat. Add 1 tablespoon each of scallions and ginger. Stir-fry 1 minute to flavor oil. Add lobster pieces and cook until lobster turns red, about 3 minutes, turning to be sure that all parts are cooked. Remove lobster and discard oil, but do not clean wok.

3. Return lobster to wok, add remaining scallions and ginger, soy sauce, sherry, and chicken broth. Cover and cook over high heat 5 minutes, turning lobster pieces occasionally. With a slotted spoon, remove lobster to a platter and keep warm.

4. Return wok to high heat and boil to reduce sauce slightly. Stir dissolved cornstarch into sauce and return to a boil. Cook, stirring, until sauce thickens, about 1 minute. Sprinkle sesame oil over sauce and pour over lobster to serve.

107   SAUTEED SEA SCALLOPS

Prep: 10 minutes   Cook: 9 to 10 minutes   Serves: 2

½ pound sea scallops
¼ cup vegetable oil
3 scallions—1 whole, 2 cut into 2-inch pieces
2 cups Vegetable Stock (page 28), Chinese Chicken Stock (page 27), or reduced-sodium canned chicken broth
1 tablespoon rice vinegar
2 teaspoons soy sauce
1 tablespoon dry sherry
1 teaspoon cornstarch
¼ cup sliced cucumber
¼ cup sliced carrot
¼ cup sliced bamboo shoots
8 slices of fresh ginger

1. If scallops are very large, cut in half horizontally.

2. In a wok, heat 2 tablespoons oil over high heat. Add whole scallion and cook until bright green, about 2 seconds. Add stock and vinegar and bring to a boil. Reduce to a simmer and cook 5 minutes. Discard scallion.

3. Add scallops and simmer until they turn opaque and are just done, 30 to 45 seconds. With a slotted spoon, remove scallops to a plate. Strain stock and reserve ¼ cup. Add soy sauce, sherry, and cornstarch and stir to blend. Set sauce aside.

4. Wipe out wok with paper towels and return to high heat. Add remaining 2 tablespoons oil and heat to smoking. Add cucumber, carrot, bamboo shoots, scallion pieces, and ginger. Stir-fry until vegetables are tender but still crisp, about 2 minutes. Add reserved sauce to wok. Stir to blend well, return to a boil, and cook until sauce thickens, about 1 to 2 minutes. Add scallops, toss to heat and mix well, and serve.

108   FISH FILLETS IN WINE SAUCE
Prep: 15 minutes   Cook: 14 to 18 minutes   Serves: 4

2 pounds fish fillets (such as cod, bass, tilefish, bluefish)	1 garlic clove, minced
1 teaspoon salt	1 scallion, minced
¼ teaspoon pepper	2 teaspoons minced fresh ginger
½ cup dry white wine	½ cup chicken broth
¾ cup flour	2 tablespoons soy sauce
2 eggs, beaten	2 teaspoons cornstarch
½ cup vegetable oil	2 teaspoons Asian sesame oil

1. Remove any small bones from fish. Cut fillets into 2 x 3-inch pieces. Season with salt and pepper. Sprinkle 2 tablespoons wine over fish. Let stand 10 minutes.

2. Pour half of flour onto a plate. Dip fish pieces in flour, shake off excess, and dip in egg. Coat again with remaining flour.

3. In a large skillet, heat 3 tablespoons vegetable oil over medium-high heat. Add half of fish and cook, turning once, until golden on both sides and just opaque throughout, 3 to 4 minutes. Do not crowd pan. Remove to a plate lined with paper towels. Repeat, adding more oil, until all fish is cooked. Pour out oil and wipe wok with paper towels.

4. Return wok to high heat. Add 1 tablespoon oil, garlic, scallion, and ginger and stir-fry until aromatic, about 10 seconds. Add remaining wine, broth, and soy sauce. Simmer 5 minutes.

5. In a small bowl, dissolve cornstarch in 1 tablespoon cold water and add to wok. Bring to a boil and cook, stirring, until sauce thickens, about 1 minute. Add sesame oil, then gently slide fish pieces into wok. Simmer gently until fish is heated through, 1 to 2 minutes. Serve at once.

109 SQUID RINGS WITH PEPPER STRIPS
Prep: 10 minutes   Cook: 3 minutes   Serves: 4

2 pounds fresh squid
1 teaspoon salt
3 tablespoons vegetable oil
½ cup red bell pepper strips
½ cup green bell pepper strips
1 fresh jalapeño pepper,
      seeded and thinly sliced
3 slices of fresh ginger,
      shredded

3 scallions, cut into 2-inch
      lengths
3 tablespoons soy sauce
3 tablespoons dry white wine
1 tablespoon fish sauce (*nuoc
      nam*)
1 tablespoon fresh lime juice
¼ cup cilantro leaves

1. Clean squid and cut into rings. Toss with salt.

2. In a wok, heat oil over high heat until smoking. Add squid, bell pepper strips, jalapeño rings, ginger, and scallions. Stir-fry, tossing constantly, until squid turns white and opaque, about 2 minutes. Remove to a plate.

3. Return wok to high heat. Add soy sauce, wine, fish sauce, and lime juice; stir to mix. Return squid and vegetables to wok. Toss to heat through and blend, about 30 seconds. Remove from heat. Stir in cilantro leaves and serve.

Chapter 4

Chinese Stews and Braises

We usually think of Chinese food as fast stir-fried dishes. However, in this chapter we have recipes for braises and stews that take longer to cook.

You will notice that many of the dishes are called "red-braised." In Chinese culture, red is the color of happiness and good fortune, so whenever possible we like to call things red. In cooking, braises and stews that have dark soy sauce as an ingredient are called red, even though they usually look dark brown. Because these dishes involve long cooking, they are costly in terms of time; it is traditional to include at least one red-cooked dish in banquets and for formal dinners.

Not all the dishes in this chapter are red, however. Those that do not use dark soy sauce are simply braises or stews, and while they are equally delicious, they do not have a festive connotation. When offered as everyday food, braises and stews are often served as a single main course, with white rice, and perhaps a vegetable, to make up a complete meal. These recipes can also be integrated into a typical multidish Chinese menu to provide diversity from stir-frying.

I think you will find this chapter very useful, because while many of the dishes require long cooking, the preparation time is usually minimal. Best of all, many of these recipes can be cooked ahead of time, sometimes even frozen, and reheated.

110   EMPRESS CHICKEN
Prep: 15 minutes   Cook: 45 to 46 minutes   Serves: 6

To reduce the fat in this dish, remove the chicken skin before cooking. If you do so, fry the chicken only 3 minutes before adding the liquids.

6 dried Chinese mushrooms	½ cup dry sherry
2 tablespoons vegetable oil	½ cup dark soy sauce
2 teaspoons minced fresh ginger	1 tablespoon brown sugar
¼ cup minced scallions	1 cup sliced bamboo shoots
1 (3-pound) chicken, cut up into bite-size pieces	1 tablespoon cornstarch

1. In a small bowl, soak dried mushrooms in ½ cup warm water until soft, about 10 minutes. Drain, reserving mushroom water. Remove and discard mushroom stems.

2. In a large saucepan, heat oil over medium heat. Add ginger and scallions and stir-fry until aromatic, about 30 seconds. Add chicken and cook, turning, until light golden, about 5 minutes. Add sherry and cook 3 minutes. Add soy sauce, brown sugar, bamboo shoots, reserved mushrooms, and reserved mushroom water. Cover and simmer over low heat until chicken is tender, about 35 minutes. (Dish may be prepared up to this point up to 2 days ahead and refrigerated or frozen.)

3. Just before serving, in a small bowl, mix cornstarch with ¼ cup cold water. Add to chicken, bring to a boil, and cook, stirring, until sauce thickens, 1 to 2 minutes.

111   CHICKEN CURRY
Prep: 20 minutes   Cook: 38½ minutes   Serves: 4

The Chinese have adopted curry from Malaysia. They love this mildly sweet, coconut-flavored curry because it goes so well with rice.

3 pounds cut-up chicken or chicken parts	3 tablespoons curry powder
3 tablespoons vegetable oil	2 cups unsweetened coconut milk
2 garlic cloves, minced	1 cup Chinese Chicken Stock (page 27) or reduced-sodium canned broth
1 scallion, minced	
1 slice of fresh ginger, minced	
1 medium onion, minced	Salt and pepper

1. Heat a dry wok over medium heat. Add chicken pieces skin side down and cook, turning once until lightly browned, about 5 minutes. Remove to plate and discard any fat chicken has thrown off.

2. Add oil, garlic, scallion, ginger, and onion to wok and stir-fry over medium heat until onion is softened, about 3 minutes. Add curry powder and stir-fry until aromatic, about 30 seconds; be careful not to burn. Return chicken to wok. Add coconut milk and chicken stock. Bring to a boil, reduce heat to low, and simmer until chicken is tender and sauce is reduced and thickened, about 30 minutes. If curry dries out too much during cooking, add 1 or 2 tablespoons of water. Season with salt and pepper to taste.

---

112   LEMON CHICKEN
Prep: 10 minutes   Chill: 3 hours   Cook: 24 to 33 minutes   Serves: 6

This dish is very popular in Hong Kong, where the use of liquor, such as gin, in a marinade is also common. The fresh lemon flavor marries well with the chicken. Strips of lemon zest can be used as a garnish.

3 **pounds chicken thighs**	¼ **cup lemon juice**
1 **teaspoon salt**	⅓ **cup chicken broth**
2 **tablespoons dark soy sauce**	1 **teaspoon sugar**
3 **tablespoons gin**	1 **tablespoon Asian sesame oil**
¼ **cup minced fresh ginger**	1 **teaspoon cornstarch**
3 **tablespoons oil**	**Salt**
2 **teaspoons lemon zest**	

1. If desired, debone chicken thighs, but leave skin on. Combine salt, soy sauce, and gin and rub all over chicken pieces. Cover and marinate in refrigerator 3 hours.

2. In a small saucepan, combine minced ginger with ¼ cup water. Simmer until water is reduced by half and tastes strongly of ginger, about 3 to 4 minutes. Strain and discard ginger.

3. In a wok, heat ginger water and oil. Remove chicken pieces from marinade; reserve marinade. Add chicken pieces to wok and cook over medium heat until browned, 5 to 7 minutes. Add reserved marinade, lemon zest, lemon juice, chicken broth, sugar, and sesame oil. Bring to a boil, reduce to a simmer, and cook chicken until tender, 15 to 20 minutes. Remove to a platter and keep warm.

4. In a small bowl, dissolve cornstarch in 2 tablespoons cold water. Add to sauce, return to a boil, and cook, stirring, until sauce thickens, 1 to 2 minutes. Season with salt to taste, pour over chicken, and serve.

113   DISTILLED CHICKEN
Prep: 20 minutes   Cook: 1½ to 2 hours   Serves: 6

Traditionally, this dish from Yunnan is cooked in a special casserole with a funnel in the middle. When the steam condenses, it drips back into the dish, forming the clear liquid and succulent chicken that is characteristic of this recipe. If you do not have a Yunnan pot, a flameproof casserole can be used. Improvise by propping up the cover to trap more steam than normal.

6 dried Chinese mushrooms
2 ounces Smithfield ham
3 pounds chicken breasts, cut into bite-size pieces
⅓ cup dry sherry

4 slices of fresh ginger, shredded
2 scallions, minced
1 teaspoon salt

1. In a small bowl, soak mushrooms in ½ cup warm water until soft, about 15 minutes. Remove mushrooms; discard liquid. Cut off and discard stems. Cut ham into matchstick pieces.

2. Place chicken in a Yunnan pot or flameproof casserole. Arrange mushrooms over chicken pieces. Sprinkle ham around chicken. Add sherry, ginger, scallions, and salt.

3. Cover casserole and place in a wok. Fill wok with enough water to cover bottom of casserole by 2 inches. Bring water to a boil, reduce heat to low, and simmer until chicken is very tender and a flavorful broth has been distilled into casserole dish. This should take about 1½ to 2 hours. Replenish water in wok as necessary.

4. Skim off fat and serve chicken directly from casserole.

114   OYSTER-FLAVORED DRUMSTICKS
Prep: 10 minutes   Cook: 22 minutes   Serves: 6

2 tablespoons vegetable oil
2 teaspoons minced fresh ginger
1 garlic clove, minced
1 scallion, minced
2 pounds chicken drumsticks

2 tablespoons oyster sauce
2 tablespoons dry sherry
1 tablespoon dark soy sauce
½ cup chicken broth
2 teaspoons cornstarch

1. In a wok, heat oil over high heat. Add ginger, garlic, and scallion and stir-fry until aromatic, about 30 seconds. Add drumsticks, oyster sauce, sherry, soy sauce, and chicken broth. Bring to a boil, reduce heat, and simmer until chicken is tender, about 20 minutes.

2. In a small bowl, blend cornstarch with 2 tablespoons cold water. Stir into wok, return to a boil, and cook, stirring until sauce thickens and just coats drumsticks, 1 to 2 minutes. Serve at once.

115 DUCK BRAISED WITH BAMBOO SHOOTS, CHESTNUTS, AND MUSHROOMS

Prep: 20 minutes   Cook: 1¼ to 1½ hours   Serves: 6

1 (4- to 5-pound) duck
6 dried Chinese mushrooms
1 cinnamon stick
½ teaspoon whole cloves
½ teaspoon fennel seeds
1 star anise
1 teaspoon Szechuan
  peppercorns
1 piece of dried tangerine peel

2 scallions, minced
2 tablespoons minced fresh
  ginger
½ cup sliced bamboo shoots
1 cup peeled chestnuts
½ cup dry sherry
¼ cup mushroom soy sauce
¼ cup light soy sauce

1. Trim duck of excess fat and cut into bite-size pieces. Soak mushrooms in warm water until soft, about 15 minutes. Drain, reserving liquid. Remove and discard stems. In a piece of cheesecloth, wrap cinnamon stick, cloves, fennel seeds, star anise, Szechuan peppercorns, and tangerine peel to form a spice bag.

2. In a large heavy saucepan or flameproof casserole, cook pieces of duck skin side down, over medium-high heat, in batches without crowding until browned, about 10 minutes per batch. Remove to a plate.

3. Pour off all but 1 tablespoon fat from pan and return to medium heat. Add minced scallions and ginger. Cook until aromatic, about 30 seconds. Return duck to saucepan. Add mushroom caps, reserved mushroom liquid, bamboo shoots, chestnuts, sherry, mushroom soy sauce, light soy sauce, spice bag, and enough water to cover duck. Bring to a boil, reduce heat, cover, and simmer until duck is tender, 45 minutes to 1 hour. Skim off any fat and serve.

116   RED-BRAISED DUCK

Prep: 10 minutes   Cook: 52 to 70 minutes   Serves: 4 to 6

1 (4½- to 5-pound) duck
1 tablespoon vegetable oil
1 tablespoon Szechuan peppercorns
1 whole star anise
1 cinnamon stick
2 small pieces of dried tangerine peel
½ teaspoon fennel seeds
2 cups dark soy sauce

1 cup unsalted Chinese Chicken Stock (page 00) or reduced-sodium canned broth
¼ cup dry sherry
2 slices of fresh ginger
4 scallions, cut into 2-inch pieces
¼ cup brown sugar

1. Trim all excess fat from duck. In a wok, heat oil over medium-high heat. Add duck and cook, turning carefully, until browned all over, 7 to 10 minutes. Remove duck and drain off fat from wok.

2. Tie Szechuan peppercorns, star anise, cinnamon stick, tangerine peel, and fennel seeds in a piece of cheesecloth to make a spice bag.

3. Return duck to wok. Add soy sauce, stock, sherry, ginger, scallions, brown sugar, and spice bag. Bring liquid to a simmer, cover, and braise duck until tender and juices run clear when thigh is pricked, 45 minutes to 1 hour.

4. Remove duck from sauce. Skim fat from top of sauce in wok. Cut wings, legs, and thighs from duck. Remove breast meat from bone and slice. Arrange duck pieces on a platter and serve with a little sauce drizzled over duck.

117   BRAISED DUCK WITH LEEKS

Prep: 15 minutes   Cook: 1 hour 9 minutes to 1 hour 12 minutes
Serves: 4

1 (4- to 5-pound) duck
½ cup dry sherry
1 cup dark soy sauce
2 cups Chinese Chicken Stock (page 27) or reduced-sodium canned broth
¼ cup brown sugar

2 scallions
4 slices of fresh ginger
1 teaspoon Chinese five-spice powder
½ teaspoon coriander seeds
8 leeks, white part only
2 teaspoons cornstarch

1. Trim duck of excess fat and cut into serving pieces. Heat a wok over medium heat, add duck, a few pieces at a time, and cook, turning, until brown, 5 to 7 minutes. With a slotted spoon, transfer duck pieces to large saucepan or flameproof casserole.

2. Add sherry, bring to a boil, and cook 3 minutes. Add soy sauce, chicken stock, brown sugar, scallions, ginger, five-spice powder, and coriander seeds. Return to a boil, reduce heat to low, cover, and simmer duck 40 minutes.

3. Meanwhile, cut leeks in half lengthwise and rinse well. Add to duck and cook until leeks are tender, about 20 minutes longer.

4. Remove duck with leeks to a serving platter. Skim off fat from sauce. Strain 1 cup sauce into a small saucepan. In a small bowl, dissolve cornstarch in 2 tablespoons cold water. Add to sauce, bring to a boil, and cook, stirring, until sauce thickens, 1 to 2 minutes. Spoon sauce over duck and serve.

118 RED-BRAISED QUAIL
Prep: 15 minutes   Cook: 28 to 29 minutes   Serves: 4

Quail are available with the carcass removed, leaving only the wings and leg bones; these are known as semiboned. Be sure to order them from the butcher, as they are a bother to bone yourself. For extra flavor, you can substitute the cooking liquid from Pressed Anise Beef (page 134) for the soy sauce and spices in this recipe.

8 **Chinese (Napa) cabbage leaves**	1 **tablespoon Szechuan peppercorns**
⅓ **pound salt pork, cut into 8 slices**	1 **cup mushroom soy sauce**
8 **semiboned quail**	1 **tablespoon brown sugar**
2 **tablespoons star anise**	1 **teaspoon cornstarch**
1 **cinnamon stick**	1 **tablespoon brandy**

1. In a large saucepan of boiling water, cook cabbage leaves until wilted, about 2 minutes. Cool in a bowl of ice water. Wrap each piece of salt pork in a cabbage leaf, roll up, and place inside quail. Cross quail legs and tuck into cavity to make a neat shape.

2. Make a spice bag by wrapping star anise, cinnamon stick, and Szechuan peppercorns in cheesecloth. In a wok or large flameproof casserole, combine spice bag, soy sauce, brown sugar, and 4 cups water. Bring to a boil, reduce heat, cover, and simmer 10 minutes. Add quail and cook until tender, about 15 minutes. Remove to a serving platter and cover to keep warm.

3. In a small saucepan, combine ½ cup cooking liquid from wok with cornstarch and brandy. Bring to a boil and cook, stirring, until thickened, 1 to 2 minutes. Spoon sauce over quail and serve.

119 RED-BRAISED BEEF
Prep: 10 minutes   Cook: 45 minutes to 1 hour   Serves: 6

This dish improves if prepared ahead of time and reheated. It also freezes beautifully.

1 tablespoon vegetable oil	2 scallions, minced
3 pounds beef chuck, cut into 1½-inch cubes	½ cup dry sherry
	3 tablespoons dark soy sauce
1 tablespoon minced fresh ginger	1 whole star anise
	1 tablespoon sugar

1. In a saucepan, heat oil over high heat until just smoking and brown beef cubes. Add minced ginger and scallions and stir-fry until aromatic, about 30 seconds.

2. Add sherry, soy sauce, star anise, sugar, and 1 cup of water. Bring to a boil, reduce heat to low, and simmer until meat is tender when pricked with a fork, 45 minutes to 1 hour. There should be about one-third of cooking juices left. If there is more, remove meat and boil liquid over high heat to reduce. Serve meat in juices.

---

120 LONG-SIMMERED BEEF
Prep: 10 minutes   Cook: 2½ to 2¾ hours   Serves: 6

This is a dish beloved by the Chinese for its healthy properties and simplicity. Try it once, and you'll be hooked too!

3 pounds brisket or shin of beef	½ teaspoon whole black peppercorns
2 leeks	6 carrots, peeled
4 slices of fresh ginger	6 turnips, peeled and quartered
2 scallions	½ cup Wild Pepper Mix (page 25)
4 cups Chinese Chicken Stock (page 27) or reduced-sodium canned broth	

1. Cut beef into 4 large pieces. Trim leeks, saving a few green tops, and rinse well. Place beef in a large flameproof casserole. Add leek greens, ginger, scallions, chicken stock, black peppercorns, 1 carrot, and enough water to cover. Bring to a simmer.

2. Remove casserole from heat and set it in a wok one-third full of water. Bring water in wok to a boil, reduce heat to low, and simmer for 2 hours. Refill water in wok as necessary.

3. Meanwhile, cut carrots on a diagonal into pieces about 1 inch thick. Slice white parts of leek. Add carrots, leeks, and turnips to casserole and cook until beef and vegetables are tender, 30 to 45 minutes.

4. Remove meat from broth, slice, and arrange on a platter with vegetables. Skim off fat from broth. Spoon a little broth over meat. Serve with side dishes of wild pepper mix for dipping meat into. Remaining broth should be served in individual bowls.

121 YANG CHOW LION'S HEAD
Prep: 20 minutes   Cook: 1 hour 10 minutes   Serves: 6

This is one of the more popular festive "red-simmered" dishes, which signify good fortune to the Chinese. Often prepared in the home for the Chinese New Year, lion's head improves if made ahead of time and reheated.

4 dried Chinese mushrooms	2 teaspoons cornstarch
1 tablespoon tree ears	½ teaspoon granulated sugar
¼ cup bamboo shoots	1 teaspoon salt
1½ pounds coarsely ground pork	1 teaspoon pepper
2 scallions, finely minced	2 tablespoons vegetable oil
2 tablespoons minced fresh ginger	4 cups shredded Chinese (Napa) cabbage
1 egg, lightly beaten	1 cup Chinese Chicken Stock (page 27) or reduced-sodium canned broth
2 tablespoons dark soy sauce	
2 tablespoons dry sherry	2 teaspoons brown sugar

1. In separate bowls, soak mushrooms and tree ears in warm water until soft, about 15 minutes. Drain and stem mushrooms, reserving liquid. Drain tree ears and discard liquid. Coarsely chop mushrooms, tree ears, and bamboo shoots.

2. In a large bowl, mix ground pork, chopped mushrooms, tree ears, and bamboo shoots. Add scallions, ginger, egg, 1 tablespoon of soy sauce, 1 tablespoon of sherry, 1 teaspoon of cornstarch, granulated sugar, salt, and pepper. Form into 4 large meatballs.

3. In a wok, heat 1 tablespoon oil over medium heat. Add meatballs and cook, turning gently, until brown all over, about 5 minutes. Remove to a large flameproof casserole with a cover. These are the lion's heads.

4. Heat remaining tablespoon of oil in wok, add cabbage, and stir-fry over medium-high heat until just wilted, about 3 minutes. Spread over meatballs. This is the lion's mane.

5. In a small bowl, mix chicken stock with brown sugar and remaining 1 tablespoon each soy sauce and sherry. Pour over lion's heads, bring to a simmer, and cook 1 hour.

6. In a small bowl, mix remaining teaspoon of cornstarch with ¼ cup cold water. Uncover casserole and stir in cornstarch mixture. Return to a boil and cook, stirring, until thickened, 1 to 2 minutes. This dish may be prepared 1 day ahead and reheated. Everyone should be served a piece of meatball with cabbage and sauce.

122   SIMMERED PORK WITH LOTUS ROOT
Prep: 10 minutes   Cook: 2 hours 10 minutes   Serves: 6

This simple brothy dish is considered good for your health. We would have it at least once every lotus root season.

3 **pounds pork butt or belly**
2 **pounds lotus root, peeled**
1 **scallion**
2 **slices of fresh ginger**

10 **peppercorns**
2 **tablespoons pearl barley**
   Soy Vinegar Dip (page 18)

1. In a large saucepan or stockpot, place pork and lotus root. Cover with cold water. Bring to a boil, reduce heat to low, and simmer, skimming off any scum that rises to the top, 10 minutes.

2. Add scallion, ginger, and peppercorns. Continue to simmer on low heat 1 hour. Add barley and simmer 1 hour longer, or until pork is easily pierced with a fork.

3. To serve, remove pork and lotus root from broth. Slice and arrange on a platter. Serve with soy vinegar dip on the side. Skim fat off broth and ladle into individual bowls.

123   RED BEAN CURD, PORK, AND TARO
Prep: 15 minutes   Cook: 48 to 50 minutes   Serves: 6

This is my mother's recipe for a quick, easy home-style dish. It can be prepared a day in advance and reheated. The red bean curd gives the dish a distinctive taste. Serve with white rice.

2 **garlic cloves, minced**
2 **tablespoons red bean curd**
   (nam yue)
2 **tablespoons vegetable oil**
3 **pounds pork butt**
   (shoulder), trimmed and
   cut into 2-inch cubes

¼ **cup dry sherry**
2 **pounds taro, peeled and cut**
   into 1½-inch chunks
   Salt and pepper

1. In a small bowl, mash garlic with red bean curd.

2. In a wok or large flameproof casserole, heat oil until just smoking. Add pork and cook over medium heat, turning, until browned, 5 to 7 minutes. Add garlic and red bean curd mixture. Stir-fry, tossing to coat pork, about 1 minute. Add sherry and cook 2 minutes.

3. Add taro and enough water to cover meat and vegetables. Bring to a boil, reduce heat to low, cover, and cook until meat is tender and taro can be pierced with a fork, about 40 minutes. Season with salt and pepper to taste.

124 BRAISED BEAN THREADS, PORK, AND VEGETABLES

Prep: 20 minutes   Cook: 30 minutes   Serves: 6

6 ounces bean threads
1 tablespoon tree ears
6 dried Chinese mushrooms
2 tablespoons vegetable oil
½ pound boneless pork, cut into thin strips
2 tablespoons mushroom soy sauce
2 tablespoons dry sherry
1 cup Chinese Chicken Stock (page 27) or reduced-sodium canned broth

3 medium carrots, peeled and cut diagonally into ½-inch-thick slices
4 medium turnips, peeled and quartered
1 pound bok choy, cut into 1-inch pieces
2 leeks (white and tender green), sliced
1 teaspoon pepper
Salt

1. In separate bowls, soak bean threads and tree ears in warm water until soft, about 15 minutes. Drain and discard water. In another bowl, soak mushrooms in ½ cup warm water until soft. Drain, reserving liquid. Remove and discard stems.

2. In a wok, heat oil over medium-high heat. Add pork and stir-fry until pork loses its pink color, about 3 minutes. Add soy sauce, sherry, mushroom liquid, and stock. Bring to a boil, simmer 1 minute, and add mushrooms, tree ears, carrots, turnips, bok choy, and leeks. Simmer 5 minutes.

3. Add bean threads and return to a boil. Reduce heat, cover, and simmer until vegetables are soft, about 20 minutes. Add pepper and season with salt to taste. Remove from heat and spoon into a large tureen to serve.

125 OXTAIL STEW

Prep: 20 minutes   Cook: 3½ to 4 hours   Serves: 6

4 pounds oxtails, trimmed
⅓ cup soy sauce
2 cups Rich Meat Stock (page 28) or canned beef broth
6 slices of fresh ginger
1 tablespoon tomato paste
1 tablespoon oyster sauce

⅓ cup dry sherry
1 teaspoon sugar
2 tablespoons Szechuan peppercorns, crushed
1 teaspoon coriander seeds
¼ cup cilantro leaves
2 tablespoons cider vinegar

1. In a large flameproof casserole, place oxtails in one layer. Add soy sauce, stock, ginger, tomato paste, oyster sauce, sherry, sugar, Szechuan peppercorns, and coriander seeds. Bring to a boil, reduce heat to low, cover, and simmer gently until oxtails are tender and falling apart, about 3½ to 4 hours. Stir occasionally and turn meat once after 1½ hours.

2. Skim off fat from surface. Stir in cilantro leaves and vinegar.

126   RED-BRAISED FISH STEAKS

Prep: 10 minutes   Cook: 17 to 20 minutes   Serves: 6

1 cup dark soy sauce
½ cup dry sherry
2 tablespoons sugar
6 scallions, cut into 2-inch
     pieces
6 slices of fresh ginger, finely
     shredded

1 teaspoon finely shredded
     fresh orange zest
2 teaspoons Szechuan
     peppercorns
6 fish steaks (halibut, cod, or
     swordfish), cut 1 inch
     thick

1. In a large skillet, combine soy sauce, sherry, sugar, half of scallions and shredded ginger, orange zest, Szechuan peppercorns, and 1 cup of water. Bring to a boil, reduce heat to low, and simmer, covered, 10 minutes.

2. Add fish steaks, return to a simmer, cover, and cook over medium-low heat until fish is opaque throughout, 7 to 10 minutes. With a slotted spoon, transfer fish to a serving platter. Sprinkle remaining scallions and ginger over fish. Drizzle with a little sauce.

127   BEAN CURD CASSEROLE

Prep: 20 minutes   Cook: 32 minutes   Serves: 6

2 pounds firm bean curd
2 ounces bean threads
10 dried Chinese mushrooms
1 tablespoon vegetable oil
6 slices of fresh ginger
4 ounces ham, cut into
     matchstick pieces
1 cup sliced bamboo shoots

2 carrots, peeled and sliced
½ pound bok choy, washed
     and shredded lengthwise
4 scallions, cut into 2-inch
     pieces
2 tablespoons dry sherry
⅓ cup soy sauce
   Salt and pepper

1. Drain bean curd and cut into 2-inch squares. Soak bean threads in warm water until soft, about 15 minutes. Drain and cut into 2-inch lengths. Soak mushrooms in 1 cup warm water until soft, about 15 minutes. Drain, reserving water. Remove and discard stems.

2. In a casserole, heat oil over medium heat. Add ginger slices and cook until light brown, about 1 minute. Add ham and cook 1 minute. Add bean curd, mushrooms, mushroom water, bean threads, bamboo shoots, carrots, bok choy, scallions, sherry, soy sauce, and enough water to cover. Bring to a boil, reduce heat, cover, and simmer 30 minutes. Season with salt and pepper to taste.

128 STEWED LAMB WITH GARLIC, GINGER, AND VEGETABLES

Prep: 25 minutes   Cook: 2 hours   Serves: 6

2 pounds boneless leg of lamb, well trimmed
6 tablespoons vegetable oil
1 medium onion, quartered
5 garlic cloves, crushed
6 slices of fresh ginger, minced
¼ cup dark soy sauce
2 tablespoons yellow bean sauce
⅓ cup dry sherry
2 teaspoons sugar
½ teaspoon pepper
6 carrots
4 leeks
2 small red potatoes

1. Cut lamb into 2-inch cubes. In a wok or large flameproof casserole, heat oil over high heat until just smoking. Add half of lamb and stir-fry until browned, 5 to 7 minutes. Remove to a plate. Repeat with remaining lamb.

2. Pour off all but 2 tablespoons of oil. Return to heat, add onion, and stir-fry over medium heat until wilted, about 3 minutes. Add garlic and ginger and stir-fry until aromatic, about 30 seconds. Return meat to wok, add soy sauce, bean sauce, sherry, sugar, pepper, and 1 cup water. Stir to blend. Bring to a boil, reduce heat to low, and simmer until meat is tender, about 1½ hours.

3. Meanwhile, peel carrots and slice diagonally. Clean leeks and slice. Cut potatoes into quarters. Add vegetables to stew, return to a simmer, and cook until soft, about 30 minutes.

Chapter 5

Especially Hot and Spicy

I loved writing this chapter, because like so many Americans today, I definitely love hot food. And whether you call it Hunan or Szechuan, Chinese cooking is filled with great spicy dishes. Although fire-breathers could plan a whole menu from the recipes in this chapter, they are meant to be used together with a selection from elsewhere in the book to make up interesting menus with balanced flavors.

In Chinese cooking, the "hot" comes from a variety of ingredients: fresh and dried hot chile peppers—whole and crushed into flakes; chile paste, often labeled "Szechuan chile paste with garlic"; cayenne; and hot oil, or Chile Oil (see recipe on page 23). Fresh ginger, too, contributes a zippy bite.

Because this chapter is intended for people who really enjoy hot food, the quantities of chile, cayenne, or chile paste called for will definitely give the dishes a bite. If you like your food a little milder, don't hesitate to cut down on any of the spicy ingredients in a recipe. You will still find the dish enticingly delicious.

---

129 HOT AND SPICY CHICKEN DRUMSTICKS
Prep: 10 minutes   Cook: 21 to 27 minutes   Serves: 6 to 8

2 tablespoons vegetable oil	24 chicken drumsticks
2 teaspoons minced fresh ginger	¼ cup dark soy sauce
2 garlic cloves, minced	2 tablespoons dry sherry
2 scallions, minced	1 teaspoon black pepper
6 fresh or dried hot chile peppers	1 teaspoon sugar
	1 teaspoon cornstarch

1. In a wok or large flameproof casserole, bring oil to smoking point over medium heat. Add ginger, garlic, scallions, and chile peppers. Stir-fry until aromatic, about 30 seconds. Add chicken drumsticks, soy sauce, sherry, black pepper, and sugar. Stir to mix well. Bring to a boil, reduce heat, cover, and simmer until chicken is tender, 20 to 25 minutes. With tongs remove drumsticks to a platter.

2. In a small bowl, blend cornstarch with 2 tablespoons cold water. Add to sauce in wok, bring to a boil, and cook, stirring, until sauce thickens, 1 to 2 minutes. Pour over chicken drumsticks and serve.

130 SHREDDED COLD CHICKEN WITH HOT PEANUT DRESSING

Prep: 20 minutes   Cook: 6 to 7 minutes   Serves: 4 to 6

1 cold White Poached
   Chicken (page 182)
3 tablespoons chunky peanut
   butter
3 tablespoons vegetable oil
½ to 1 teaspoon cayenne
1 teaspoon minced fresh
   ginger

1 garlic clove, minced
1 scallion, minced
3 tablespoons Asian sesame
   oil
1 tablespoon cider vinegar
2 tablespoons soy sauce
6 Boston lettuce leaves

1. Skin and bone chicken. With your fingers, shred chicken meat and set aside. In a small bowl, combine peanut butter with ¼ cup warm water. Stir to blend well.

2. In a small saucepan, combine vegetable oil, cayenne, ginger, garlic, and scallion. Cook over low heat until hot and aromatic, 1 to 2 minutes. Stir in peanut butter mixture, sesame oil, vinegar, and soy sauce. Simmer 5 minutes.

3. In a mixing bowl, toss shredded chicken with hot dressing. Remove to a platter and serve on lettuce leaves.

131 MA LA CHICKEN

Prep: 15 minutes   Stand: 10 minutes   Cook: 9 to 14 minutes
Serves: 4

"Ma la" means spicy hot, and this dish lives up to its name. Serve with plenty of white rice.

1 pound skinless, boneless
   chicken breasts, cut into
   1-inch cubes
1 egg white
1 tablespoon dry sherry
½ cup chicken broth
2 tablespoons soy sauce
2 teaspoons cider vinegar
½ teaspoon cayenne
½ teaspoon black pepper
2 teaspoons cornstarch

½ cup vegetable oil
2 garlic cloves, minced
1 scallion, minced
2 teaspoons minced fresh
   ginger
1 medium green bell pepper,
   cut into ½-inch dice
6 small fresh red or green
   chile peppers, seeded and
   thinly sliced

1. In a small bowl, toss chicken with egg white and sherry. Let stand 10 minutes.

2. In another bowl, mix together chicken broth, soy sauce, vinegar, cayenne, black pepper, and cornstarch.

3. In a wok, bring oil to smoking point over medium heat. Add chicken pieces and cook until chicken is white throughout, 3 to 5 minutes. Remove with a slotted spoon and drain on paper towels. Repeat. Pour off all but 2 tablespoons of oil.

4. Return wok to high heat. Add garlic, scallion, and ginger and stir-fry until aromatic, about 10 seconds. Add green pepper and sliced chiles and stir-fry until slightly softened, 1 to 2 minutes. Whisk liquid ingredients and add to wok. Add chicken pieces, return to a boil, and cook, stirring, until sauce has thickened and coats chicken pieces, about 2 minutes.

---

132 SPICY CHICKEN WITH PEANUTS AND BAMBOO SHOOTS

Prep: 20 minutes   Cook: 6 to 8 minutes   Serves: 4

1 **pound skinless, boneless chicken breasts**	¼ **cup peanuts**
1 **egg white**	¼ **cup sliced bamboo shoots, cut into matchsticks**
1 **tablespoon plus 1 teaspoon cornstarch**	½ **cup chicken broth**
3 **tablespoons vegetable oil**	1 **tablespoon dry sherry**
2 **scallions, minced**	1 **tablespoon soy sauce**
1 **tablespoon minced fresh ginger**	1 **teaspoon sugar**
4 **garlic cloves, minced**	1 **tablespoon chile paste**
	2 **tablespoons Asian sesame oil**

1. Cut chicken into ½-inch cubes. In a small bowl, blend egg white, 2 teaspoons cornstarch, and 2 teaspoons water. Add chicken and toss to coat. Let stand 10 minutes.

2. In a wok, heat vegetable oil over high heat. Add scallions, ginger, and garlic. Stir-fry until aromatic, about 30 seconds. Add chicken cubes and stir-fry until chicken turns white, 3 to 5 minutes. Add peanuts and stir-fry 1 minute, being careful not to burn them. Add bamboo shoots, chicken broth, sherry, soy sauce, sugar, and chile paste.

3. In a small bowl, blend remaining 2 teaspoons cornstarch with 2 tablespoons cold water. Add to wok, bring to a boil, and cook, stirring, until sauce thickens, 1 to 2 minutes. Toss to blend well. Remove from heat, stir in sesame oil, and serve.

133 SPICY CHICKEN WITH TANGERINE PEEL

Prep: 20 minutes   Stand: 20 minutes   Cook: 5 to 8 minutes
Serves: 4

1 skinless, boneless chicken breast, cut into thin shreds
2 tablespoons cornstarch
½ teaspoon salt
3 pieces dried tangerine peel
3 tablespoons vegetable oil
3 slices of fresh ginger, minced
2 garlic cloves, minced

2 scallions, minced
3 small dried hot red peppers
2 tablespoons soy sauce
1 tablespoon dry sherry
1 tablespoon cider vinegar
2 teaspoons sugar
¼ cup chicken broth
1 teaspoon shredded orange zest

1. In a bowl, toss chicken with 1 tablespoon of cornstarch and salt. Let stand 20 minutes. Meanwhile, soak tangerine peel in ¼ cup hot water until soft, about 15 minutes. Remove peel and reserve water. Cut tangerine peel into fine shreds.

2. In a wok, heat oil over medium heat. Add ginger, garlic, scallions, hot red peppers, and shredded tangerine peel. Stir-fry until aromatic, about 30 seconds. Add chicken and stir-fry until chicken turns white, 3 to 5 minutes. Add soy sauce, sherry, vinegar, sugar, chicken broth, orange zest, and reserved tangerine water.

3. In a small bowl, blend remaining tablespoon of cornstarch with ¼ cup cold water. Add to wok, bring to a boil, and cook, stirring, until sauce thickens, 1 to 2 minutes. Remove to a serving platter.

134 CHICKEN CUBES WITH CASHEWS AND CHILES

Prep: 10 minutes   Cook: 8 to 9 minutes   Serves: 4

1 pound skinless, boneless chicken breast, cut into ½-inch cubes
1 egg white
1 tablespoon cornstarch
¼ cup vegetable oil
¼ cup cashew nuts
4 small dried hot red peppers

1 teaspoon minced fresh ginger
1 scallion, minced
2 teaspoons chile paste
1 tablespoon soy sauce
1 tablespoon dry sherry
¼ cup chicken broth

1. In a small bowl, toss chicken cubes with egg white, 1 teaspoon cornstarch, and 1 teaspoon oil.

2. In a wok, heat remaining oil until just smoking. Add cashews and hot red peppers and stir-fry 1 minute. With a slotted spoon, remove to a plate. Add chicken and cook over medium heat, stirring often, until chicken is just white throughout, about 3 minutes. Remove from wok.

3. Add ginger and scallion to wok and stir-fry over medium heat until aromatic, about 30 seconds. Add chile paste, soy sauce, sherry, and chicken broth. Reduce heat to low and simmer 2 minutes.

4. In a small bowl, blend remaining 2 teaspoons cornstarch with 2 tablespoons water. Add to wok, bring to a boil, and cook, stirring, until sauce thickens, 1 to 2 minutes. Return chicken, cashews, and hot red peppers to wok. Stir-fry over medium heat until hot. Remove to a serving plate.

135 HUNAN BRAISED BEEF ON A BED OF SPINACH

Prep: 20 minutes   Cook: 53 to 68 minutes   Serves: 6

3 tablespoons vegetable oil	1 whole star anise
1 tablespoon minced fresh ginger	1 cinnamon stick
	5 small dried hot red peppers
3 pounds beef chuck, cut into 1½-inch cubes	½ cup dry sherry
	3 tablespoons dark soy sauce
2 scallions, cut into 2-inch lengths	4 pounds fresh spinach

1. In a wok, heat 1 tablespoon of oil over high heat until just smoking. Add minced ginger and stir-fry until aromatic, about 10 seconds. Add beef cubes and cook, stirring, until lightly browned, about 5 minutes. Remove beef to a large saucepan or flameproof casserole.

2. Add scallions, star anise, cinnamon stick, hot red peppers, sherry, soy sauce, and 1 cup water. Bring to a boil, reduce heat to low, and simmer until beef is tender and sauce has reduced by two-thirds, 45 minutes to 1 hour.

3. Meanwhile, wash and dry spinach in a salad spinner. When beef is done, heat remaining 2 tablespoons oil in a wok over high heat and stir-fry spinach until just wilted, about 3 minutes.

4. Remove spinach to a serving platter, pour beef and sauce over bed of spinach, and serve.

136 SPICY BLACK BEAN BEEF WITH ASPARAGUS

Prep: 15 minutes   Cook: 7 to 8 minutes   Serves: 4 to 6

1   pound asparagus
2   pounds flank steak
1   tablespoon dark soy sauce
2   teaspoons dry sherry
1   tablespoon cornstarch
2   tablespoons fermented
     black beans
2   garlic cloves, minced
3   tablespoons vegetable oil

2   teaspoons minced fresh
     ginger
2   scallions, minced
¼   cup Rich Meat Stock (page
     28) or canned beef broth
1   tablespoon oyster sauce
1   teaspoon sugar
2   teaspoons Asian sesame oil

1. Cut asparagus on a diagonal into 2-inch pieces. Cut flank steak lengthwise into 3-inch-wide strips and cut strips crosswise into ¼-inch slices. In a bowl, toss steak with soy sauce, sherry, and cornstarch. Rinse black beans to remove excess salt. In a small bowl, mash beans with garlic and 2 teaspoons of vegetable oil.

2. In a wok, heat remaining vegetable oil over medium heat. Add asparagus and stir-fry until tender but still crisp, about 3 minutes. With a slotted spoon, remove to a plate.

3. Return wok to high heat until smoking. Add ginger, scallions, and black bean mixture. Stir-fry until aromatic, about 30 seconds. Add beef and cook until browned around the edges but still pink inside, 2 to 3 minutes.

4. Add stock, oyster sauce, sugar, and asparagus. Stir-fry over high heat until sauce is hot and blended, about 1 minute. Remove from heat. Sprinkle with sesame oil and serve.

137 HOT AND SPICY SHREDDED BEEF

Prep: 15 minutes   Cook: 8 to 10 minutes   Serves: 4

1   pound fillet of beef
1   tablespoon cornstarch
1   teaspoon salt
¼   cup plus 2 tablespoons
     vegetable oil
4   slices of fresh ginger, finely
     shredded
2   carrots, peeled and finely
     shredded

2   scallions, cut into 2-inch
     pieces
2   tablespoons soy sauce
1   tablespoon hoisin sauce
1   tablespoon yellow bean
     sauce
2   tablespoons chile paste
2   tablespoons dry sherry
2   teaspoons sugar
2   teaspoons Asian sesame oil

1. Slice beef into ¼-inch-thick slices. Cut slices into 2 x ¼-inch shreds. In a bowl, toss beef shreds with cornstarch, salt, and 1 tablespoon oil.

2. In a wok or skillet, heat remaining oil. Add beef shreds, spreading them over surface in a single layer. Cook over medium heat, stirring, until meat is well browned, 5 to 7 minutes. With a slotted spoon, remove meat to plate. Discard all but 2 tablespoons oil.

3. Return wok to medium-high heat. Add ginger, carrots, and scallions and stir-fry 1 minute. Return beef to wok and stir-fry, tossing to mix well, 1 minute.

4. Add soy sauce, hoisin sauce, bean sauce, chile paste, sherry, and sugar. Continue to stir-fry, tossing, to blend sauce with meat and vegetables, about 1 minute. Remove from heat. Add sesame oil, stir to blend, and serve.

138   DOUBLE-COOKED SZECHUAN PORK
Prep: 15 minutes   Cook: 39 minutes   Serves: 4 to 6

Traditionally, belly pork is used for this recipe, but as butt or shoulder has less fat and is more readily available, I have used this cut.

2 **pounds pork butt (shoulder), with some fat left on**	1 **tablespoon dry sherry**
2 **tablespoons fermented black beans**	2 **tablespoons soy sauce**
	1 **tablespoon chile paste**
3 **tablespoons vegetable oil**	1 **tablespoon hoisin sauce**
3 **garlic cloves, minced**	½ **teaspoon tomato paste or ketchup**
3 **scallions, minced**	2 **teaspoons sugar**

1. In a large saucepan, cover pork with water, bring to a boil, reduce heat, and simmer for 30 minutes. Drain and cut meat into ¼-inch-thick slices. Cut slices into 2 x 3-inch pieces.

2. Rinse black beans to remove excess salt. Place in a small bowl and mash lightly.

3. In a wok or large skillet, heat 2 tablespoons of oil over medium heat. Add pork pieces in a single layer. Brown 2 minutes on each side. With a slotted spoon, remove to a plate. Discard oil and wipe out wok with paper towels.

4. Return wok to heat, add remaining 1 tablespoon oil, and heat to smoking. Add garlic, scallions, and black beans. Stir-fry over medium heat until aromatic, about 30 seconds. Add sherry, soy sauce, chile paste, hoisin sauce, tomato paste, sugar, and ¼ cup water. Bring to a boil and cook 3 minutes.

5. Return pork to wok and cook until pork is heated through, turning to coat well, about 2 minutes. Remove to a serving platter.

139 PORK CUBES IN HOT SWEET SAUCE
Prep: 15 minutes   Cook: 8 to 15 minutes   Serves: 4

1 pound boneless pork loin	2 teaspoons minced fresh
2 teaspoons cornstarch	ginger
½ teaspoon salt	2 tablespoons soy sauce
¾ teaspoon pepper	1 tablespoon hoisin sauce
3 tablespoons vegetable oil	1 tablespoon chile paste
2 garlic cloves, minced	2 tablespoons dry white wine
	Pinch of sugar

1. Trim pork and cut into 1-inch cubes. In a bowl, toss pork with cornstarch, salt, and pepper.

2. In a wok, heat oil until just smoking. Add pork and stir-fry over high heat until meat loses its pink color, 3 to 5 minutes. Remove to a plate. Add garlic and ginger to wok and stir-fry until aromatic, about 10 seconds. Add soy sauce, hoisin sauce, chile paste, wine, sugar, and ¼ cup water. Bring to a boil.

3. Return pork to wok. Reduce heat to low and simmer until pork is tender, 5 to 10 minutes.

140 HOT AND SPICY STEWED PORK
Prep: 20 minutes   Cook: 37 to 42 minutes   Serves: 6

6 dried Chinese mushrooms	½ cup sliced water chestnuts
2 tablespoons vegetable oil	2 tablespoons dry sherry
1 tablespoon minced fresh	½ cup mushroom soy sauce
ginger	½ teaspoon cayenne
2 scallions, minced	6 small dried hot red peppers
3 pounds pork butt	1 tablespoon sugar
(shoulder), trimmed and	1 teaspoon black pepper
cut into 2-inch cubes	1 cinnamon stick
½ cup sliced bamboo shoots	

1. In a small bowl, soak mushrooms in ½ cup warm water until soft, about 15 minutes. Drain, reserving liquid. Remove stems and discard. Cut caps into quarters.

2. In a wok or saucepan, heat oil until smoking. Add ginger and scallions. Stir-fry over medium heat until aromatic, about 30 seconds. Add pork cubes and cook until brown, about 5 minutes.

3. Add mushroom caps, bamboo shoots, and water chestnuts. Stir-fry 1 minute. Add sherry, mushroom soy sauce, cayenne, hot red peppers, sugar, black pepper, cinnamon stick, and reserved mushroom liquid. Bring to a boil, reduce heat to low, cover, and simmer until pork is fork-tender, 30 to 35 minutes.

141 VELVET PORK SLICES IN CHILE SAUCE

Prep: 15 minutes   Stand: 15 minutes   Cook: 8 to 9 minutes
Serves: 4

1 pound pork tenderloin
1 egg white
2 teaspoons cornstarch
½ teaspoon salt
3 tablespoons vegetable oil
1 cup snow peas (about
   2 ounces)
1 tablespoon minced fresh
   ginger

1 tablespoon chile paste
2 teaspoons soy sauce
1 tablespoon yellow bean
   sauce
¼ cup chicken broth
2 teaspoons sugar
1 tablespoon Asian sesame oil

1. Cut pork tenderloin into ¼-inch-thick slices. In a medium bowl, toss pork slices with egg white, cornstarch, 1 teaspoon salt, and 1 teaspoon vegetable oil to coat evenly. Let stand at room temperature 15 minutes.

2. Meanwhile, bring a medium saucepan of salted water to a boil. Add snow peas and cook just until they turn bright green, about 5 *seconds.* Drain and rinse under cold running water.

3. In a wok, heat remaining vegetable oil to smoking. Add ginger and stir-fry over medium-high heat until aromatic, about 30 seconds. Add pork and stir-fry until lightly browned but still slightly pink inside, about 3 minutes.

4. Add chile paste, soy sauce, bean sauce, broth, and sugar. Bring to a boil, reduce heat, and simmer, tossing to mix, 2 minutes. Add snow peas and stir-fry until heated through, 1 to 2 minutes. Remove from heat, drizzle with sesame oil, and serve.

142 SUPER SPICY SPARERIBS

Prep: 10 minutes   Stand: 6 hours   Cook: 25 minutes   Serves: 6

1 rack baby spareribs (about
   2½ pounds), cut in half
   lengthwise
¼ cup hoisin sauce
1 tablespoon chile paste
¼ cup soy sauce

1 tablespoon Asian sesame oil
¼ cup honey
1 teaspoon salt
3 small dried hot red peppers,
   crumbled

1. Set ribs in a roasting pan. Blend together hoisin sauce, chile paste, soy sauce, sesame oil, honey, salt, and crumbled peppers. Pour over ribs and turn to coat well. Cover and refrigerate 6 hours. Return to room temperature before cooking.

2. Preheat oven to 450°F. Place ribs in oven and roast, basting often and turning once or twice, until ribs are tender, about 25 minutes.

3. Remove ribs from oven. Let stand 10 minutes, then cut between ribs to separate. Place on a serving platter. Skim off fat from surface of roasting juices and pour over ribs.

143   FISH-FLAVORED SHREDDED PORK
Prep: 20 minutes   Stand: 25 minutes   Cook: 5 minutes   Serves: 4

This Szechuan dish is prepared with the pungent flavors used for fish, thus its name. It doesn't have any fish in it at all.

1   pound boneless pork loin
½   teaspoon cornstarch
½   teaspoon salt
3   tablespoons vegetable oil
1   tablespoon fermented black
     beans
4   garlic cloves, minced
4   slices of fresh ginger,
     minced

2   or 3 small dried red hot
     peppers, crumbled
3   scallions, minced
½   cup sliced bamboo shoots
2   tablespoons soy sauce
2   tablespoons dry sherry
2   tablespoons cider vinegar
2   teaspoons sugar

1. Trim pork of any excess fat and cut meat into matchstick shreds. In a bowl, toss pork with cornstarch, salt, and 1 tablespoon oil. Let stand 25 minutes.

2. Rinse black beans to remove excess salt. In a small bowl, combine black beans, minced garlic, and ginger.

3. In a wok or skillet, heat remaining 2 tablespoons oil until just smoking. Add pork and stir-fry over high heat to brown lightly, about 2 minutes. Add black bean mixture, hot red peppers, and scallions. Stir-fry over medium heat until aromatic, about 30 seconds. Add bamboo shoots and toss to mix. Add soy sauce, sherry, vinegar, and sugar. Bring to a boil and cook over medium heat 2 minutes, stirring to blend well. Remove from heat and serve.

144   SPICY BEAN CURD WITH GROUND PORK
Prep: 15 minutes   Cook: 3 to 4 minutes   Serves: 4

½   pound ground pork
1   tablespoon dry white wine
1   tablespoon plus 1 teaspoon
     cornstarch
½   teaspoon salt
½   teaspoon pepper
2   tablespoons vegetable oil
1   scallion, minced

¼   teaspoon Szechuan
     peppercorns, crushed
1   teaspoon soy sauce
1   teaspoon chile paste
¼   teaspoon sugar
1   pound firm bean curd, cut
     into ½-inch cubes

1. In a small bowl, blend pork with wine, 1 teaspoon of cornstarch, salt, and pepper. Let stand 10 minutes. In another small bowl, dissolve remaining 1 tablespoon cornstarch in ¼ cup cold water.

2. Heat oil in a wok until just smoking. Add pork mixture, scallions, and Szechuan peppercorns and stir-fry over medium heat 1 to 2 minutes to blend. Add soy sauce, chile paste, and sugar. Stir-fry 1 minute. Add diced bean curd and stir gently.

3. Stir cornstarch and water mixture to blend and add to wok. Bring to a boil and cook, stirring, until sauce thickens, about 1 minute. Serve hot.

145   SZECHUAN SPICY LAMB

Prep: 20 minutes   Stand: 30 to 40 minutes   Cook: 10 to 11 minutes
Serves: 4 to 6

1½ pounds boneless leg of lamb
¼   cup soy sauce
1   tablespoon cornstarch
1   tablespoon plus 1 teaspoon
     minced fresh ginger
¼   cup plus 2 teaspoons
     vegetable oil
4   dried Chinese mushrooms
2   tablespoons tree ears
3   garlic cloves, minced

3   scallions, minced
5   small dried hot red peppers
¼   cup coarsely chopped water
     chestnuts
1   carrot, shredded
3   tablespoons dry sherry
1   tablespoon cider vinegar
½   to 1 teaspoon cayenne
1   tablespoon sugar
1   tablespoon Asian sesame oil

1. Cut lamb into ¼-inch-thick slices and then into matchstick-size pieces. In a medium bowl, toss lamb and 1 tablespoon soy sauce, 2 teaspoons cornstarch, 1 teaspoon minced ginger, and 2 teaspoons vegetable oil. Let stand at room temperature 30 to 40 minutes.

2. In a small bowl, soak mushrooms in ¼ cup warm water until soft, about 15 minutes. Drain, reserving liquid. Remove and discard stems. Cut caps into shreds. In another bowl, soak tree ears in warm water until soft, about 10 minutes. Drain, rinsing off grit if necessary. Discard water.

3. In a wok, heat remaining ¼ cup vegetable oil over medium-high heat. Add lamb and stir-fry until browned, about 5 minutes. With a skimmer or slotted spoon, remove to a plate. Add remaining ginger, garlic, scallions, and dried hot peppers to wok. Stir-fry over high heat until aromatic, about 20 seconds. Add mushrooms, tree ears, water chestnuts, and carrot. Stir-fry until soft, about 2 minutes.

4. Return lamb to wok. Add remaining soy sauce, sherry, vinegar, cayenne, and sugar. Bring to a boil and cook 1 minute.

5. In a small bowl, blend remaining 1 teaspoon cornstarch with reserved mushroom liquid. Add to wok. Return to a boil and cook, stirring, until sauce thickens, 1 to 2 minutes. Continue tossing meat and vegetables to mix and coat well. Remove from heat. Add sesame oil, stir to blend, and serve.

146 SLIVERED LAMB WITH TURNIPS AND CARROTS

Prep: 15 minutes   Cook: 10 minutes   Serves: 6

2 pounds boneless leg of lamb
1 egg white
1 tablespoon cornstarch
⅓ cup vegetable oil
4 slices of fresh ginger, finely shredded
4 scallions, finely shredded
2 carrots, peeled and shredded

4 small turnips, peeled and cut into matchstick pieces
3 tablespoons dry white wine
2 tablespoons soy sauce
1 tablespoon chile paste
1 tablespoon yellow bean sauce

1. Trim any excess fat from lamb and cut meat into matchstick slivers. In a medium bowl, toss lamb with egg white, cornstarch, and 1 tablespoon oil until evenly coated.

2. In a wok or skillet, heat remaining oil over medium-high heat. Add lamb slivers and spread out in one layer. Cook, tossing frequently, until browned, about 5 minutes. With a slotted spoon, remove to a plate. Discard all but 2 tablespoons oil.

3. Return wok to medium heat. Add ginger and scallions and stir-fry until aromatic, about 30 seconds. Add carrots and turnips and stir-fry 2 minutes. Add wine, soy sauce, chile paste, bean sauce, and 3 tablespoons water. Return meat to wok. Bring to a boil and cook, stirring, until meat is hot and well coated with sauce, about 2 minutes. Remove to a serving platter.

147 SHRIMP IN SPICY BLACK BEAN SAUCE

Prep: 15 minutes   Cook: 6 to 7 minutes   Serves: 4

1 pound medium shrimp, shelled and deveined
1 egg white
2 teaspoons cornstarch
1 tablespoon fermented black beans
3 garlic cloves, minced
¼ cup plus 1 tablespoon vegetable oil

1 tablespoon minced fresh ginger
¼ cup diced red bell pepper
2 to 3 jalapeño peppers, seeded and thinly sliced
2 tablespoons soy sauce
1 tablespoon dry white wine
1 scallion, minced

1. In a small bowl, toss shrimp with egg white and 1 teaspoon cornstarch until evenly coated. Rinse black beans to remove excess salt. In a small bowl, mash beans with garlic and 1 tablespoon of oil.

2. In a wok, heat remaining ¼ cup oil until just smoking over medium heat. Add shrimp and stir-fry until pink, about 3 minutes. Remove to a plate. Pour off all but 2 tablespoons oil.

3. Return wok to high heat. Add black bean mixture and stir-fry until aromatic, about 30 seconds. Add ginger, red bell pepper, and jalapeño peppers. Stir-fry 1 minute. Return shrimp to wok. Add soy sauce, wine, and 2 tablespoons water.

4. In a small bowl, blend remaining cornstarch with 2 tablespoons cold water and add to wok. Bring to a boil and cook, stirring, until sauce thickens, 1 to 2 minutes. Remove from heat, sprinkle with scallion, and serve.

---

148 SPICY VELVET SHRIMP WITH CUCUMBER AND PEAS

Prep: 20 minutes   Stand: 10 minutes   Cook: 7 to 8 minutes
Serves: 4

1 **pound large shrimp, shelled and deveined**	2 **scallions, minced**
1 **egg white**	6 **small dried hot red peppers**
2 **teaspoons cornstarch**	½ **teaspoon cayenne**
1 **teaspoon soy sauce**	½ **cup peas, cooked fresh or thawed frozen**
¼ **cup plus 2 tablespoons vegetable oil**	2 **cucumbers, peeled, seeded, and cut into ½-inch dice**
2 **teaspoons minced fresh ginger**	2 **tablespoons dry white wine**
	3 **tablespoons chicken broth**

1. In a medium bowl, toss shrimp with egg white, 1 teaspoon of cornstarch, and soy sauce. Let stand 10 minutes.

2. In a wok, heat oil until just beginning to smoke. Add shrimp and cook over medium heat, tossing, until shrimp begins to turn pink, about 3 minutes. With a slotted spoon, remove shrimp to plate. Pour off all but 2 tablespoons of oil.

3. Return wok to medium heat. Add ginger, scallions, hot red peppers, and cayenne. Stir-fry until aromatic, about 30 seconds. Add peas and cucumber cubes and stir-fry until hot, about 1 minute.

4. In a small bowl, combine wine, broth, and remaining 1 teaspoon cornstarch. Add to wok, bring to a boil, and cook, stirring, until sauce thickens, 1 to 2 minutes. Return shrimp to wok. Toss to coat and heat through. Remove from heat and serve.

149 SPICY SHRIMP AND FRAGRANT MELON BALLS

Prep: 20 minutes   Stand: 20 minutes   Cook: 10 to 11 minutes
Serves: 4

Honeydew melon lends a fragrance to this Hong Kong-style dish.

1 pound large shrimp, shelled and deveined	1 slice of fresh ginger
1 egg, beaten	8 small dried hot red peppers
2 tablespoons cornstarch	1 cup honeydew melon balls
¼ teaspoon salt	1 tablespoon soy sauce
¼ cup plus 3 tablespoons vegetable oil	1 tablespoon ketchup
	1 tablespoon dry sherry
	2 teaspoons sugar

1. In a bowl, toss shrimp, egg, cornstarch, salt, and 1 tablespoon oil. Let stand 20 minutes.

2. In a wok, heat 5 tablespoons oil until just smoking. Add shrimp in batches and cook over medium heat, turning, until shrimp are golden and crisp, about 3 minutes per batch. Remove to paper towels. Discard oil.

3. Return wok to medium heat. Add 1 tablespoon oil and heat until just smoking. Add ginger and crumble 1 hot red pepper into wok. Stir-fry until ginger is brown, 1 to 2 minutes. Discard ginger. Add remaining whole hot red peppers and cook over medium heat 30 seconds. Add melon balls and stir-fry 30 seconds. Add soy sauce, ketchup, sherry, sugar, and ¼ cup water. Bring to a boil, reduce heat, and simmer 2 minutes. Add shrimp. Toss to coat well and heat shrimp. Remove to a serving platter.

150 KUNG PAO SHRIMP

Prep: 15 minutes   Stand: 20 minutes   Cook: 9 to 14 minutes
Serves: 4

1 pound medium shrimp, shelled and deveined	3 garlic cloves, minced
1 egg	4 small dried hot red peppers, crumbled
3 tablespoons cornstarch	¼ cup peanuts, raw or dry-roasted
½ teaspoon salt	
¼ cup plus 2 tablespoons vegetable oil	2 tablespoons dry sherry
3 scallions, minced	2 tablespoons rice vinegar
3 slices of fresh ginger, minced	2 tablespoons sugar
	1 tablespoon Asian sesame oil

1. In a medium bowl, toss shrimp with egg, 2 tablespoons of cornstarch, and salt. Let stand 20 minutes or longer.

2. In a wok, heat vegetable oil until smoking. Add shrimp in 2 batches and stir-fry over high heat until pink, 3 to 5 minutes per batch. Remove from wok to paper towels. Discard all but 2 tablespoons oil.

3. Return wok to high heat. Add scallions, ginger, garlic, and crumbled hot red peppers. Stir-fry until aromatic, about 30 seconds. Add peanuts and stir-fry 1 minute. Add sherry, vinegar, sugar, and 3 tablespoons water.

4. In a small bowl, blend remaining 1 tablespoon cornstarch with ¼ cup cold water. Add to sauce and bring to a boil. Cook, stirring, until sauce thickens, 1 to 2 minutes. Add shrimp, toss to coat with sauce, and heat through. Drizzle with sesame oil, stir to blend, and serve.

---

151   SPICY CLAMS
Prep: 20 minutes   Cook: 7 to 12 minutes   Serves: 4

4 dozen clams	3 tablespoons vegetable oil
2 tablespoons fermented	3 scallions, minced
black beans	1 tablespoon chile paste
3 garlic cloves, minced	¼ cup dry white wine

1. With a stiff brush, scrub clams under cold running water. Drain in a colander. Rinse black beans to remove excess salt. In a small bowl, mash beans with garlic and 1 tablespoon of oil.

2. In a wok, heat remaining 2 tablespoons oil over medium heat. Add black bean mix, scallions, and chile paste and stir-fry until aromatic, about 30 seconds. Add white wine and ¼ cup water. Cook 1 minute.

3. Add clams, bring to a boil, and cover. Cook until clams open, 5 to 10 minutes. Discard any clams that do not open. Uncover and toss to coat well with sauce. Remove to a serving bowl.

---

152   FRIED SQUID WITH SPICY SALT
Prep: 15 minutes   Cook: 3 minutes per batch   Serves: 4 to 6

The spicy salt here is contained in the Wild Pepper Mix.

2 pounds squid, cleaned	2 small dried hot red peppers,
½ cup flour	crushed
½ cup cornstarch	2 teaspoons Wild Pepper Mix
2 cups vegetable oil	(page 25)

1. Cut cleaned squid into rings about ¼ inch thick. Drain in a colander. In a bowl, sift together flour and cornstarch.

2. In a wok, heat oil over medium-high heat to 375°F, or until a cube of bread browns in 1 minute. Toss squid rings in flour mixture until well coated. Cook in batches without crowding until squid rings are golden and crisp, about 3 minutes per batch. Drain on paper towels.

3. Discard oil, but do not clean wok. Add crushed hot red peppers and wild pepper mix. Toss over high heat 30 seconds. Add squid rings and continue tossing to coat with pepper mix. Remove from heat and serve hot.

153   MA LA FISH
Prep: 15 minutes   Cook: 7 minutes   Serves: 4

1½ pounds firm white fish
    fillets, such as tilefish, red
    snapper, or cod,
    ¾ to 1 inch thick
½ cup flour
½ cup cornstarch
½ teaspoon salt
¾ teaspoon black pepper
¼ cup plus 3 tablespoons
    vegetable oil
2 teaspoons minced fresh
    ginger

2 garlic cloves, minced
2 scallions, minced
2 tablespoons soy sauce
½ to 1 teaspoon cayenne
2 tablespoons dry white wine
¼ cup chicken broth
¼ cup peas, cooked fresh or
    thawed frozen
1 tablespoon Asian sesame oil

1. Check fish for any small bones and remove them with pincers. Cut fish into 3-inch square pieces. In a bowl, combine flour, cornstarch, salt, and black pepper. Add fish and toss gently to coat pieces well.

2. In a wok, heat 6 tablespoons vegetable oil until just smoking. Add fish and cook over medium heat, turning once, until crisp and golden, about 2 minutes per side. Remove to paper towels to drain. Pour off oil and wipe out wok with paper towels.

3. Return wok to high heat and add remaining 1 tablespoon vegetable oil. Add ginger, garlic, and scallions and cook until aromatic, about 30 seconds. Add soy sauce, cayenne, wine, and broth. Bring to a boil, add fish, reduce heat, and simmer 1 minute. Add peas and cook 1 minute longer. Remove from heat. Drizzle in sesame oil and serve.

154   HOT AND SOUR POACHED FISH
Prep: 10 minutes   Cook: 10 minutes   Serves: 6

2 cups Chinese Chicken Stock
    (page 27) or reduced-
    sodium canned broth
¼ cup dry white wine
3 tablespoons soy sauce
2 tablespoons cider vinegar
½ teaspoon cayenne
1 tablespoon Asian sesame oil
½ teaspoon sugar
1 tablespoon cornstarch

2 pounds firm white fish
    fillets, cut into 2 x 3-inch
    pieces
2 scallions, cut into 2-inch-
    long shreds
1 tablespoon finely shredded
    fresh ginger
1 teaspoon black pepper
3 tablespoons vegetable oil

1. In a small nonreactive saucepan, combine chicken stock, wine, soy sauce, vinegar, cayenne, sesame oil, and sugar. Bring to a boil, reduce heat, and simmer 5 minutes. In a small bowl, mix cornstarch with ¼ cup cold water. Stir into sauce, return to a boil, and cook, stirring, until thickened, about 1 minute. Remove from heat and cover to keep warm.

2. In a wok, bring 10 cups water to a boil. Reduce to a gentle simmer, add fish, and poach until just white throughout, about 3 minutes. With a skimmer or slotted spoon, remove fish to a serving platter with deep sides. Sprinkle shredded scallions, ginger, and black pepper over fish.

3. In a small saucepan, heat vegetable oil until smoking. Immediately drizzle over fish, scallions, and ginger. Pour warm sauce over fish and serve at once.

155   FISH AND HOT WILLOW SAUCE
Prep: 20 minutes   Cook: 9 to 14 minutes   Serves: 4 to 6

¼ cup flour
¼ cup plus 2 teaspoons cornstarch
½ teaspoon salt
½ teaspoon pepper
2 pounds firm-textured white fish fillets about 1 inch thick, such as cod, snapper, halibut
¼ cup plus 2 tablespoons oil
1½ tablespoons minced fresh ginger
3 garlic cloves, minced

3 scallions, minced
2 sweet gherkin pickles, minced
2 tablespoons diced green bell pepper
2 tablespoons diced red bell pepper
2 tablespoons soy sauce
3 tablespoons rice vinegar
2 tablespoons dry sherry
½ to 1 teaspoon cayenne
1 tablespoon sugar

1. Sift together flour, ¼ cup cornstarch, salt, and pepper. Spread out on a plate. Check fish for any little bones. Remove with pincers. Cut fish fillets into 2 x 3-inch pieces. Dredge fish in flour mixture to coat well.

2. In a wok or large skillet, heat 3 tablespoons oil over medium heat. Add half of fish fillets and cook, turning once, until golden, 3 to 5 minutes. Remove to paper towels to drain. Add another 2 tablespoons oil to wok and cook remaining fish. Discard oil and clean out wok with paper towels. Arrange fish on a serving platter and cover with foil to keep warm.

3. Return wok to medium heat. Add remaining 1 tablespoon oil and heat to smoking. Add ginger, garlic, scallions, gherkins, and green and red pepper and stir-fry until aromatic, about 30 seconds. Add soy sauce, vinegar, sherry, cayenne, and sugar.

4. In a small bowl, blend remaining 2 teaspoons cornstarch with 3 tablespoons water. Add to sauce, bring to a boil, and cook, stirring, until thickened, 1 to 2 minutes. Pour over fish and serve.

156 VELVET SCALLOPS, CHILES, AND PEAS

Prep: 20 minutes   Cook: 7 minutes   Serves: 4

1 pound sea scallops
1 egg white
1 teaspoon cornstarch
2 tablespoons vegetable oil
2 teaspoons minced fresh
  ginger
1 scallion, minced

6 small dried hot red peppers
1 (10-ounce) package frozen
  tiny peas, thawed
¼ cup Vegetable Stock (page
  28) or canned broth
1 tablespoon dry white wine
½ teaspoon pepper

1. In a medium bowl, toss scallops with egg white and cornstarch until evenly coated. Let stand 10 minutes at room temperature.

2. In a wok, heat oil to smoking. Add ginger, scallion, and hot red peppers. Stir-fry over medium heat until aromatic, about 30 seconds. Add peas and cook 2 minutes.

3. Add scallops and stir-fry until they begin to turn opaque, about 2 minutes. Add stock, wine, and pepper. Stir-fry, tossing, 2 minutes longer. Transfer to a serving platter and serve.

157 COD STEAK WITH BLACK BEANS AND HOT CHILES

*Prep: 10 minutes   Cook: 10 to 15 minutes, or 5 minutes in microwave
Serves: 4*

When prepared in a microwave, this dish is quick and easy, but it still tastes authentically Chinese.

1 tablespoon fermented black
  beans
1 tablespoon vegetable oil
2 teaspoons minced fresh
  ginger

2 cod steaks, cut 1 inch thick
  (about 1½ pounds)
2 teaspoons soy sauce
1 tablespoon minced scallion
2 or 3 fresh hot chiles, seeded
  and minced

1. Rinse black beans to remove excess salt and soak in warm water for 5 minutes; drain. In a small bowl, mash beans slightly with oil and minced ginger.

2. Arrange cod steaks on a heatproof plate and spread mashed black bean mixture evenly on fish. Drizzle soy sauce over fish and sprinkle with minced scallion and hot chiles. Place plate in a bamboo steamer basket and cover with lid.

3. Fill a wok one-third full of water, bring to a simmer, and place bamboo basket over water. Steam over medium heat until fish is opaque throughout, 10 to 15 minutes. Or cover with microwave-safe plastic wrap and microwave on High until fish just flakes, about 5 minutes.

158   CRUNCHY VERY SPICY BEAN CURD SQUARES

Prep: 15 minutes   Cook: 10 minutes   Serves: 4

4 bean curd squares	1 tablespoon soy sauce
2 cups vegetable oil	1 tablespoon chile paste
1 scallion, minced	1 tablespoon cornstarch
2 teaspoons minced fresh ginger	2 teaspoons Asian sesame oil
2 garlic cloves, minced	
1 cup Chinese Chicken Stock (page 27) or reduced-sodium canned broth	

1. Cut bean curd squares into 4 quarters. In a wok, heat vegetable oil over medium-high heat to 375°F, or until a bread cube browns in 1 minute. Deep-fry bean curd until puffed and golden, about 5 minutes. Drain on paper towels.

2. Discard all but 1 tablespoon of oil. Return wok to medium heat. Add scallion, ginger, and garlic and stir-fry until aromatic, about 30 seconds. Add chicken stock, soy sauce, and chile paste. In a small bowl, blend cornstarch with ¼ cup cold water. Add to wok and bring to a boil. Cook, stirring, until sauce thickens, about 2 minutes.

3. Add bean curd squares and gently stir to coat with hot sauce. Remove from heat, drizzle with sesame oil, stir to mix, and serve.

159   QUICK HOT BEAN SPROUTS

Prep: 5 minutes   Cook: 3 minutes   Serves: 4 to 6

This dish is so quick it can almost be done in the time it takes to read this recipe.

2 pounds fresh bean sprouts	2 teaspoons chile paste
1 tablespoon vegetable oil	Salt
1 slice of fresh ginger	
2 teaspoons Chile Oil (page 23)	

1. Rinse bean sprouts and dry in a salad spinner or colander.

2. In a wok, heat vegetable oil until smoking. Add ginger and stir-fry over high heat until brown, 1 to 2 minutes; discard. Add chile oil and chile paste to wok. Stir-fry a few seconds, stirring to mix well. Add bean sprouts and stir-fry over high heat until wilted and coated with seasonings, about 1 minute. Season with salt to taste and serve.

160 GREEN BEANS IN PORK SAUCE

Prep: 20 minutes   Cook: 13 to 14 minutes   Serves: 6

Although you can use fried green beans in this sauce, this recipe uses boiled beans, thus reducing fat content considerably for the diet-conscious.

1 pound green beans, trimmed	1 scallion, minced
1 tablespoon vegetable oil	½ pound lean ground pork
3 garlic cloves, minced	2 tablespoons chile paste
2 teaspoons minced fresh ginger	¼ cup chicken broth
	2 teaspoons soy sauce
	2 teaspoons cornstarch

1. In a large pot of boiling salted water, cook green beans until tender but still firm, about 5 minutes. Drain and rinse under cold running water to cool; drain well.

2. In a wok, heat oil over medium heat until just smoking. Add garlic, ginger, and scallion and stir-fry until aromatic, about 30 seconds. Add ground pork and stir-fry until pork loses its pink color, tossing to break up any lumps of meat, about 5 minutes.

3. Add chile paste, chicken broth, and soy sauce. Bring to a boil and simmer 1 minute. In a small bowl, dissolve cornstarch in 2 tablespoons cold water. Add to sauce, return to a boil, and cook, stirring, until sauce thickens, 1 to 2 minutes. Add green beans and toss to blend and heat through.

161 HOT AND SOUR CABBAGE

Prep: 5 minutes   Cook: 18 minutes   Serves: 6

1 head Chinese (Napa) cabbage, about 1½ pounds	1 tablespoon soy sauce
3 tablespoons vegetable oil	2 tablespoons rice vinegar
1 slice of fresh ginger	2 teaspoons Asian sesame oil
1 tablespoon chile paste	Salt
½ cup chicken broth	1 small dried hot red pepper, crumbled

1. Wash cabbage. Remove and discard coarse outer leaves. Shred remaining cabbage thinly.

2. In a wok, bring vegetable oil to smoking point over high heat. Add ginger slice and stir-fry until brown, 1 to 2 minutes; discard ginger. Add cabbage and stir-fry 1 minute. Add chile paste, broth, soy sauce, vinegar, and sesame oil. Reduce heat to medium and cook, stirring occasionally, until cabbage is wilted, about 15 minutes.

3. Season with salt to taste. With a slotted spoon transfer cabbage to a serving platter and sprinkle crumbled chile pepper on top.

162 CAULIFLOWER AND BROCCOLI TOSSED IN HOT AND SOUR SAUCE

Prep: 25 minutes   Cook: 12 to 16 minutes   Serves: 6 to 8

1 head of cauliflower	2 tablespoons cider vinegar
1 bunch of broccoli	¼ cup chicken broth
1 tablespoon vegetable oil	1 to 1½ teaspoons cayenne
1 slice of fresh ginger	1 teaspoon black pepper
2 tablespoons soy sauce	2 teaspoons Asian sesame oil

1. Trim cauliflower and cut into florets. Cut stems from broccoli florets and discard. In a large pot of boiling salted water, cook cauliflower florets until just tender, 3 to 5 minutes. Add broccoli florets to boiling water and cook until just tender, about 3 minutes. Scoop out with a skimmer or slotted spoon, transfer to a colander, and rinse under cold running water; drain well.

2. In a wok or saucepan, heat vegetable oil to smoking. Add ginger and cook until brown, about 1 minute; discard ginger. Add soy sauce, vinegar, broth, cayenne, black pepper, and sesame oil. Bring to a boil, reduce heat, and simmer 2 minutes.

3. Add cauliflower and broccoli and toss until hot and flavors have been absorbed, 3 to 5 minutes. Remove to a bowl and serve hot.

163 BLISTERED SPICY GREEN BEANS

Prep: 20 minutes   Cook: 4 to 6 minutes   Serves: 4 to 6

1 tablespoon fermented black beans	2 cups plus 2 teaspoons vegetable oil
1 tablespoon chile paste	1 pound green beans, trimmed
3 garlic cloves, minced	½ cup chicken broth
1 teaspoon minced fresh ginger	Salt

1. In a small bowl, lightly mash black beans, chile paste, garlic, ginger, and 2 teaspoons oil. Rinse green beans and dry thoroughly with paper towels.

2. In a wok, heat remaining 2 cups oil to 375°F, or until a cube of bread browns in 1 minute. Carefully add green beans and cook over high heat, stirring, until they blister, 3 to 5 minutes. Drain on paper towels. Discard oil, but do not wipe out wok.

3. Reheat wok over medium heat. Add black bean mixture a~ ' aromatic, about 10 seconds. Add chicken broth and bring Return green beans to wok. Toss to blend and heat well. Se taste and serve.

GGPLANT IN SPICY GARLIC MEAT SAUCE

rep: 15 minutes   Cook: 20 minutes   Serves: 4 to 6

_____ean ground pork
1 tablespoon plus 2 teaspoons
    dark soy sauce
1 tablespoon cornstarch
4 small, narrow Japanese
    eggplants or 1 small
    regular eggplant
3 tablespoons vegetable oil

2 teaspoons minced fresh
    ginger
1 scallion, minced
4 garlic cloves, minced
¼ cup chicken broth
1 tablespoon chile paste
2 teaspoons sugar
2 teaspoons Asian sesame oil

1. In a small bowl, combine ground pork with 2 teaspoons dark soy sauce and 1 teaspoon cornstarch. Blend well. Cut unpeeled eggplants crosswise on a diagonal into ½-inch-thick slices. (If using regular eggplant, cut lengthwise in half first.)

2. In a wok, bring 2 teaspoons of vegetable oil to smoking point over medium heat. Add ginger, scallion, and garlic. Stir-fry until aromatic, about 30 seconds. Add pork and stir-fry until pork loses its pink color, about 3 minutes. Remove to a plate.

3. Add remaining vegetable oil to wok and heat to smoking. Add eggplant and stir-fry over medium-high heat, tossing, until lightly browned, about 5 minutes. Return pork to wok. Add broth, chile paste, sugar, and remaining 1 tablespoon soy sauce. Bring to a boil, stirring to mix. Reduce heat and cook until eggplant is tender, about 10 minutes.

4. In a small bowl, blend remaining 2 teaspoons cornstarch with 2 tablespoons cold water. Add to wok, bring to a boil, and cook, stirring, until sauce thickens, 1 to 2 minutes. Remove from heat. Drizzle with sesame oil and serve.

165   COLD BEAN CURD AND BEAN SPROUTS WITH CHILE OIL AND CILANTRO

Prep: 15 minutes   Stand: 15 minutes   Cook: none   Serves: 4 to 6

1 garlic clove, minced
⅓ cup Chile, Black Bean, and
    Garlic Oil (page 23)
1 pound firm bean curd, cut
    into 1-inch cubes

1 pound fresh bean sprouts
½ cup cilantro leaves
2 fresh jalapeño peppers,
    seeded and thinly sliced
2 scallions, minced

1. In a small bowl, combine garlic with chile oil. Pour 2 tablespoons over bean curd, toss gently, and let stand 15 minutes or longer.

In a medium bowl, toss together bean sprouts, cilantro leaves, jalapeño ers, and scallions. Pour remaining dressing over vegetables. Toss to ll. Top with cold bean curd and serve. Toss vegetables with bean ble.

Chapter 6

The Chinese Way with Vegetables

In Chinese cooking, there is a tradition rich in the use of vegetables and vegetarian products, such as bean curd, and no meal is ever served without a vegetable dish. Today in America, too, vegetables are prized for their healthful vitamins, minerals, and fiber and for the complex carbohydrates they provide. So I thought it useful to include a separate chapter just for vegetables.

The variety of vegetables used in Chinese cooking can seem bewildering, but these days, quite a few are available in the produce sections of large supermarkets. Many of the green vegetables come from the cabbage family, the most familiar ones being Napa, or Chinese, cabbage and bok choy. Besides leafy green vegetables, Chinese use bean sprouts, baby eggplant, jicama (also used in Mexican cooking), fresh water chestnuts, long beans, snow peas, gourds, squashes, and melons, as well as a large variety of root vegetables, such as taro and yams. Western vegetables, such as carrots, celery, tomatoes, potatoes, green beans, and cucumbers, are also embraced enthusiastically.

For all these different vegetables, there are a variety of tempting ways to prepare them in stir-fries, braises, and steamed dishes. Some of these recipes, such as Vegetable Mu Shu, Crusty Bean Curd Squares in Black Bean Sauce, or Braised Vegetable Medley, make excellent main courses. Others, such as Ginger-Braised Carrots, Long Beans and Peanuts with Garlic, and Stir-Fried Silk Squash, make excellent side dishes.

In China, there is a grand tradition of vegetarian cooking stemming from Buddhist monks who used bean curd as a staple of their cooking for its high protein content. Many of these recipes, which are scattered throughout the book, treat some form of bean curd as a "mock food"—mock duck or mock fish. This chapter includes over a dozen recipes for bean curd, among them an unusual Tea-Smoked Bean Curd.

To round out our vegetable lover's chapter, I have included an assortment of cold vegetables and salad dishes, such as Silver and Gold Salad, Shredded Vegetable Salad, and the simple Bean Sprout Salad.

166   FRESH VEGETABLE BUDDHA'S DELIGHT

Prep: 30 minutes   Cook: 10 to 13 minutes   Serves: 8

2 ounces bean threads
½ cup snow peas
1 cup broccoli florets
1 tablespoon vegetable oil
1 slice of fresh ginger
½ cup sliced mushrooms
½ cup sliced bamboo shoots
1 cup sliced water chestnuts

1 carrot, peeled and cut into
    fine 1-inch shreds
1 celery rib, cut into fine
    1-inch shreds
1 tablespoon soy sauce
⅓ cup chicken broth
1 tablespoon cornstarch
½ teaspoon pepper

1. Soak bean threads in warm water until softened, about 10 minutes. Drain and cut into 2-inch lengths.

2. Meanwhile, in a large saucepan, bring 3 quarts of salted water to a boil. Add snow peas and cook until they turn bright green, about 5 *seconds*. Remove with a slotted spoon and rinse under cold running water. Add broccoli florets to boiling water and cook until florets turn bright green, 2 to 3 minutes. Drain and rinse under cold water to cool. Drain snow peas and broccoli.

3. Heat oil in a wok until just smoking over medium heat. Add ginger slice and cook until brown, 1 to 2 minutes. Remove and discard ginger. Add snow peas, broccoli, mushrooms, bamboo shoots, water chestnuts, carrot, and celery. Stir-fry until vegetables are tender, about 5 minutes. Add bean threads and stir to mix well.

4. In a small bowl, whisk together soy sauce, chicken broth, cornstarch, and pepper. Add to wok, toss to mix, and return sauce to a boil. Cook until sauce thickens and naps vegetables, 1 to 2 minutes.

167   BEAN SPROUT SALAD

Prep: 10 minutes   Cook: none   Serves: 6

1 pound fresh bean sprouts
¼ cup minced scallions
2 tablespoons rice vinegar
2 tablespoons vegetable oil
2 tablespoons Asian sesame
    oil

1 tablespoon soy sauce
½ teaspoon sugar
½ teaspoon grated fresh ginger
½ teaspoon Chile Oil
    (page 23)

1. Rinse and drain bean sprouts. Toss bean sprouts with scallions and set aside.

2. In a small bowl, whisk together vinegar, vegetable oil, sesame oil, soy sauce, sugar, grated ginger, and chile oil. Pour over bean sprout mixture just before serving.

168 QUICK TOSSED BEAN SPROUTS WITH CHIVES

Prep: 5 minutes   Cook: 1 to 2 minutes   Serves: 4 to 6

This dish is quicker to prepare than to describe. Garlic chives may be used instead of regular chives, if they are available.

4 cups fresh bean sprouts	1 tablespoon Asian sesame oil
1 cup 2-inch lengths chives	4 garlic cloves, bruised
3 tablespoons vegetable oil	½ teaspoon salt

1. Wash bean sprouts and dry in a salad spinner or colander; pat with paper towels. In a large bowl, toss bean sprouts with chives so they are evenly mixed.

2. In a wok, combine vegetable oil and sesame oil. Heat over medium heat. Add garlic and cook until aromatic, about 30 seconds. Remove and discard.

3. Turn heat to high. Add bean sprouts and chives and toss quickly just until heated through, 30 to 60 seconds. Do not overcook. Season with salt and serve.

169 BAMBOO SHOOTS WITH SPINACH GREENS

Prep: 10 minutes   Cook: 3 to 4 minutes   Serves: 4

2 cups tightly packed spinach leaves	1 tablespoon vegetable oil
1 cup sliced bamboo shoots	1 tablespoon minced scallion
2 teaspoons cornstarch	2 teaspoons minced fresh ginger
½ cup chicken broth	Salt and pepper

1. Cut spinach leaves into thin ribbons. Rinse bamboo shoots with hot water. In a small bowl, blend cornstarch with broth.

2. In a wok, heat oil over medium heat. Add scallion and ginger and stir-fry until aromatic, about 30 seconds. Add bamboo shoots and stir-fry 1 minute.

3. Add spinach ribbons and toss to mix well. Add cornstarch mixture and bring to a boil. Cook, stirring, until thickened, 1 to 2 minutes. Season with salt and pepper to taste.

170   GREEN BEANS WITH BLACK BEAN SAUCE

Prep: 20 minutes   Cook: 9 to 11 minutes   Serves: 6

1 pound green beans	½ teaspoon minced fresh
1 tablespoon fermented	ginger
black beans	1 tablespoon vegetable oil
3 garlic cloves, minced	½ cup chicken broth

1. In a large saucepan of boiling salted water, cook green beans until crisp-tender, 5 to 7 minutes. Drain and rinse under cold running water. Drain well.

2. Rinse black beans to remove excess salt. In a small bowl, mash beans with garlic, ginger, and oil.

3. In a wok set over medium heat, stir-fry black bean mixture until aromatic, 5 to 10 seconds. Add chicken broth, bring to a boil, and cook until reduced to ⅓ cup, about 3 minutes. Add green beans, toss to mix, heat through, and serve.

171   SESAME ASPARAGUS SPEARS

Prep: 20 minutes   Cook: 5 to 7 minutes   Serves: 4 to 6

This is an East-West combination of asparagus and sesame that works beautifully with either an American or Chinese meal.

2 bunches asparagus	½ teaspoon salt
1 tablespoon toasted sesame	½ teaspoon freshly ground
seeds	pepper
1 tablespoon rice vinegar	2 tablespoons olive oil
1 teaspoon Dijon mustard	1 tablespoon Asian sesame oil
1 teaspoon finely minced	
fresh ginger	

1. Peel asparagus and lay in a large skillet. Cover with salted water, bring to a boil, reduce heat to low, and simmer until asparagus is tender, 5 to 7 minutes. Drain and lay on a serving platter. Sprinkle with sesame seeds.

2. In a small bowl, blend together vinegar, mustard, ginger, salt, and pepper. Whisk in olive oil and sesame oil. Pour dressing over asparagus. Serve warm or at room temperature.

172 OYSTER SAUCE BROCCOLI
Prep: 15 minutes   Cook: 5 minutes   Serves: 6

1 pound broccoli
1 tablespoon vegetable oil
1 teaspoon minced fresh
  ginger

3 tablespoons oyster sauce
1 teaspoon sugar
2 teaspoons brandy
2 teaspoons Asian sesame oil

1. Cut florets from broccoli stems and set aside. Peel stems and cut into 2 x ½-inch sticks. In a large saucepan of boiling salted water, cook broccoli sticks and florets until they turn a bright green color, about 2 minutes. Drain and rinse under cold running water; drain well.

2. In a wok, heat vegetable oil until just smoking. Add ginger and broccoli and stir-fry over medium heat until broccoli is tender, about 2 minutes.

3. Add oyster sauce, sugar, brandy, and 2 tablespoons water. Toss with broccoli to heat through. Remove from heat. Drizzle with sesame oil, stir to mix well, and serve.

173 SWEET AND SOUR CABBAGE
Prep: 15 minutes   Cook: 9 to 11 minutes   Serves: 6

1 large head of Chinese
  (Napa) cabbage
2 tablespoons vegetable oil
1 large onion, sliced
2 tablespoons soy sauce

2 tablespoons dry white wine
2 tablespoons cider vinegar
2 tablespoons sugar
1 small dried hot red pepper

1. Wash cabbage; remove coarse outer leaves and discard. Cut remaining cabbage leaves into 2½-inch-wide pieces.

2. In a wok or large flameproof casserole, heat oil over medium heat. Add onion and stir-fry until softened, 3 to 5 minutes. Add cabbage and stir-fry 1 minute.

3. Add soy sauce, wine, vinegar, sugar, whole hot red pepper, and ¼ cup water. Reduce heat and simmer, stirring occasionally, until cabbage is tender, about 5 minutes.

GINGER-BRAISED CARROTS

Prep: 10 minutes   Cook: 19 to 26 minutes   Serves: 4

roll-cut these carrots, they will be perfect. Rolling-cut simply means that you slice a peeled carrot on a diagonal, roll the carrot one-third over, and slice again. Repeat the roll and slice. You will get a triangular-shaped piece of carrot. Repeat this motion until the carrot is all cut. Chinese believe that this three-sided shape allows more flavor to be absorbed. I have Westernized this recipe a little by adding a bit a of butter at the end.

1 tablespoon vegetable oil	2 tablespoons fresh lemon
1 medium onion, minced	juice
2 tablespoons minced fresh	½ teaspoon salt
ginger	½ teaspoon pepper
2 scallions, minced	½ cup chicken broth
2 pounds carrots, peeled and	1 tablespoon butter
roll-cut into 1-inch pieces	3 tablespoons minced cilantro

1. In a wok or large saucepan, heat oil over medium heat. Add onion and cook until softened, 3 to 5 minutes. Add ginger and scallions and cook until aromatic, about 30 seconds. Add carrots, lemon juice, salt, pepper, and chicken broth. Reduce heat to medium-low, cover, and cook until carrots are tender, 15 to 20 minutes. If carrots get too dry, add 1 to 2 tablespoons of water to pan.

2. Just before serving, fold in butter and minced cilantro.

175 JICAMA, LONG BEANS, AND CHERRY TOMATO SALAD

Prep: 20 minutes   Cook: 8 minutes   Serves: 6 to 8

1 pound long beans, cut into	2 tablespoons Asian sesame
2-inch lengths	oil
2 tablespoons rice vinegar	1 jicama, about 2 pounds,
1 garlic clove, minced	peeled and cut into
1 teaspoon salt	2 x ¼-inch strips
½ teaspoon pepper	2 pint baskets of cherry
⅓ cup safflower oil	tomatoes

1. In a large pot of boiling salted water, cook long beans until tender but still crisp, about 8 minutes. Drain and rinse under cold running water until cool.

2. In a bowl, combine vinegar, garlic, salt, and pepper. Whisk in safflower oil and sesame oil. In 3 separate bowls, toss long beans, jicama, and cherry tomatoes in dressing.

3. On a round serving platter, mound long beans in center. Arrange jicama around beans and tomatoes around jicama to form a tricolored platter.

176 LONG BEANS AND PEANUTS WITH GARLIC

Prep: 20 minutes   Cook: 9 to 11 minutes   Serves: 6

Long beans, sometimes called yard-long beans or asparagus beans, come in two varieties: dark green and pale green. There is no difference in flavor or in how they are cooked.

2 pounds long beans, cut into 2-inch pieces	1 tablespoon soy sauce
1 cup dry-roasted peanuts	1 teaspoon sugar
2 tablespoons vegetable oil	½ teaspoon chile paste
¼ teaspoon cayenne	1 tablespoon dry sherry
½ teaspoon paprika	¼ cup vegetable or chicken
4 garlic cloves, minced	broth
	½ teaspoon salt

1. In a large pot of boiling salted water, cook long beans until crisp-tender, 5 to 7 minutes. Drain and rinse under cold running water.

2. In a small bowl, toss peanuts with 2 teaspoons of oil, cayenne, and paprika.

3. In a wok, heat remaining oil over medium heat. Add garlic and stir-fry until aromatic, about 30 seconds. Add soy sauce, sugar, chile paste, sherry, and broth. Simmer 1 minute.

4. Add long beans, stirring to mix well. Cook, stirring, until beans are warm, about 2 minutes. Add peanuts and salt. Toss to blend and serve.

177 SLOW-COOKED CHINESE CABBAGE

Prep: 15 minutes   Cook: 1 hour   Serves: 4

1 head of Chinese (Napa)
    cabbage (about
    1½ pounds)
	1 tablespoon vegetable oil

	1 tablespoon Asian sesame oil

2 cups Chinese Chicken Stock
    (page 27) or reduced-
    sodium canned broth
	¼ teaspoon salt

	¼ teaspoon pepper
	¼ teaspoon sugar

1. Separate cabbage leaves and rinse well. Cut leaves in half crosswise. Cut stalk ends lengthwise into 3 pieces. Cut leafy sections in same way but keep separate.

2. In a large saucepan, combine chicken stock, vegetable oil, sesame oil, salt, pepper, and sugar. Bring to a boil, reduce heat to low, and layer stalk ends of cabbage on bottom of saucepan. Layer leafy sections on top of stalk layer. Cover and simmer over low heat 1 hour.

3. With a slotted spoon, remove cabbage to serving bowl. Mound in center of dish and spoon broth around cabbage to serve.

178   MUSHROOM-FILLED POTATO BALLS

Prep: 20 minutes   Cook: 18 minutes   Makes: about 48

6 dried Chinese mushrooms
½ cup plus 1 tablespoon
    vegetable oil
1 teaspoon minced fresh
    ginger
1 pound fresh white
    mushrooms, sliced

1 tablespoon dark soy sauce
1 tablespoon dry sherry
1 teaspoon sugar
    Mashed Potato Dough
    (recipe follows)
½ cup flour

1. In a small bowl, soak dried mushrooms in ½ cup warm water until soft, about 15 minutes. Drain, reserving liquid. Remove and discard stems.

2. In a medium skillet, heat 1 tablespoon oil over medium heat. Add ginger and cook until fragrant, about 10 seconds. Add sliced fresh mushrooms and Chinese mushroom caps and cook, stirring, 3 minutes. Add soy sauce, sherry, sugar, and reserved mushroom liquid. Reduce heat to low and simmer until mushrooms are tender and most of liquid is absorbed, about 10 minutes. Transfer mixture to a food processor and finely mince. Remove to a bowl and let cool.

3. Pinch off a walnut-size piece of potato dough and roll into a ball between palms. Flatten with heel of hand into a 3-inch pancake. Fill with a scant 1 teaspoon of mushroom filling. Crimp together and roll to seal. Continue until all dough and filling are used up. Roll balls in ½ cup flour.

4. In a large skillet, heat remaining ½ cup oil over medium heat. Add filled balls and cook, rolling them about to cook evenly, until golden, about 5 minutes. Drain briefly on paper towels. Serve hot. Potato balls can be cooked ahead of time and reheated in a warm oven.

179   MASHED POTATO DOUGH

Prep: 10 minutes   Cook: 15 to 20 minutes
Makes: about 2 cups dough

1 pound baking potatoes
1 teaspoon salt
2 tablespoons butter

1 cup plus 2 tablespoons flour
2 eggs

1. Peel potatoes and cut into 1½-inch chunks. In a medium saucepan, bring potatoes and enough cold water to cover to a boil. Reduce heat and simmer until potatoes are tender and just beginning to break up, 10 to 15 minutes. Drain and mash potatoes with a large fork or masher.

2. In another medium saucepan, combine 1 cup water, salt, and butter. Bring to a boil and immediately add 1 cup of flour all at once. Stir with a wooden spoon until mixture pulls away from sides of saucepan and forms a thin film on bottom of saucepan, about 5 minutes. Remove from heat and let cool slightly, about 5 minutes.

3. Beat in eggs, 1 at a time. Add mashed potatoes and blend well. Dust work surface with remaining 2 tablespoons flour. Turn out dough and knead until smooth.

180 SNOW PEAS WITH WATER CHESTNUTS
Prep: 10 minutes   Cook: 4 minutes   Serves: 6

This dish can be eaten hot or at room temperature, which makes it a really useful quick vegetable dish.

4 **cups snow peas (about** **1 pound)**	½ **teaspoon sugar**
2 **tablespoons vegetable oil**	½ **teaspoon salt**
1 **cup water chestnuts**	2 **teaspoons sesame seeds**

1. In a large pot of boiling salted water, cook snow peas until they turn bright green, about 5 seconds. Drain immediately and rinse under cold running water to cool. Drain well.

2. In a wok, heat oil over medium heat. Add water chestnuts and snow peas and stir-fry until hot, about 1 minute. Add sugar and salt. Stir-fry 2 minutes.

3. Remove to a serving dish. Sprinkle sesame seeds on top and serve.

181 SPINACH WITH BEAN CURD CHEESE
Prep: 10 minutes   Cook: 3½ to 5½ minutes   Serves: 4

If you go to an Asian market, you will probably see water spinach, or *ong choi*. Buy some and try it in this recipe.

3 **pounds spinach or** *ong choi*	1 **tablespoon bean curd cheese**
2 **tablespoons vegetable oil**	(*fu yue*)
1 **slice of fresh ginger, minced**	**Salt**

1. Rinse and dry spinach. Remove any tough stems.

2. In a wok, heat oil over medium heat. Add ginger and stir-fry until aromatic, about 30 seconds. Add bean curd cheese and 2 tablespoons water. Stir to break up. Add spinach and cook, tossing, until spinach is wilted, 3 to 5 minutes. Season with salt to taste and serve.

182   OIL-WILTED GARLICKY SPINACH
Prep: 10 minutes   Cook: 3 to 4 minutes   Serves: 4

Here the spinach must be completely dry to avoid any splattering of oil. Rinse the leaves ahead of time, spin dry if possible, and then spread out on a towel to finish drying.

3 **pounds fresh spinach**	5 **garlic cloves, mashed**
¼ **cup vegetable oil**	½ **teaspoon salt**

1. Discard any tough stems from spinach. Pat with paper towels if not completely dry.

2. In a wok, heat oil to just smoking over high heat. Add garlic and cook until light brown, 1 to 2 minutes; remove and discard garlic.

3. Add spinach to wok, being careful not to splatter oil. Turn briskly until spinach wilts, about 2 minutes. Season with salt. Remove and serve.

183   STIR-FRIED SILK SQUASH
Prep: 10 minutes   Cook: 6 to 7 minutes   Serves: 6

When buying silk squash, look for firm squash. A good test is to hold one end and whip it back and forth gently. A fresh squash should not break too easily.

3 **silk squash**	1 **tablespoon dry sherry**
1 **tablespoon vegetable oil**	1 **teaspoon sugar**
1 **tablespoon minced scallion**	2 **teaspoons cornstarch**
2 **tablespoons soy sauce**	

1. Peel silk squash and cut diagonally into 2-inch pieces. There should be about 6 cups.

2. In a wok, heat oil until just smoking. Add scallion and stir-fry 2 seconds. Add silk squash and stir-fry over medium heat until tender, about 5 minutes.

3. In a small bowl, whisk together soy sauce, sherry, sugar, cornstarch, and 2 tablespoons cold water. Add to wok, bring to a boil, and cook, stirring, until mixture thickens and coats squash, 1 to 2 minutes.

184 SAUTEED SWEET POTATOES WITH SAUCE AND GINGER

Prep: 10 minutes   Cook: 31 to 38 minutes   Serves: 6

Try this Asian treatment of a traditional American vegetable at Thanksgiving for a different potato dish. You can add some bits of bacon for a richer dish.

1 tablespoon vegetable oil
1 medium onion, minced
1 teaspoon minced fresh
   ginger
4 large sweet potatoes, peeled
   and cut into 1-inch cubes

2 tablespoons soy sauce
½ teaspoon pepper
¼ cup brown sugar

1. In a large saucepan, heat oil over medium heat. Add onion and cook until softened, 3 to 5 minutes. Add ginger and cook until fragrant, about 10 seconds. Add sweet potato cubes, soy sauce, pepper, and 2 cups water. Cover, reduce heat to low, and cook, stirring occasionally, until potatoes are tender, 25 to 30 minutes. If potatoes get too dry before they are tender, add 1 to 2 tablespoons water.

2. Uncover and sprinkle brown sugar over sweet potatoes. Raise heat to medium and cook, stirring constantly, until sugar melts and coats potatoes, about 3 minutes.

185 BRAISED TARO ROOT

Prep: 10 minutes   Cook: 45 to 46 minutes   Serves: 4 to 6

Chinese are fond of taro, which is a starchy root. Little ones are often simply boiled and dipped in sugar. If you like, you can braise some pork cubes along with the taro in this recipe.

1 large taro
2 tablespoons vegetable oil
2 garlic cloves, crushed
1 tablespoon yellow bean
   sauce

2 tablespoons dry sherry
2 tablespoons dark soy sauce
2 teaspoons sugar

1. Peel taro and cut into 2-inch chunks. You should have about 3 cups.

2. In a wok or saucepan, heat oil over medium heat. Add garlic and stir-fry until aromatic, about 10 seconds. Add bean sauce, sherry, soy sauce, sugar, and 1½ cups water. Bring to a simmer.

3. Add taro chunks, stirring to mix them in. Reduce heat to low, cover, and cook until taro is tender and has absorbed flavor of sauce, about 45 minutes. Stir occasionally and add more water if dish becomes too dry.

186 BRAISED CHINESE MUSHROOMS
Prep: 20 minutes   Cook: 11 minutes   Serves: 4

2 ounces dried Chinese mushrooms	1 tablespoon soy sauce
½ pound fresh shiitake mushrooms	1 teaspoon sugar
2 tablespoons vegetable oil	¼ teaspoon salt
1 teaspoon minced fresh ginger	1 tablespoon dry sherry

1. In a bowl, soak dried mushrooms in ½ cup warm water for 10 to 15 minutes, until they are soft. Drain, reserving water. Remove and discard stems. Wipe shiitake mushrooms with a damp paper towel to remove any grit. Remove stems and discard.

2. In a wok, heat oil over medium heat until just smoking. Add minced ginger and fresh shiitake mushrooms. Stir-fry 1 minute. Add soaked mushrooms, reserved mushroom water, soy sauce, sugar, salt, and sherry. Reduce heat to low and simmer, covered, until mushrooms have absorbed almost all liquid, about 10 minutes. Remove from heat and serve warm or cold.

187 RAINBOW VEGETABLES
Prep: 15 minutes   Cook: 6 minutes   Serves: 6

The fresh crunch of these vegetables contrasts with the soft rice stick noodles, texture differences that delight the Chinese palate.

½ pound rice stick noodles (mei fun)	½ pound snow peas
1 pound bok choy	2 tablespoons vegetable oil
3 carrots, peeled	1 slice of fresh ginger
2 red bell peppers	Salt and pepper

1. In a large bowl, soak rice stick noodles in warm water until soft, 10 to 15 minutes; drain.

2. Trim bok choy and rinse thoroughly in cold water. Cut off green leaves and shred them. Cut white stems into ½-inch-thick sticks. Cut carrots into similar-size sticks. Stem and seed red peppers and cut into 2 x ½-inch strips. Cut snow peas into matchstick-size pieces.

3. In a wok, heat oil over medium heat. Add ginger and brown 1 minute; discard. Add bok choy stems and carrots and stir-fry 1 minute. Add red peppers and snow peas and stir-fry 1 minute longer. Add rice stick noodles and cook, tossing to mix well, until noodles are hot, about 3 minutes. Stir in shredded bok choy leaves. Season with salt and pepper to taste and serve.

188   VEGETABLE MU SHU

Prep: 20 minutes   Cook: 7 to 8 minutes   Serves: 4

4 dried Chinese mushrooms
6 tablespoons vegetable oil
4 eggs, beaten
6 water chestnuts, coarsely chopped
6 squares Marinated Pressed Bean Curd (page 124), cut into thin matchsticks
¼ cup sliced bamboo shoots
2 tablespoons soy sauce
1 tablespoon dry sherry
1 tablespoon cornstarch
1 teaspoon sugar
1 teaspoon pepper
½ cup bean sprouts
4 scallions, minced
2 tablespoons minced fresh ginger
8 Mu Shu Pancakes (page 210) or 6-inch flour tortillas
Hoisin sauce

1. Soak mushrooms in ½ cup warm water until soft, about 15 minutes. Remove, reserving water. Cut off and discard stems. Cut caps into thin shreds.

2. In a wok, bring 3 tablespoons oil to smoking point over medium heat. Add eggs and cook, stirring, until just set, about 3 minutes. Remove to a plate.

3. Add remaining oil to wok and heat over medium heat. Add mushrooms, water chestnuts, bean curd sticks, and bamboo shoots. Stir-fry 2 minutes.

4. In a small bowl, combine soy sauce, sherry, cornstarch, sugar, pepper, and reserved mushroom water. Add to wok, bring to a boil, and cook until sauce thickens, 1 to 2 minutes. Add bean sprouts and stir-fry until wilted, about 1 minute. Return eggs to wok and stir to blend. Remove from heat and stir in scallions and ginger.

5. Serve mu shu vegetables rolled in warm pancakes spread with hoisin sauce.

189   BRAISED VEGETABLE MEDLEY
Prep: 15 minutes   Cook: 22 to 27 minutes   Serves: 6 to 8

4 ounces bean threads
2 tablespoons tree ears
8 dried Chinese mushrooms
1 tablespoon vegetable oil
2 teaspoons minced fresh
    ginger
½ cup sliced bamboo shoots
1 cup fresh corn kernels

½ cup canned straw
    mushrooms
3 tablespoons mushroom soy
    sauce
½ cup Vegetable Stock (page
    28) or chicken broth
2 teaspoons Asian sesame oil
Salt and pepper

1. In separate bowls, soak bean threads and tree ears in warm water until soft, about 15 minutes. Drain bean threads and cut into 6-inch lengths. Drain tree ears and trim off any hard bits.

2. Meanwhile, in a third bowl, soak dried mushrooms in ½ cup warm water until soft, about 15 minutes. Drain mushrooms, reserving liquid. Remove and discard stems. Slice caps into matchsticks.

3. In a wok, bring vegetable oil to smoking point over medium heat. Add ginger and stir-fry until aromatic, about 15 seconds. Add tree ears, soaked mushrooms, bamboo shoots, corn kernels, and straw mushrooms. Stir-fry, tossing, 1 minute. Add soy sauce, stock, and reserved mushroom water. Add bean threads, stirring to mix well.

4. Reduce heat to low, cover, and simmer until flavors have blended, 20 to 25 minutes. Stir in sesame oil, season with salt and pepper to taste, and serve.

190   SILVER AND GOLD SALAD
Prep: 20 minutes   Cook: 1 minute   Serves: 6

4 ounces bean threads
    (cellophane noodles)
½ cup rice vinegar
1 tablespoon sugar
1 teaspoon salt

1 large daikon, peeled and
    finely shredded
6 carrots, peeled and finely
    shredded
1 small dried hot red pepper,
    crushed

1. Soak bean threads in a bowl of warm water until soft, about 15 minutes. Drain and cut into 6-inch lengths. In a small saucepan, cover bean threads with fresh cold water, bring to a boil, reduce heat, and simmer 1 minute. Drain and rinse under cold running water. Drain noodles well and transfer to a large bowl.

2. In a small bowl, combine rice vinegar, sugar, and salt. Stir to dissolve sugar. Add daikon and carrots to noodles, pour on dressing, and toss to blend. Turn into a serving bowl and scatter crushed pepper over salad.

191 SHREDDED VEGETABLE SALAD
Prep: 20 minutes   Cook: 1 minute   Serves: 8

2 ounces bean threads
  (cellophane noodles)
2 teaspoons Asian sesame oil
1 cup shredded carrots
1 cup shredded zucchini

1 cup shredded cucumbers
1 cup shredded celery
1 cup Sesame Vinaigrette
  (page 25)

1. Soak bean threads in a bowl of warm water until softened, about 15 minutes. Drain and cut into 2-inch pieces. Place cut noodles in a small saucepan, cover with fresh water, bring to a boil, and simmer 1 minute. Drain and rinse under cold running water. Drain noodles and transfer to a large bowl. Drizzle on sesame oil and toss to coat.

2. Add shredded carrots, zucchini, cucumbers, and celery to noodles. Pour on sesame vinaigrette, toss, and serve.

192 BEAN THREAD AND CUCUMBER SALAD
Prep: 15 minutes   Cook: 1 minute   Serves: 4

2 ounces bean threads
  (cellophane noodles)
2 tablespoons minced
  scallions
3 tablespoons soy sauce
¼ cup rice vinegar
2 tablespoons Asian sesame
  oil

2 tablespoons vegetable oil
1 tablespoon minced fresh
  ginger
1 teaspoon minced garlic
¼ cup chicken broth
¼ to ½ teaspoon cayenne
1 cucumber, peeled, seeded,
  and shredded

1. Soak bean threads in a bowl of warm water until soft, about 10 minutes; drain. Cut into 2-inch lengths. In a small saucepan, cook bean threads in enough water to cover until just soft, about 1 minute. Drain and rinse under cold running water.

2. In a small bowl, whisk together 1 tablespoon minced scallion with soy sauce, vinegar, sesame oil, vegetable oil, ginger, garlic, chicken broth, and cayenne.

3. Toss bean threads in half of dressing and arrange on a serving plate. Spread cucumber shreds over bean threads and pour remaining dressing over cucumber. Sprinkle remaining 1 tablespoon minced scallion on top.

193 CRUSTY BEAN CURD SQUARES IN BLACK BEAN SAUCE

Prep: 15 minutes   Cook: 14 minutes   Serves: 4

4 squares of firm bean curd
1 tablespoon fermented black
    beans
2 garlic cloves, minced
½ cup vegetable oil

3 celery ribs, cut into ¼-inch
    dice
1 tablespoon soy sauce
1 scallion, minced

1. Cut bean curd into 1-inch cubes. Dry on paper towels. Rinse black beans to remove excess salt; drain well. Mash beans with garlic.

2. In a wok, heat oil over medium-high heat to 375°F, or until a bread cube browns in 1 minute. Fry bean curd cubes in 2 batches until golden, about 5 minutes per batch. Remove with a slotted spoon and drain on paper towels. Pour off all but 1 tablespoon oil.

3. Return wok to heat, add black bean mixture, and stir-fry over medium heat until aromatic, about 30 seconds. Add celery and stir-fry until slightly softened, about 2 minutes. Add bean curd, soy sauce, and 2 tablespoons water. Bring to a boil and toss to mix well. Sprinkle with minced scallion, stir to mix, and serve.

194 STIR-FRIED BEAN CURD

Prep: 5 minutes   Cook: 2 to 3 minutes   Serves: 4

2 tablespoons vegetable oil
1 scallion, cut into 1-inch
    pieces
¼ teaspoon salt

1 pound firm bean curd, cut
    into 1-inch cubes
2 tablespoons soy sauce
½ teaspoon pepper

1. In a wok, heat oil until just smoking. Add scallion and salt and stir-fry over medium heat until aromatic, about 10 seconds.

2. Add bean curd cubes, soy sauce, and pepper. Cook over medium heat, tossing gently, until heated through, 2 to 3 minutes. Serve.

195   BEAN CURD WITH SCRAMBLED EGGS
Prep: 10 minutes   Cook: 5 minutes   Serves: 4 to 6

1 pound firm bean curd
4 eggs, beaten
2 tablespoons soy sauce
½ teaspoon black pepper
¼ teaspoon cayenne
¼ cup chicken or vegetable
   stock

1 tablespoon vegetable oil
1 slice of fresh ginger
2 scallions, minced
½ cup tiny frozen peas

1. Cut bean curd into ½-inch cubes. In a bowl, combine eggs, 1 tablespoon soy sauce, black pepper, cayenne, and stock. Beat to blend well.

2. In a wok or medium saucepan, heat oil over medium heat. Add ginger and stir-fry until light brown, about 1 minute; discard. Add scallions and peas. Cook, stirring, 1 minute. Reduce heat to low. Add bean curd and remaining 1 tablespoon soy sauce. Cook, stirring gently to mix well. Add eggs and cook, stirring to break eggs up, until they are just set, about 3 minutes. Serve at once.

196   RED-BRAISED BEAN CURD WITH MUSHROOMS AND BAMBOO SHOOTS
Prep: 20 minutes   Cook: 15 to 20 minutes   Serves: 6

8 dried Chinese mushrooms
1 cup dark soy sauce
1 whole star anise
1 teaspoon Szechuan
   peppercorns
2 slices of fresh ginger

2 scallions, cut into 2-inch
   pieces
2 pounds firm bean curd, cut
   into 2-inch squares
½ cup sliced bamboo shoots

1. Soak mushrooms in 1 cup warm water until soft, about 15 minutes. Drain, reserving water. Remove and discard stems.

2. In a large saucepan or flameproof casserole, combine soy sauce, star anise, Szechuan peppercorns, ginger, scallions, and reserved mushroom water. Bring to a boil; reduce to a simmer.

3. Add mushrooms, bean curd, and bamboo shoots. Return to a boil and reduce heat to low. Cover and simmer until bean curd has absorbed flavor, 15 to 20 minutes.

197   BEAN CURD AND VEGETABLE KEBABS
Prep: 30 minutes   Stand: 30 minutes   Cook: 15 minutes   Serves: 4

6 squares of Marinated
   Pressed Bean Curd (recipe
   follows)
¼ cup olive oil
¼ cup dry white wine
1 tablespoon dark soy sauce
1 teaspoon black pepper
1 teaspoon fresh minced
   thyme or ½ teaspoon
   dried

Few drops of Tabasco
1 medium onion, cut into
   2-inch squares
2 red bell peppers, cut into
   2-inch squares
24 water chestnuts
1 medium eggplant, peeled
   and cut into 2-inch cubes
3 medium zucchini, cut into
   2-inch-thick lengths

1. Soak 24 (10-inch) bamboo skewers in cold water for 30 minutes. Cut marinated bean curd squares into 4 quarters each. In a glass baking dish, combine olive oil, wine, soy sauce, pepper, thyme, and Tabasco. Add bean curd, onion, bell peppers, water chestnuts, eggplant, and zucchini. Toss gently to coat and marinate 30 minutes at room temperature. Thread 1 piece each bean curd, onion, red pepper, water chestnut, eggplant, and zucchini onto each skewer. Reserve.

2. Transfer marinade to a small saucepan. Bring to a boil, reduce heat, and simmer 5 minutes.

3. Preheat broiler or outdoor grill. Grill kebabs, turning often and basting with marinade, until vegetables are tender, about 10 minutes. Serve remaining marinade poured over kebabs.

198   MARINATED PRESSED BEAN CURD
Prep: 5 minutes   Cook: 5 minutes   Stand: overnight
Makes: 6 squares

¼ cup dark soy sauce
¼ cup dry white wine
1 tablespoon rice vinegar
1 whole star anise

½ teaspoon fennel seeds
   Pressed Bean Curd (recipe
   follows)

1. In a small nonreactive saucepan, combine soy sauce, wine, vinegar, star anise, fennel seeds, and 1 cup water. Bring to a boil, reduce heat to low, cover, and simmer 5 minutes. Strain, reserving liquid.

2. Lay bean curd in a glass dish and pour marinade over squares. Cover and refrigerate overnight, turning once. Remove from marinade and serve as is, hot or cold, or use in cooking.

199 PRESSED BEAN CURD

Prep: 5 minutes   Stand: 30 minutes   Cook: none   Makes: 6 squares

Because bean curd, or tofu, is a staple of the Chinese vegetarian diet, we have many ways of changing its texture to provide diversity. Being bland, bean curd also absorbs flavors easily. This recipe results in very firm-textured bean curd that can be used in several different ways.

**6 squares of bean curd or
    1 pound firm bean curd**

1. If you are using a 1-pound block of bean curd, slice this into 6 pieces. Lay damp cheesecloth on a cutting board. Arrange bean curd slices or squares on board, cover with more damp cheesecloth, and place another board over bean curd. Lay boards on a kitchen drain board and tilt toward sink. Weight down with cans or a bowl filled with water. Let stand 30 minutes or longer. The water in the bean curd will press out, resulting in a very firm bean curd.

2. Pressed bean curd can be kept refrigerated 2 or 3 days.

200 BEAN CURD STICKS WITH MUSHROOMS

Prep: 10 minutes   Cook: 9 minutes   Serves: 4

Pressed Bean Curd (page 125)
1 tablespoon vegetable oil
2 scallions, minced
1 teaspoon minced fresh ginger
1 garlic clove, minced
6 ounces fresh white mushrooms, sliced

6 ounces fresh shiitake mushrooms, sliced
2 tablespoons soy sauce
2 tablespoons chicken or vegetable broth or water
2 tablespoons dry sherry
1 teaspoon pepper
1 tablespoon lemon juice

1. Cut bean curd squares into ¼-inch-thick slices; then cut slices into matchsticks.

2. In a wok or skillet, bring oil to smoking point over medium heat. Add scallions, ginger, and garlic. Stir-fry until aromatic, about 10 seconds. Add white and shiitake mushrooms and stir-fry 2 minutes. Add bean curd sticks and stir gently to blend. Add soy sauce, broth, sherry, and pepper.

3. Bring to a boil, reduce heat, and simmer, uncovered, 5 minutes, stirring occasionally. Add lemon juice and cook 1 minute longer.

201 BAKED VEGETARIAN BEAN CURD POCKETS

Prep: 20 minutes   Cook: 35 to 37 minutes   Serves: 4 to 6

4 dried Chinese mushrooms
¼ teaspoon tree ears
2 squares of Pressed Bean Curd (page 125), coarsely chopped
1 tablespoon vegetable oil
1 scallion, minced
1 teaspoon minced fresh ginger
1 garlic clove, minced

2 cups bean sprouts
1 carrot, peeled and shredded
1 celery rib, shredded
1 tablespoon plus 2 teaspoons soy sauce
½ teaspoon pepper
8 squares of fresh firm bean curd
1 tablespoon Asian sesame oil
1 teaspoon cornstarch

1. In separate bowls, soak mushrooms and tree ears in warm water until soft, about 15 minutes. Drain mushrooms, reserving ¼ cup liquid. Remove and discard stems. Coarsely chop caps. Drain tree ears and discard water. Chop coarsely. In a medium bowl, mix together chopped pressed bean curd, mushrooms, and tree ears.

2. In a large nonstick skillet, heat vegetable oil over medium heat. Add scallion, ginger, and garlic and cook until aromatic, about 30 seconds. Add bean sprouts, carrot, celery, 2 teaspoons soy sauce, and pepper. Cook until vegetables are wilted, 5 to 7 minutes. Remove from heat and let cool slightly. Stir into pressed bean curd mixture to make filling.

3. Preheat oven to 350°F. Cut fresh bean curd squares in half on a diagonal to form 16 triangles. Scoop out a little pocket in center of cut side and stuff with filling. Lay triangles in a baking dish.

4. In a small bowl, blend remaining soy sauce, sesame oil, ¼ cup mushroom liquid, and cornstarch. Pour over bean curd triangles. Bake until bean curd is hot and sauce has thickened slightly, about 30 minutes.

202   SMOKED BEAN CURD WITH OYSTER SAUCE AND VEGETABLES

Prep: 20 minutes   Cook: 5 to 10 minutes   Serves: 4 to 6

6 dried Chinese mushrooms
3 tablespoons oyster sauce
2 tablespoons sherry
1 tablespoon soy sauce
1 teaspoon sugar
½ teaspoon pepper
2 tablespoons vegetable oil
2 teaspoons minced fresh ginger
6 squares of Tea-Smoked Bean Curd (recipe follows), cut into ½-inch cubes

½ pound bok choy, stems cut into sticks, leaves shredded
1 cup sliced bamboo shoots
1 (15-ounce) can baby corn, drained
1 (15-ounce) can straw mushrooms, drained
2 teaspoons Asian sesame oil

1. In a small bowl, soak dried mushrooms in 1 cup warm water until soft, about 15 minutes. Drain, reserving liquid. Remove and discard stems. In another small bowl, stir together oyster sauce, sherry, soy sauce, sugar, pepper, and reserved mushroom water.

2. In a wok, heat vegetable oil over medium heat until just smoking. Add ginger and stir-fry until aromatic, about 30 seconds. Add smoked bean curd, dried mushrooms, bok choy, bamboo shoots, baby corn, and straw mushrooms. Stir to mix well. Add combined sauce mixture. Reduce heat to low, cover, and simmer until bean curd has absorbed flavor, 5 to 10 minutes. Remove from heat. Drizzle with sesame oil and serve.

203   TEA-SMOKED BEAN CURD

Prep: 5 minutes   Cook: 15 minutes   Makes: 6 squares

½ cup sugar
½ cup flour

½ cup black tea leaves
6 squares of firm bean curd

1. Line a wok with aluminum foil. Sprinkle a layer of sugar, then a layer of flour over it, and lastly a layer of tea leaves. Place a metal rack in wok and arrange bean curd squares on rack.

2. Line metal wok lid with enough foil to form an overhang. Heat wok over medium heat until you see a wisp of smoke. Cover and crimp foil to seal tightly. Smoke bean curd until brown, about 15 minutes. Turn off heat. Let stand 5 minutes for smoke to dissipate, then uncover. Bean curd may be smoked 2 or 3 days in advance and stored well wrapped in refrigerator before using.

Chapter 7

Banquet Dishes

Because food is so important in Chinese culture, there is a whole category of cooking known as banquet cooking. These dishes usually involve elaborate presentation, rare and expensive ingredients, and/or longer preparation and cooking methods. Sometimes inexpensive ingredients are used, but then these are usually cooked by a slow process. Contrasting and balancing flavors and the look of a dish is something you will find emphasized in banquet dishes. Soups are made using homemade stocks as a base, so that even simple clear soups have a richness not usual in everyday broths. This is important to remember when preparing Shark's Fin Soup and Sizzling Rice Soup.

At banquets and formal dinners, dishes are served sequentially, or one at a time. Sometimes the cooking methods are simple, but the dramatic presentations make the dishes suitable for a banquet; for example, Winter Melon Pond, Squirrel Fish, and Chrysanthemum Squid. A typical menu would begin with an appetizer plate, often cold like Jellyfish Salad, and proceed with several stir-fried or small dishes, rising to a crescendo with a big banquet soup, such as Shark Fin Soup. Then on to the more formally presented, opulent banquet dishes like our Hoisin-Glazed Roast Chicken with Sweet Rice Stuffing.

Typically, a sweet soup might be served as a course somewhere in the middle of the feast. Modern practice, however, has put the sweet course at the end. It is also appropriate to plan a banquet menu where only one type of food makes up all the courses. A perfect example would be a Peking Duck dinner, where the duck skin would be served in pancakes, then a duck stir-fry would follow, with duck soup as a finale. Sometimes complete seafood menus are also used and in vegetarian cuisine, every dish would be made with vegetables or bean curd. Since elaborate presentations are such a key part of banquet dishes, this is a chance to use your best dinnerware and let your imagination run free when garnishing your platters.

Of course, for most of us, preparing a banquet of eight to ten dishes can be off-putting. Don't hesitate to try any of these wonderful dishes one at a time or as part of a simple menu. Do as the Chinese do and buy one or two dishes from Chinatown, such as a beautiful glazed roast duck or a rack of ribs. Then make one or two of the special dishes and integrate these into a formal dinner with a side dish of vegetables and a simple salad. If you are more adventurous, combine several banquet dishes for a great buffet.

Just remember to mix up your cooking methods, so you are not stuck in the kitchen cooking too many stir-fries. A soup, a roast, a red-braised dish (see "Chinese Stews and Braises," page 71) would make a perfect buffet with a noodle or rice dish and a salad. For a dramatic, special dinner just do a firepot dinner with sauces, or a Peking Duck dinner. Once you try one or two of these dishes, you will see how easy it is to mix banquet dishes into your regular cooking.

204   SIZZLING RICE SOUP

Prep: 20 minutes   Cook: 16 to 17 minutes   Serves: 8 to 10

The rice squares in this recipe sizzle when the hot soup is poured over them—thus, the name of the soup.

6 dried Chinese mushrooms	1 piece of dried tangerine
½ cup sliced bamboo shoots	peel, about 1 inch round
1 tablespoon vegetable oil	Salt and pepper
2 eggs, beaten	12 (2-inch) squares Sizzling
6 cups Rich Meat Stock (page	Rice (recipe follows)
28) or reduced-sodium	
canned chicken broth	

1. Soak dried mushrooms in 1 cup warm water until soft, about 15 minutes. Drain, reserving mushroom water. Remove and discard stems. Cut mushroom caps into matchstick-size strips. Cut bamboo shoot slices into similar-size strips.

2. In a 6- to 7-inch skillet or crepe pan, heat oil. Pour in just enough beaten egg to form a thin crepe. Cook without turning over medium heat until crepe is set but not brown, 1 to 2 minutes. Remove from skillet and repeat until all egg is used up. Roll up egg crepes and cut into ¼-inch ribbons.

3. In a large saucepan, bring stock to a boil. Add tangerine peel, reduce heat to medium, and simmer 5 minutes. Add reserved mushrooms and mushroom water, bamboo shoots, and egg ribbons. Simmer 10 minutes. Season with salt and pepper to taste.

4. Place sizzling rice squares in a soup tureen or individual bowls and pour hot soup over them. Serve immediately as rice sizzles.

205   SIZZLING RICE
Prep: 3 minutes   Stand: 33 to 35 minutes
Cook: 1½ hours plus 3 to 5 minutes   Makes: 28 (2-inch) squares

These rice squares are used in the famous soup, but also for seafood "sizzle platters." They can be made in advance, cooled completely, and stored in an airtight tin for several weeks. Lightly salted, they also make a good snack for children.

1½ cups long-grain white rice	2 cups peanut oil
2 cups cold water	

1. Preheat oven to 350°F. Soak rice in cold water for 30 minutes. Lightly grease a 15 x 10-inch baking pan.

2. Place rice and water in baking pan and cover tightly with foil. Bake 30 minutes.

3. Reduce oven temperature to 300°F. Uncover pan and continue baking rice 1 hour longer. Let cool, then unmold and cut into 2-inch squares.

4. In a wok, heat oil to 375°, or until a bread cube turns brown in 1 minute. Deep-fry rice squares, a few at a time, until puffed and lightly golden, 3 to 5 minutes. Drain on paper towels.

206   SHRIMP IN BROTH WITH SIZZLING RICE
Prep: 30 minutes   Cook: 18 minutes   Serves: 6

½ pound medium shrimp	2 teaspoons dry sherry
4 cups Chinese Chicken Stock	1 scallion, minced
(page 27) or reduced-	Salt and pepper
sodium canned broth	6 Sizzling Rice squares
1 slice of fresh ginger	(page 131)
1 teaspoon soy sauce	

1. Shell and devein shrimp, reserving shrimp shells.

2. In a medium saucepan, combine chicken stock, shrimp shells, and ginger. Bring to a boil, reduce heat, and simmer 10 minutes. Strain and discard shells and ginger. Return broth to saucepan.

3. Add soy sauce, sherry, and scallion. Simmer 5 minutes. Add shrimp and cook until shrimp just turn pink, about 3 minutes. Season with salt and pepper to taste.

4. Place a sizzling rice square in each individual soup bowl and pour hot soup into bowl. Rice should sizzle. Serve immediately.

207   WINTER MELON POND

Prep: 2 hours   Cook: 3 to 4 hours   Serves: 10

This is another instance where presentation is everything—a simple soup served in a spectacular manner. The winter melon is decorated by carving dragons, good luck characters, and so forth on the skin; then the hollow melon is filled with soup and steamed.

A winter melon pond is always presented whole, and the soup is served directly from it, together with pieces of tender melon scooped from the inside. For those less artistic, a template cut out on heavy paper works well as a stencil for the design. The hardest part of this dish is to figure out how to steam a whole melon. Before you buy your winter melon, take a few measurements so you will choose one that will fit your largest pot.

1 winter melon, about 12 pounds	½ pound lean boneless pork, cut into thin shreds
2 pieces of dried tangerine peel	4 ounces Smithfield ham, shredded
10 dried Chinese mushrooms	½ cup sliced bamboo shoots, shredded
4 ounces bean threads	
2½ quarts Chinese Chicken Stock (page 27)	½ cup coarsely chopped water chestnuts
2 tablespoons dry sherry	½ cup canned ginkgo nuts *
½ pound skinless, boneless chicken breast, cut into thin shreds	2 tablespoons soy sauce
	1 teaspoon pepper
	Salt

1. Cut top off melon and set aside. Scoop out seeds and stringy parts. Carve design on outside. Carving may be done 1 day in advance.

2. In 3 separate bowls, soak tangerine peel, mushrooms, and bean threads in warm water until soft, about 15 minutes. Drain tangerine peel and cut into thin shreds. Drain mushrooms, reserving liquid. Remove and discard stems. Cut caps into shreds. Drain bean threads and cut into 6-inch pieces.

3. Place melon on a shallow bowl and place bowl on a large dish towel, which will serve as a sling. Place a steaming rack in the bottom of a very large pot. Fill pot with enough water to come to bottom of melon, and bring to a boil. Place melon in its sling on steaming rack in pot.

4. In a large saucepan, bring stock, sherry, and reserved mushroom liquid to a boil. Pour into winter melon. Add tangerine peel, mushrooms, chicken, pork, ham, bamboo shoots, water chestnuts, gingko nuts, soy sauce, and pepper. Stir to break up meat and combine ingredients. Replace melon lid. Cover melon with another dish towel and cover pot with a lid. Steam melon over low heat until soft, 3 to 4 hours. Add bean threads to soup during last 15 minutes. Uncover and season with salt to taste.

5. Remove melon to a deep-sided serving dish. Serve soup and scooped-out pieces of melon at table.

---

* *Available in Asian markets*

208 SHARK FIN SOUP

Prep: 10 minutes   Stand: 6 hours   Cook: 23 to 29 minutes
Serves: 6 to 8

Shark fin is one of the famous banquet texture foods. Processed until it has no flavor of its own, it must be served in a flavorful dish that enhances the silky texture. In this soup, the shark fin is combined with another famous textured food of Chinese cuisine: velvet chicken. Shark fin comes in different degrees of processing. We use a variety that looks silvery and shiny and has been cleaned, so it requires less soaking time. Be warned: This is an expensive ingredient and is typical of an opulent theme when served at a banquet.

4 **ounces shark fin (page 6)**	3 **egg whites**
5 **scallions, 4 whole, 1 minced**	¼ **cup plus 1 tablespoon dry**
4 **slices of fresh ginger**	**sherry**
8 **cups Chinese Chicken Stock**	2 **tablespoons cornstarch**
(page 27)	1 **tablespoon vegetable oil**
4 **ounces skinless, boneless**	**Salt**
chicken breast	

1. Soak shark fin in cold water 6 hours. Remove as much tough cartilage as possible and retain "needles" of fin. Drain well.

2. In a large saucepan, combine 6 cups cold water, 4 whole scallions, and sliced ginger. Add shark fin, bring to a boil, reduce heat, and simmer 10 minutes. Drain in a fine strainer and rinse under cold running water.

3. Return shark fin to saucepan. Add 2 cups of chicken stock, bring to a boil, and cook until almost all stock is absorbed, 10 to 15 minutes. Remove from heat.

4. In a food processor, finely mince chicken with egg whites. Add 1 tablespoon of sherry. Pulse to combine well. Remove to a bowl. In a small bowl, blend cornstarch with ¼ cup cold water.

5. In a wok or large saucepan, heat oil. Add minced scallion and stir-fry over medium heat until aromatic, about 30 seconds. Add remaining 6 cups stock, remaining ¼ cup sherry, and shark fin. Whisk cornstarch and water to blend. Add to stock, bring to a boil, and cook, stirring, until soup is thickened 2 to 3 minutes. Add chicken and immediately stir to break up chicken. Cook over low heat until chicken turns white, about 30 seconds. Season with salt to taste. Remove from heat and serve.

209   DUCK SOUP
Prep: 10 minutes   Cook: 35 minutes   Serves: 6

Traditionally this soup is served as a last course with Peking Duck.

8 cups Chinese Chicken Stock (page 27) or reduced-sodium canned broth
Duck carcass, reserved from Peking Duck (page 142)
1 slice of fresh ginger
1 scallion
1 tablespoon dry sherry
1 tablespoon soy sauce
1 pound soft bean curd, cut into ½-inch dice
2 cups shredded Chinese (Napa) cabbage
Salt and pepper

1. In a large stockpot, combine chicken stock, duck carcass, ginger, and scallion. Bring to a boil, reduce heat, and simmer until stock is flavorful, about 30 minutes. Strain; discard bones and vegetables.

2. Return stock to pot. Add sherry, soy sauce, bean curd, and cabbage. Bring to a boil, reduce heat, and simmer until hot, about 5 minutes. Remove from heat. Season with salt and pepper to taste.

210   PRESSED ANISE BEEF
Prep: 15 minutes   Cook: 2¾ hours   Press: overnight   Serves: 8

This is a delicious appetizer that makes the long cooking and pressing well worthwhile. Pressed beef is usually served as part of a cold meat appetizer platter. You can combine it with smoked chicken, white cooked chicken, slices of ham, braised mushrooms, or other dishes.

2 cups dark soy sauce
¼ cup Szechuan peppercorns
½ cup star anise
2 cinnamon sticks
2 tablespoons brown sugar
2½ pounds lean chuck or brisket, trimmed and cut into a rectangular shape

1. In a saucepan or flameproof casserole large enough to hold meat, combine soy sauce, Szechuan peppercorns, star anise, cinnamon sticks, brown sugar, and 10 cups of water. Bring to a boil, reduce heat to low, cover, and simmer 15 minutes to infuse liquid with flavor.

2. Add meat to saucepan, return to a boil, reduce heat to low, cover, and simmer until meat is fork tender, about 2½ hours.

3. Remove meat from cooking liquid. Let cool, wrap in plastic wrap, and set on a plate. Cover with another plate and weight down, with heavy cans. Refrigerate overnight.

4. Slice pressed meat as thinly as possible, arrange on a platter, and serve as an appetizer.

211   JELLYFISH SALAD

Prep: 25 minutes   Stand: 30 minutes   Cook: 12 minutes
Serves: 6 to 8

In banquet cuisine, there are texture foods that are prized by gourmets. A chef's talents are showcased in their preparation as they have no taste of their own, and must be enhanced with other flavors to be delectable. Jellyfish is one of these foods. It is dried and salted. The preparation involves removing any fishy flavor and the end result is something unique. Whenever I have served this, guests come back for more.

1 (14-ounce) package salted dried jellyfish
1 skinless, boneless chicken breast half (4 to 5 ounces)
2 garlic cloves, crushed through a press
½ teaspoon salt
¼ teaspoon sugar
½ cup rice vinegar
4 scallions, cut into 2-inch pieces
1 cup finely shredded Chinese (Napa) cabbage

1. Rinse jellyfish in several changes of cold water. In a bowl, soak jellyfish in warm—not hot—water until soft and translucent, about 30 minutes. Drain well. Roll up jellyfish and cut into ¼-inch ribbons. Refrigerate 10 minutes.

2. Meanwhile, place chicken in a small saucepan. Add lightly salted water to cover. Bring to a simmer, reduce heat to medium-low, and cook until just white in center, about 12 minutes. Let chicken cool in liquid. Tear into shreds.

3. In a small bowl, mash garlic with salt and sugar. Whisk in vinegar. Set dressing aside.

4. In a large bowl, toss jellyfish, scallions, and cabbage. Remove 3 tablespoons dressing to a medium bowl. Toss jellyfish and vegetables in remaining dressing. Mound on a serving platter. Cover and refrigerate 15 minutes. Just before serving, add chicken to reserved dressing, toss, and lay over jellyfish-vegetable mix.

212   LONG LIFE NOODLES IN EGG SAUCE
Prep: 10 minutes   Cook: 14 to 15 minutes   Serves: 6

In China, eggs are associated with long life. Noodles, specifically long life noodles, are always served at birthday banquets, and as according to Chinese custom the New Year is everyone's birthday, these noodles are ideal for a festive New Year's dinner. The noodles, or *lu mein*, in this dish are served in individual bowls with equal amounts of sauce and one or two condiments sprinkled on top.

1 **pound thin fresh noodles**	3 **tablespoons cornstarch**
2 **cups Chinese Chicken Stock**	2 **eggs, well beaten**
(page 27) or reduced-	1 **teaspoon freshly ground**
sodium canned broth	**pepper**
¼ **cup dark soy sauce**	2 **teaspoons Asian sesame oil**
1 **whole star anise**	¼ **cup shredded ham**
3 **tablespoons dry sherry**	2 **scallions, shredded**

1. In a large pot of rapidly boiling water, cook noodles until just tender but still firm, about 3 minutes. Drain and divide among 6 bowls. Cover to keep warm.

2. In a medium saucepan, combine ½ cup water, stock, soy sauce, star anise, and sherry. Bring to a boil, reduce heat, and simmer 10 minutes. Dissolve cornstarch in ½ cup cold water and stir into sauce. Bring to a boil, stirring, until thickened, 1 to 2 minutes.

3. Remove from heat and immediately stir in beaten eggs with a fork to form thin threads. Season with pepper and sesame oil. Spoon over noodles, sprinkle with ham and scallions, and serve.

213   OLD AND NEW EGGS
Prep: 10 minutes   Cook: 15 to 20 minutes   Serves: 4

One-hundred-year-old eggs *(pay dahn)* are actually eggs preserved in alkaline ash. The ash turns the egg white to a jellylike brown, and the yolk develops a greenish color. Its distinctive flavor, almost like strong cheese, is an acquired taste. They are often served simply quartered, with soy drizzled over them. This is a more interesting way to try these eggs.

3 **100-year-old eggs** *	1 **tablespoon vegetable oil**
3 **fresh eggs**	1 **tablespoon soy sauce**
3 **tablespoons chicken broth**	1 **tablespoon Asian sesame oil**
½ **teaspoon salt**	1 **scallion, finely minced**

1. Clean "mud" off old eggs. Rinse shells, crack, and peel. With a stainless steel knife, finely dice eggs. In a small bowl, gently beat fresh eggs, trying not to form too much foam. Stir in chicken broth and salt.

2. Grease a shallow 7- or 8-inch heatproof bowl well with oil. Place diced "old" eggs on bottom of bowl. Pour on beaten "new" eggs. Set bowl in a bamboo steamer, cover, and set in a wok.

3. Fill wok one-third full of water. Bring water to a boil, reduce heat to medium-low, and steam eggs until set, 15 to 20 minutes. Remove from heat, let cool slightly, and unmold eggs. Cover and refrigerate until cold.

4. Slice eggs and arrange in overlapping layers on a serving plate. Drizzle with soy sauce and sesame oil. Scatter minced scallion over eggs. This dish should be served cold.

*Available in Asian markets

---

214 DRUNKEN CHICKEN

Prep: 10 minutes   Chill: 2 hours plus overnight   Cook: 25 minutes
Stand: 20 minutes   Serves: 4 to 6

This simple but succulent poached chicken is usually served cold as a first course. It gets its name from the sherry in which it is soaked. Since it is best marinated overnight, be sure to cook this dish a day ahead.

1 (3-pound) whole chicken
2 teaspoons minced fresh
    ginger
1½ teaspoons salt
¼ teaspoon Chinese five-spice
    powder

2 scallions, cut into 2-inch
    lengths
4 cups dry sherry

1. Rinse chicken inside and out under cold running water; pat dry with paper towels. In a small bowl, combine minced ginger, salt, and five-spice powder. Rub chicken inside and out with seasoning mixture. Refrigerate 2 hours.

2. Place chicken on a heatproof plate. Surround with scallions. Fill a wok one-third full of water. Bring water to a boil, then reduce to a simmer. Place a rack in the wok and place plated chicken on rack. Cover wok and steam chicken over medium heat for 25 minutes. Without lifting lid, turn off heat and let chicken stand in covered wok for 20 minutes. The retained heat will finish cooking chicken.

3. When chicken is cool, cut into quarters. Discard scallions. Place chicken parts and juices that have accumulated on plate in a glass dish and cover with sherry. Marinate chicken overnight in refrigerator, turning occasionally.

4. To serve, remove chicken from sherry, cut into bite-size pieces, and mound on serving platter.

215 SAVORY PRESSED BEAN CURD SLIVERS

Prep: 10 minutes   Stand: 10 minutes   Cook: 3 minutes   Serves: 6

The preparation of this appetizer dish removes excess starch from the bean curd slivers.

Pressed Bean Curd	1 **tablespoon sugar**
(page 125)	1 **tablespoon Asian sesame oil**
Boiling water	1 **teaspoon finely minced**
¼ **cup dark soy sauce**	**fresh ginger**

1. Place pressed bean curd squares in a medium saucepan of simmering water. Over low heat, simmer 3 minutes; drain.

2. Cut bean curd squares horizontally into ¼-inch-thick slices. Stack slices and cut into fine matchstick-size slivers. Place slivers in a heatproof bowl. Pour boiling water over bean curd. Let stand 10 minutes. Drain and repeat twice.

3. In a small bowl, combine soy sauce, sugar, and sesame oil. Stir to dissolve sugar. Add minced ginger.

4. Pour dressing over drained bean curd slivers. Toss gently to mix and mound on a plate. Serve cold or at room temperature.

216 SALT-BAKED CHICKEN

Prep: 20 minutes   Cook: 1 hour   Serves: 4

1 **(3-pound) whole chicken**	2 **tablespoons soy sauce**
8 **scallions, cut into 2-inch**	2 **tablespoons vodka**
pieces	2 **boxes (6 pounds) coarse**
8 **slices of fresh ginger,**	**(kosher) salt**
shredded	

1. Trim chicken, rinse under cold running water, and wipe dry with paper towels, inside and out. In a small bowl, combine scallions, ginger, soy sauce, and vodka. Rub mixture all over chicken, inside and out.

2. Preheat oven to 450°F. In a wok, heat salt over medium heat, tossing to warm evenly. Pour salt into a deep ovenproof casserole. Bury chicken in salt, being sure to cover chicken completely. Sprinkle a little water over salt to form a crust. Place in oven and cook 1 hour. Remove from oven and let stand 10 minutes.

3. To serve, break crust and uncover chicken. The chicken will not taste too salty, but succulent and delicious.

217 HOISIN-GLAZED ROAST CHICKEN WITH SWEET RICE STUFFING

Prep: 30 minutes   Cook: 1 hour 40 minutes   Stand: 15 minutes
Serves: 6 to 8

6 dried Chinese mushrooms	¼ cup cooked small shrimp
1½ cups glutinous rice	¼ cup dry-roasted peanuts
2 cups Chinese Chicken Stock (page 27) or reduced-sodium canned broth	1 teaspoon salt
	½ teaspoon pepper
	2 teaspoons vegetable oil
¼ cup dry sherry	1 (4-pound) whole chicken
2 teaspoons minced fresh ginger	¼ cup hoisin sauce
	2 tablespoons soy sauce
4 scallions, minced	1 teaspoon Asian sesame oil
¼ cup diced ham	¼ cup dry white wine
¼ cup coarsely chopped water chestnuts	1 bunch of watercress
2 Chinese sausages *(lop cheung)*, diced	

1. In a small bowl, soak mushrooms in ½ cup warm water until soft, about 15 minutes. Remove mushrooms, reserving liquid. Cut off and discard stems. Slice caps into thin shreds.

2. Rinse rice with cold water. In a medium saucepan, combine rice, stock, sherry, and reserved mushroom liquid. Bring to a boil, reduce heat, cover, and cook until rice is tender and liquid is absorbed, about 20 minutes.

3. Remove from heat. Add ginger, scallions, ham, water chestnuts, sausage, shrimp, peanuts, salt, and pepper. Toss gently with a fork to combine. Let cool 10 minutes. With 2 teaspoons vegetable oil, grease a roasting pan large enough to hold chicken.

4. Preheat oven to 350°F. Fill cavity of chicken with rice stuffing. Close with a skewer. Place chicken in roasting pan. In a small bowl, blend hoisin sauce, soy sauce, and sesame oil.

5. Pour wine over chicken and roast 20 minutes. Baste chicken with hoisin glaze. Continue to roast basting chicken every 15 minutes until juices in thickest part of thigh run clear and golden when pricked with a knife, about 1 hour longer. Remove to a serving platter. Let stand 15 minutes.

6. To serve, garnish platter with watercress. Carve chicken at table and spoon out stuffing.

218   BRAISED GIZZARDS IN OYSTER SAUCE
Prep: 15 minutes   Cook: 55 minutes   Serves: 4 to 6

1 pound chicken gizzards
1 cup Chinese Chicken Stock
   (page 27) or reduced-
   sodium canned broth
2 scallions—1 whole,
   1 minced

1 slice of fresh ginger plus
   ½ teaspoon minced
2 teaspoons vegetable oil
2 tablespoons oyster sauce
1 teaspoon sugar
1 tablespoon Asian sesame oil

1. Trim gizzards and cut in half. In a saucepan, combine gizzards with stock, whole scallion, and ginger slice. Bring to a boil, cover, reduce heat to medium-low, and simmer until gizzards are tender, about 40 minutes. Remove from heat.

2. In a wok, heat vegetable oil until just smoking. Add minced scallion and minced ginger. Stir-fry over high heat until aromatic, about 30 seconds. Add oyster sauce, sugar, gizzards, and any stock remaining in pan. Bring to a boil, reduce heat, and simmer until gizzards have absorbed flavor and sauce has reduced slightly, about 15 minutes. Drizzle with sesame oil and serve.

219   CHICKEN CONGEE
Prep: 10 minutes   Cook: 1½ to 2 hours   Serves: 8

Congee, also called *jook* by the Cantonese, is usually served for breakfast. It is often made with plain water and flavored with various toppings, which are mixed into the gruel individually. This recipe makes a richer, chicken-flavored congee. As children, we were often served this simple, comforting dish when we were sick—a Chinese version of the proverbial chicken soup that cured everything. If you have a slow cooker, congee can be prepared overnight for breakfast or brunch.

1 (3-pound) whole chicken
1 cup long-grain rice
10 cups cold water

Salt
Congee Sauce (recipe
   follows)

1. In a heavy-bottomed stockpot, bring chicken, rice, and water to a boil. Reduce heat to low and simmer until chicken is tender and rice breaks up to form a thick gruel, about 1½ to 2 hours. Stir gently occasionally to prevent rice sticking and burning. Season with salt to taste. Remove chicken and cut into bite-size pieces.

2. To serve, spoon rice congee into individual serving bowls and top with chicken pieces. Drizzle sauce over chicken pieces.

220 CONGEE SAUCE
Prep: 5 minutes   Cook: none   Makes: ½ cup

2 tablespoons soy sauce
2 tablespoons Asian sesame
   oil
1 tablespoon rice vinegar
1 teaspoon sugar

½ teaspoon freshly ground
   pepper
2 scallions, minced
2 tablespoons finely shredded
   fresh ginger

In a small bowl, whisk together soy sauce, sesame oil, vinegar, sugar, and pepper. Stir in scallions and ginger.

221 CANTONESE CRISPY ROAST DUCK
Prep: 15 minutes   Stand: 2 hours   Cook: 55 to 75 minutes
Stand: 15 minutes   Serves: 4

A preliminary dunking in hot water is the Chinese secret to a crispy duck divulged in this simple recipe.

1 (4- to 5-pound) duck
½ tablespoon salt
1 teaspoon Chinese five-spice
   powder

1 tablespoon honey
1 tablespoon soy sauce

1. In a large pot, bring 5 quarts of water to a boil. Remove from heat and dunk duck briefly in hot water. Drain and dry thoroughly with paper towels.

2. In a small bowl, mix salt and five-spice powder. Rub all over duck. Place duck on a roasting rack set in a shallow roasting pan, and let duck air-dry in a cool place until skin feels like parchment, about 3 to 5 hours. Placing duck in front of a fan can reduce drying time to 2 hours.

3. Preheat oven to 450°F. In another small bowl, mix honey, soy sauce, and 3 tablespoons water. With a pastry brush, paint duck all over with this glaze. Roast duck until brown, about 10 to 15 minutes. Reduce oven temperature to 350° and continue roasting duck 45 minutes to 1 hour, basting every 15 minutes with honey-soy glaze. Duck is done when juices run clear when pricked in thickest part of thigh.

4. Remove duck from oven. Let stand 15 minutes. Cut wings, legs, and thighs from duck. Remove breast meat from bone and slice. Arrange duck pieces on a platter and serve.

222 PEKING DUCK

Prep: 30 minutes   Stand: 2 hours   Cook: 1½ hours
Serves: 4 to 6

Peking duck is one of the truly great dishes in Chinese cooking. It can be served as one course in a banquet, or as a three-course extravaganza: first, the duck skin, wrapped in a pancake with hoisin sauce and scallion brush; then the duck meat, slivered and quickly stir-fried; and lastly, a soup made from the carcass, which ends the meal. The duck meat, however, is succulent and tender and we usually serve the skin and meat together to be wrapped in one package.

The secret to a crispy skin is all in the preparation of the duck before roasting. Air is blown between the skin and meat of a duck, which is dunked into sweetened water and air-dried until the skin feels like parchment paper. I developed this recipe using a fresh or frozen supermarket duck. If possible, a baking pan filled with sand, rather than water, should be placed under the duck to catch the fat while it is cooking.

1 (5-pound) duck, fresh or thawed frozen	1 cup hoisin sauce
1 cup honey	2 tablespoons soy sauce
24 scallions	Mu Shu Pancakes (page 210)

1. Trim duck and rinse inside and out in hot water. Pat dry with paper towels. Carefully insert fingers between skin and meat and loosen skin. With a large needle and string, sew up large cavity. Sew neck cavity as much as needed so there is only a small opening. Insert a drinking straw in neck between skin and meat. Fashion a noose just below opening. Blow as much air as possible through straw into duck to separate skin; pull noose tightly to seal air in. The duck should fill up like a balloon. If some air escapes, try to sew up leaks, but do not be too concerned.

2. Meanwhile, fill a large stockpot with 10 to 12 cups water. Add honey and bring to a boil. Turn off heat. Holding duck by the neck, briefly dunk duck once or twice, ladling some hot water over the duck as well. Do not leave duck in water too long. The dunking will wash off surface fat and tighten pores. Hang duck to dry in a cool, well-ventilated area 4 to 6 hours, until skin feels like parchment. Place a pan under duck to catch drippings. Drying time can be reduced to 2 hours by blowing on duck with an electric fan.

3. Trim green tops off scallions to leave white bulb and about 2 inches of pale green. With a sharp paring knife, cut 1½-inch slits into both ends of scallion stalks. Place in a bowl of ice water to crisp and curl into brushes. In a small bowl, blend hoisin sauce with soy sauce. Divide among small dishes for serving at table.

4. Remove top rack from oven. Place pan to catch drippings on bottom of oven. Preheat oven to 450°F. Replace rack and lay duck directly on rack, breast side up. Roast duck 15 minutes. Reduce heat to 350° and continue roasting duck until skin is crisp and meat is tender and no longer pink near bone, about 1 hour. Slide duck halfway out of oven and position over drip pan. Slit cavity and pour off excess fat. Remove duck to a serving platter.

5. Place pancakes in a steamer basket and steam over hot water until warm, about 10 minutes. Pancakes may be served directly from basket.

6. To serve duck, remove skin and cut into 2-inch square pieces. Place around edges of a heated platter. Slice meat and arrange in center of platter. Reserve carcass for duck soup. Diners spread hoisin sauce on pancake, place a piece of skin and meat with a scallion brush in center, and roll up into a fat cigar shape, which is eaten with fingers.

223　CRISPY SQUAB

Prep: 10 minutes　　Stand: 2 to 5 hours　　Cook: 40 to 50 minutes
Serves: 4

2 **squab, 1 pound each**	1 **teaspoon salt**
2 **tablespoons dark soy sauce**	2 **cups vegetable oil**
½ **teaspoon Chinese five-spice powder**	**Watercress sprigs**

1. Remove innards from squab. In a large saucepan, bring 6 cups of water to a boil. With tongs, dunk squab briefly in boiling water. Pat dry, inside and out, with paper towels.

2. In a small bowl, combine soy sauce with five-spice powder. Rub inside of squab with salt. Paint outside of squab with soy mixture. Place on a rack over a roasting pan and let squab dry in a cool place until skin feels like parchment, 3 to 5 hours. Placing squab before a fan will reduce drying time to 2 hours.

3. In a wok, heat oil to 375°F, or until a cube of bread browns in 1 minute. Deep-fry squab, one at a time, turning frequently, until skin is crisp and brown, squab is cooked through, and juices run clear when thigh is pricked, 20 to 25 minutes each. Remove to paper towels. Let cool 10 minutes.

4. To serve, remove wings and legs. Cut squab in half down breast and cut into bite-size pieces. Arrange on a platter, surround with watercress sprigs, and serve at room temperature.

224   FIREPOT HONG KONG STYLE
Prep: 40 minutes   Cook: at table   Serves: 6 to 8

Firepots are great for cold wintry days. You can buy a proper utensil, which has a chimney for hot coals and a moat around it to keep stock piping hot, or you can use an electric wok or deep skillet. The object is to have a cooking implement in the center of the table so each diner can use chopsticks to cook bite-size bits of meat, seafood, and vegetables, which are then dipped in different sauces. At the end of the meal, the enriched stock is served as soup.

2 ounces bean threads
½ pound skinless, boneless
   chicken breast
½ pound filet mignon
½ pound calf's liver
½ pound flounder fillets
2 lobster tails
½ pound medium shrimp,
   shelled and deveined
12 oysters
12 clams

12 mussels
1 pound shredded Chinese
   (Napa) cabbage
2 pounds spinach, washed
6 to 8 scallions
2 quarts Rich Meat Stock
   (page 28)
1 tablespoon dry sherry
½ teaspoon pepper
   Firepot Sauces (recipe
   follows)

1. In a small bowl, soak bean threads in warm water until soft, about 15 minutes. Drain and cut into 6-inch lengths. Mound in serving bowl.

2. Slice raw chicken, beef, liver, and fish as thinly as possible and arrange fanned out on separate serving plates. Shell lobster tails, slice thinly, and arrange on a serving plate with shrimp mounded in the center. Under cold running water, scrub oysters, clams, and mussels, and mound in separate bowls. Set out platters of cabbage, spinach, and scallions.

3. In a large saucepan, combine stock, sherry, and pepper. Bring to a boil and transfer to firepot.

4. To serve, place firepot with bubbling stock in the center of table surrounded by platters of ingredients. Each diner selects pieces of meat, fish, and seafood and dunks these into bubbling stock with chopsticks or a long-handled fondue fork. Cooked morsels of food are then dipped into firepot sauces of choice before eating. As the meal progresses and the stock diminishes, vegetables, bean threads, and a little more stock are added. The savory soup is served as a final course at the end of the meal.

225   FIREPOT SAUCES

Prep: 15 minutes   Stand: 1 hour   Cook: none

This recipe contains five separate dips to be served with a firepot. They are usually set out in small dishes in front of diners, so they are easily reached. You may vary them and include a hot and spicy one, if desired.

¼ cup plus 1 tablespoon
    soy sauce
1 tablespoon finely minced
    fresh ginger
1 tablespoon minced scallion
1 tablespoon minced cilantro
½ teaspoon Asian sesame oil
½ cup hoisin sauce

¼ teaspoon Tabasco
½ cup Wild Pepper Mix
    (page 25)
3 tablespoons dry mustard
¼ cup white wine vinegar
2 tablespoons finely minced
    garlic

1. In a bowl, whisk together ¼ cup of soy sauce with ginger, scallion, cilantro, and sesame oil. Divide into small dishes and serve.

2. In a small bowl, blend hoisin sauce, 1 tablespoon soy sauce, and Tabasco. Divide into small dishes and serve.

3. Divide wild pepper mix into small dishes and serve.

4. Mix dry mustard with about ⅓ cup cold water to form a watery paste. Let stand 10 minutes before serving. Thin with a little additional water if necessary.

5. In a small bowl, combine vinegar and garlic. Let stand 1 hour before serving.

226   SWEET AROMATIC ROAST PORK

Prep: 15 minutes   Stand: 2 hours   Cook: 1½ hours   Serves: 6

1 (3-pound) boneless pork leg
    or loin roast
1 tablespoon salt
1 teaspoon Chinese five-spice
    powder

¼ teaspoon ground cloves
2 tablespoons soy sauce
2 tablespoons dry sherry
2 tablespoons honey

1. Prick pork all over with tip of a knife. In a small bowl, combine salt, five-spice powder, and ground cloves. Rub all over pork. Let stand at room temperature 2 hours.

2. Preheat oven to 450°F. In a small bowl, combine soy sauce, sherry, honey, and 1 tablespoon water. Paint pork with this mixture. Place on a rack in a shallow roasting pan and roast 10 minutes. Reduce oven temperature to 350° and continue roasting, basting often with marinade, until pork is tender, about 1½ hours total. Remove pork from oven; let stand 20 minutes before carving.

227 RED ROAST PORK (CHAR SUI)
Prep: 10 minutes   Chill: 6 hours   Cook: 45 to 60 minutes
Serves: 8

This is the recipe for the roast pork strips that you see hanging in meat stores in every shop in Chinatown. If you like the traditional red color, add a few drops of red food coloring to your marinade.

4 pounds pork butt
  (shoulder), with some fat
¼ cup dark soy sauce
¼ cup hoisin sauce
¼ cup ketchup
3 tablespoons dry sherry

2 garlic cloves, minced
1 tablespoon salt
2 teaspoons Chinese five-spice
  powder
½ cup brown sugar

1. Cut pork lengthwise into long pieces, about 2½ inches thick.

2. In a medium bowl, combine soy sauce, hoisin sauce, ketchup, sherry, garlic, salt, five-spice powder, and brown sugar. Mix to blend well. Add pork and turn meat to coat well. Cover and refrigerate 6 hours.

3. Preheat oven to 350°F. Place pork strips on a rack in a shallow roasting pan. Roast in oven until pork is cooked through and tender, about 45 minutes to 1 hour, turning often and basting every 15 minutes with marinade. Discard any leftover marinade.

4. For a traditional charred look, brown pork briefly under a preheated broiler.

228 ABALONE IN OYSTER SAUCE
Prep: 10 minutes   Cook: 15 minutes   Serves: 4 to 6

1 (16-ounce) can abalone
2 teaspoons vegetable oil
1 scallion, minced
½ teaspoon minced fresh
  ginger

2 tablespoons dry sherry
2 tablespoons oyster sauce
¼ cup chicken broth
2 teaspoons Asian sesame oil

1. Remove abalone from can, rinse in warm water, and cut into thin slices.

2. In a wok or large saucepan, heat vegetable oil over medium heat until just smoking. Add scallion and ginger and stir-fry until aromatic, about 10 seconds. Add sherry, oyster sauce, and chicken broth. Bring to a boil and add abalone slices. Reduce heat and simmer until abalone is flavored and sauce thickens slightly, about 15 minutes.

3. Remove from heat. Drizzle with sesame oil, stir to blend, and serve.

229 SQUIRREL FISH

Prep: 30 minutes   Cook: 12 to 14 minutes   Serves: 6

The name of this dish relates to the "furry" effect achieved in its presentation. It takes a little effort, but with a bit of practice is really quite easy, and the end result makes it well worth it. Red snapper, sea bass, and tilefish are all good choices for this dish.

1 whole white, firm-textured fish with head, 3 to 4 pounds	2 scallions, cut into 2-inch pieces
¾ cup flour	½ cup chicken broth
¾ cup plus 1 tablespoon cornstarch	3 tablespoons cider vinegar
3 eggs	1 tablespoon soy sauce
3 cups vegetable oil	1 tablespoon Asian sesame oil
	1 slice of fresh ginger

1. Remove fish head and reserve. Fillet fish by cutting along stomach and spine up to 1 inch from tail, so that there are 2 boneless fillets, with skin, attached to tail. Carefully spread fillets on work surface without breaking off tail. With a sharp knife, score fish flesh in a diamond pattern without cutting through skin. Bring a pot of water to a boil. Remove from heat and dunk fish briefly to shrink flesh and accentuate diamond pattern. Let fish cool.

2. Mix flour with ¾ cup cornstarch and pour onto wax paper. In a wide shallow bowl, beat eggs until blended. Dip fish in beaten eggs, then coat with flour mixture.

3. In a wok, heat vegetable oil to 375°F, or until a cube of bread browns in 1 minute. Hold fish and twist fillets so flesh sides are facing out. Holding fish by tail and holding fillet ends together, carefully add fish to hot oil. Deep-fry until golden and fish is cooked through, about 5 minutes. Using 2 wide spatulas, carefully remove fish to serving platter. Flour fish head and deep-fry until crisp, about 5 minutes. Arrange on a serving platter to look like a whole fish with head on. Sprinkle with scallions.

4. In a bowl, whisk together chicken broth, vinegar, soy sauce, sesame oil, and remaining 1 tablespoon cornstarch. Pour off oil from wok. (Strain and reserve for another use, if desired.) Do not wipe out wok. Return to heat, add ginger, and stir-fry over high heat until brown, 1 to 2 minutes. Remove and discard ginger. Add sauce mixture to wok and bring to a boil, stirring, until thickened, 1 to 2 minutes. Pour over fish to serve.

230   STEAMED DRIED OYSTERS

Prep: 5 minutes   Stand: 1 hour   Cook: 5 minutes   Serves: 4

Dried oysters are a delicacy, so this dish is often served at Chinese New Year to signify prosperity. The number of oysters in the dish should add up to an even number for good luck. The cooking technique is very simple and requires hardly any time at all. In fact, the oysters could be steamed in a microwave for 3 minutes.

8 dried oysters *	1 tablespoon finely shredded
2 scallions, cut into 2-inch	ginger
shreds	¼ cup vegetable oil

1. Soak dried oysters in a bowl of warm water for 1 hour; drain. Place oysters on a heatproof plate on which they are to be served. Place plate in a bamboo steamer basket, cover, and steam 5 minutes. Remove plate from heat.

2. Sprinkle oysters with scallions and ginger.

3. In a small saucepan, heat oil until smoking, pour over oysters, and serve.

* Available in Asian markets

231   TEA LEAF SHRIMP

Prep: 20 minutes   Chill: 3 hours   Cook: 9 to 10 minutes   Serves: 4

The tender green Lung Ching or Dragon Well tea leaves used in this recipe are eaten—a most unusual feature. The tea is usually served after the meal, as it has a slight bitter quality that makes it a digestive.

1 pound medium shrimp, shelled and deveined	2 tablespoons Lung Ching tea leaves
2 egg whites	2 cups vegetable oil
2 tablespoons plus 2 teaspoons cornstarch	1 tablespoon dry sherry
1 teaspoon salt	1 teaspoon sugar

1. In a bowl, combine shrimp, egg whites, 2 tablespoons cornstarch, and ½ teaspoon salt. Cover and refrigerate 3 hours.

2. In a warmed teapot or large mug, pour 1 cup boiling water over tea leaves, cover, and let steep 5 minutes. Measure out and reserve 2 tablespoons tea. Drain off and serve remainder for drinking. Save tea leaves.

3. In a wok, heat oil over medium-high heat to 350°F, about 5 minutes. Add shrimp and cook until pink and curled, 2 to 3 minutes. Remove to paper towels to drain. Pour off oil and discard. Do not wipe out wok.

4. Return wok to heat. In a small bowl, whisk together sherry, sugar, remaining ½ teaspoon salt, 2 teaspoons cornstarch, and 2 tablespoons liquid tea. Add to wok with reserved tea leaves. Bring to a boil, add shrimp, and toss to mix and coat well. Remove from heat and serve.

232 CHRYSANTHEMUM SQUID

Prep: 20 minutes   Cook: 8 to 11 minutes   Serves: 4

This pretty name refers to the shape of the squid. In banquet cuisine, it is often the presentation that makes a dish special.

3 fresh squid (about 1 pound), cleaned
½ pound shrimp, shelled and deveined
2 ounces pork fat
1 tablespoon dry white wine
1 tablespoon plus 2 teaspoons cornstarch
1 egg white

½ teaspoon salt
1 tablespoon vegetable oil
5 heads of baby bok choy, cut lengthwise in half
¾ cup Chinese Chicken Stock (page 27) or reduced-sodium canned broth
2 teaspoons Asian sesame oil

1. Cut off tentacles from squid. Discard tentacles or reserve for another use. Cut body into four 1½-inch-wide rings. Flatten rings and cut each halfway down at even intervals to form a fringe or "petals." In a bowl, pour boiling water over squid and let stand 3 minutes; petals will curl to form flowers. Drain squid.

2. In a food processor, combine shrimp, pork fat, wine, 1 tablespoon cornstarch, egg white, and salt. Pulse to a smooth puree. Stuff squid flowers with shrimp paste and place on a heatproof plate on which they will be served.

3. In a wok, heat vegetable oil over medium-high heat. Add bok choy and cook, turning, until slightly wilted, about 2 minutes. Remove and place around squid flowers to form a ring. Place plate in a steamer basket, cover, and place basket in a wok. Fill wok one-third full of water, bring to a boil, and steam squid until filling is cooked through, 5 to 8 minutes.

4. In a small saucepan, blend stock with 2 teaspoons cornstarch and sesame oil. Bring to a boil and cook, stirring, until thickened, about 1 minute. Season with additional salt to taste. Pour over squid and vegetables and serve.

233 VEGETARIAN MOCK FISH
Prep: 20 minutes   Stand: 15 to 20 minutes
Cook: 27 to 34 minutes   Serves: 4 to 6

This dish is typical of Chinese Buddhist cooking, in which vegetarian ingredients are used to simulate meat or fish. This "fish" is served with a sweet and sour sauce, thus reproducing the flavors of sweet and sour fish.

1½ pounds Idaho potatoes, peeled and cut into chunks
½ cup Vegetable Stock (page 28) or canned broth
3 cups plus 2 tablespoons vegetable oil
Salt and pepper
4 to 6 sheets dried bean curd skin*
2 whole cloves

¼ cup cider vinegar
¼ cup sugar
1 tablespoon soy sauce
1 tablespoon cornstarch
1 slice of fresh ginger
1 tablespoon finely shredded red bell pepper
1 tablespoon shredded sliced bamboo shoots
2 scallions, cut into 2-inch pieces

1. In a saucepan, place potatoes in enough cold water to cover. Bring to a boil, reduce heat, cover, and simmer until potatoes are soft, 20 to 25 minutes. Drain and mash with stock and 2 tablespoons oil. Season with salt and pepper to taste.

2. In a flat pan, soak bean curd sheets in water to soften, about 15 to 20 minutes. Remove from water and carefully lay out on work surface, overlapping sheets. If there are any tears, overlap sheets to mend holes. Place mashed potatoes on bean curd sheets. Fold sheets and roll up to enclose potatoes. Form into a long fish shape. Mark eyes with cloves. Let roll cool to firm up.

3. In a wok, heat oil to 375°F, or until a cube of bread browns in 1 minute. Carefully lower roll into oil and deep-fry until crisp, about 3 minutes. Remove to paper towels to drain and transfer to serving platter. Pour off all but 1 tablespoon oil. (Oil may be strained and saved for another use.)

4. In a small bowl, combine vinegar, sugar, soy sauce, cornstarch, and ½ cup water. Stir to blend well. Return wok to high heat. Add ginger and stir-fry until brown, 1 to 2 minutes. Remove and discard ginger. Add shredded red pepper, bamboo shoots, and scallions. Stir-fry until slightly wilted, about 1 minute. Whisk sauce mixture to combine and add to wok. Bring to a boil; cook, stirring, until thickened, 1 to 2 minutes. Pour over roll and serve.

* *Available in Asian markets*

234 GARLIC FROG LEGS

Prep: 15 minutes   Stand: 30 minutes   Cook: 10 to 14 minutes
Serves: 4 to 6

Frog legs, or field chicken legs, as they are called in Chinese, are a great delicacy. They can be purchased fresh in fish stores in Chinatown or frozen in supermarkets.

1½ **pounds frog legs**	¼ **cup finely diced green bell**
1½ **cups dry white wine**	**pepper**
1 **egg white**	¼ **cup finely diced red bell**
3 **tablespoons soy sauce**	**pepper**
2 **tablespoons plus**	2 **tablespoons dry sherry**
2 teaspoons cornstarch	1 **tablespoon rice vinegar**
½ **cup vegetable oil**	¼ **teaspoon sugar**
6 **garlic cloves, thinly sliced**	1 **tablespoon Asian sesame oil**

1. Trim frog legs and cut in half at joint. In a bowl, toss frog legs with wine. Let stand 10 minutes, then drain. Beat egg white with 1 tablespoon soy sauce and 2 tablespoons cornstarch. Add frog legs, toss to coat, and let stand 20 minutes.

2. In a wok, heat vegetable oil over high heat to just smoking. Add frog legs and cook until white and opaque, about 5 to 8 minutes. Remove with a slotted spoon and drain on paper towels. Pour off and discard all but 2 tablespoons oil from wok.

3. Return wok to heat. Add garlic and stir-fry over medium heat until golden, about 30 seconds. Add green and red bell pepper and cook, tossing, until soft, about 2 minutes. Add frog legs and cook 1 minute.

4. In a small bowl, whisk together remaining 2 tablespoons soy sauce, sherry, vinegar, sugar, remaining 2 teaspoons cornstarch, and sesame oil. Add to wok, bring to a boil, and cook, stirring, until sauce thickens and coats legs, 1 to 2 minutes. Remove from heat and serve.

235 BUDDHA'S DELIGHT *(LO HON CHAI)*
Prep: 25 minutes   Cook: 27 minutes   Serves: 8

This classic Buddhist dish improves if prepared a day in advance. It also freezes very well. Raw peanuts can be found in Asian markets, in health food stores, and in the produce section of some supermarkets.

3 ounces dried bean curd
   sticks
¼ cup tree ears
2 ounces bean threads
1 cup vegetable oil
8 ounces fresh bean curd, cut
   into 1-inch squares
4 cups shredded Chinese
   (Napa) cabbage

½ cup shredded carrot
½ cup shredded celery
½ cup sliced bamboo shoots,
   shredded
½ cup raw peanuts
3 tablespoons soy sauce
2 tablespoons sugar
  Salt
1 tablespoon Asian sesame oil

1. In 3 separate bowls, soak bean curd sticks, tree ears, and bean threads in warm water until soft, about 15 minutes. Drain and discard water.

2. In a wok, heat vegetable oil over medium-high heat to 375°F, or until a bread cube browns in 1 minute. Deep-fry bean curd squares until golden, about 5 minutes. Remove with a slotted spoon and drain on paper towels. Pour off all but ¼ cup oil.

3. Return wok to medium heat. Add cabbage, carrot, celery, and bamboo shoots. Stir-fry 1 minute. Add peanuts, deep-fried bean curd, bean curd sticks, tree ears, bean threads, soy sauce, and sugar. Toss to mix well. Return to a boil, reduce heat to medium-low, cover, and simmer until vegetables are tender and flavors are absorbed, about 20 minutes. Season with salt to taste. Sprinkle with sesame oil and serve.

Chapter 8

Great Ways with Noodles and Rice

Noodles and rice are the basic staples of Chinese meals. Rice is preferred in the south and noodles, steamed buns, and flat breads are loved in the north, where wheat is more plentiful. Modern practice encourages more creativity in everyday cooking, so it is not uncommon nowadays to find an interaction with Indonesian, Thai, Japanese, Malaysian, and other Asian cuisines in daily Chinese meals. Consequently, you'll find a lot of variety in this chapter.

The popularity of noodles seems to be universal, and nowhere are they more loved than in China. We serve them in soups, stir-fries; we eat them hot and cold. And we make them from wheat flour, rice flour, and mung bean flour. They are satisfying as everyday food and play a significant role in festive dinners. Here you will find recipes for chow mein, lo mein, soupy noodles, hot noodles, cold noodles, rice noodles, bean threads, or cellophane noodles, even one for Thai-style noodles.

We all know that a bowl of white rice is indispensable in most Chinese meals, but in this chapter I have included recipes for several versions of the ever-popular fried rice. A few are quite simple; they use everyday ingredients we usually have on hand—eggs, scallions, bacon, peas, and ham— which are useful when you want to add a little zing to your rice. Others are more involved and include many ingredients, as in my recipes for Yang Chow Fried Rice and Confetti Rice with Pine Nuts. Customarily fried rice is a side dish, but the more elaborate ones could serve as a one-dish meal. I have also included one or two homey, comforting ways of cooking rice, as in Simple Rice and Vegetables and in soupy Sampan Rice.

Because more and more people are searching for convenience, in this chapter I have included recipes for rice or noodle dishes with a simple topping that serve as one-dish meals. Some of these recipes, such as Baked Pork Chops in Vegetable Rice Casserole and Soy Lamb Chops with Onion on Rice, are quite modern in their approach, but there is also a very traditional recipe for Chicken Rice Casserole.

For noodle lovers like me, I have included a few recipes for one-dish noodle meals, as Soupy Noodles with Fish and Spinach Wontons. Pork Cutlet with Buckwheat Noodles and Tempura Shrimp Noodles are two recipes that are Japanese inspired. Because one-dish meals are so easy, nearly all the recipes are planned for more than one person.

236   BRAISED NOODLES WITH CHICKEN

Prep: 20 minutes   Cook: 15 to 17 minutes   Serves: 4 to 6

1 pound fresh wheat flour
   noodles or thin spaghetti
   (spaghettini)
6 dried Chinese mushrooms
2 tablespoons vegetable oil
2 scallions, cut into 2-inch
   pieces
1 tablespoon shredded fresh
   ginger
½ pound skinless, boneless
   chicken breast, cut into
   ½-inch strips

¼ pound mustard greens
   or bok choy, cut into
   2 x ½-inch sticks
2 tablespoons dry sherry
3 tablespoons mushroom soy
   sauce
2 cups Chinese Chicken Stock
   (page 27) or reduced-
   sodium canned broth
2 tablespoons Asian sesame
   oil
1 tablespoon cornstarch

1. In a large pot of boiling salted water, cook noodles until just tender, about 5 minutes. Drain and rinse under cold running water; drain well. Soak mushrooms in ½ cup warm water until soft, about 15 minutes. Drain, reserving liquid. Remove and discard stems. Cut caps into shreds.

2. In a wok, heat vegetable oil until just smoking, add scallions and ginger, and stir-fry over medium heat until aromatic, about 30 seconds. Add chicken and stir-fry 1 minute. Add mustard greens or bok choy, mushrooms, sherry, soy sauce, chicken stock, and sesame oil. Bring to a boil, reduce heat to low, and simmer until chicken is tender and white throughout, about 5 minutes. With a slotted spoon, remove chicken to a plate. Keep warm.

3. In a small bowl, dissolve cornstarch in reserved ½ cup mushroom liquid. Add to sauce, bring to a boil, and cook, stirring, until thickened, about 2 minutes. Add noodles, stir, and cook until warm, 2 to 3 minutes. Add chicken pieces and ladle some sauce over chicken. Transfer to a large bowl and serve.

237   COLD NOODLES WITH PEANUT SAUCE AND CUCUMBERS

Prep: 15 minutes   Cook: 8 minutes   Chill: 1 hour   Serves: 6

1 pound fresh wheat flour
   noodles or dried thin
   spaghetti (spaghettini)
¼ cup Asian sesame oil
¼ cup soy sauce
¼ cup chunky peanut butter
2 tablespoons cider vinegar

¼ to ½ teaspoon cayenne
2 teaspoons sugar
½ teaspoon black pepper
2 garlic cloves, minced
4 cucumbers, peeled, seeded,
   and shredded

1. In a large pot of boiling water, cook noodles until tender but firm, about 8 minutes. Drain and immediately rinse under cold running water until noodles are completely cold. Drain well. Toss with 2 tablespoons sesame oil and 2 tablespoons soy sauce. Cover and refrigerate 1 hour.

2. In a small bowl, whisk together peanut butter and ¼ cup warm water until smooth. Whisk in remaining sesame oil, remaining soy sauce, vinegar, cayenne, sugar, black pepper, and minced garlic.

3. Toss chilled noodles with dressing, arrange on a serving platter, and surround with shredded cucumbers.

---

238   MEAT SAUCE NOODLES
Prep: 10 minutes   Cook: 22 to 24 minutes   Serves: 4

These noodles are cooked in a sauce, so they absorb a lot of flavor. They usually come with equal parts of sauce and noodles and are quite soupy. A great dish for cold winter evenings!

1 **pound fresh wheat flour noodles or spaghetti**	2 **tablespoons dry sherry**
2 **tablespoons vegetable oil**	2 **tablespoons oyster sauce**
1 **teaspoon minced fresh ginger**	1 **cup Rich Meat Stock (page 28) or canned beef broth**
2 **scallions, minced**	1 **teaspoon pepper**
1 **pound lean ground beef**	2 **teaspoons cornstarch**
2 **tablespoons dark soy sauce**	2 **teaspoons Asian sesame oil**

1. In a large pot of boiling water, cook noodles until just tender, 3 to 5 minutes. Drain and rinse under cold running water; drain well.

2. In a wok or saucepan, heat vegetable oil until just smoking. Add ginger and scallions and cook until aromatic, about 30 seconds. Add ground beef and stir-fry over medium heat until meat is brown, about 5 minutes. Stir to break up lumps.

3. Add soy sauce, sherry, oyster sauce, stock, and pepper. Bring to a boil, reduce heat, and simmer meat sauce 10 minutes.

4. In a small bowl, blend cornstarch with 2 tablespoons cold water. Add to sauce and bring to a boil. Cook, stirring, until sauce thickens, about 2 minutes. Add noodles and stir in. Cook until noodles are hot, about 2 minutes. Drizzle with sesame oil and serve.

239   SIMPLE TOSSED SPICY NOODLES
Prep: 15 minutes   Cook: 3 minutes   Serves: 4

These simple cold noodles are served with a twist—the dressing and vegetables are under the noodles. Each diner tosses his or her own noodles, vegetables, and dressing at the table.

1 pound fresh angel hair pasta	2 tablespoons safflower oil
2 tablespoons Chinese sesame paste	2 tablespoons Asian sesame oil
3 garlic cloves, minced	2 cups fresh bean sprouts
3 scallions, minced	1 carrot, peeled and shredded
1 tablespoon chile paste	2 tablespoons peanuts, coarsely chopped
3 tablespoons soy sauce	

1. In a large pot of boiling water, cook pasta until just tender, about 3 minutes. Drain and rinse under cold running water; drain well.

2. In a small bowl, mix sesame paste with 3 tablespoons warm water. Stir to blend into a smooth cream. Add garlic, scallions, chile paste, soy sauce, safflower oil, and sesame oil. Whisk together until smooth.

3. Divide dressing among 4 individual bowls. Add layers of bean sprouts and carrot. Top with noodles. Sprinkle with chopped peanuts and serve.

240   CHICKEN LO MEIN
Prep: 20 minutes   Cook: 9½ to 11½ minutes   Serves: 4 to 6

1 pound skinless, boneless chicken breast	1 carrot, peeled and cut into 2-inch-long matchsticks
2 teaspoons soy sauce	2 scallions, cut into 2-inch pieces
2 teaspoons cornstarch	¼ cup cooked fresh or thawed frozen peas
1 teaspoon dry sherry	½ cup chicken broth
1 pound fresh wheat flour noodles or spaghetti	½ teaspoon salt
3 tablespoons vegetable oil	½ teaspoon pepper
½ teaspoon minced fresh ginger	2 teaspoons Asian sesame oil

1. Cut chicken into thin strips about 1 inch long and ¼ inch wide. In a bowl, toss chicken pieces with soy sauce, cornstarch, sherry, and 1 teaspoon ice water.

2. In a large pot of boiling water, cook noodles until just tender, 3 to 5 minutes. Drain and rinse under cold running water. Toss in 1 tablespoon of vegetable oil and set aside.

3. In a wok, heat remaining 2 tablespoons vegetable oil. Add minced ginger and stir-fry over high heat until aromatic, about 20 seconds. Add chicken and stir-fry until white and opaque, about 3 minutes.

4. Add carrot, scallions, and peas. Cook, stirring, until carrot is slightly softened, about 2 minutes. Add broth, salt, pepper, and noodles. Toss to mix and cook until noodles are hot, about 1 minute. Remove from heat, drizzle on sesame oil, and serve.

241 PORK LO MEIN

Prep: 20 minutes   Cook: 11½ to 14½ minutes   Serves: 4

4 dried Chinese mushrooms
1 pound boneless pork loin,
    cut into thin shreds
2 teaspoons cornstarch
½ teaspoon salt
1 pound fresh wheat flour
    noodles or thin spaghetti
    (spaghettini)
2 tablespoons vegetable oil
1 slice of fresh ginger,
    shredded

2 scallions, cut into 2-inch
    pieces
¼ cup sliced bamboo shoots
1 zucchini, cut into matchstick
    pieces
2 tablespoons soy sauce
2 tablespoons oyster sauce
1 tablespoon Asian sesame oil

1. Soak mushrooms in ¼ cup warm water until soft, about 15 minutes. Drain, reserving liquid. Remove and discard stems. Cut caps into shreds. In a bowl, toss pork with cornstarch and salt.

2. Meanwhile, in a large pot of boiling water, cook noodles until just tender, 5 to 7 minutes. Drain and rinse under cold running water; drain well.

3. In a wok, heat vegetable oil until just smoking. Add ginger and stir-fry over high heat until aromatic, about 20 seconds. Add pork and stir-fry until meat loses its pink color, about 3 minutes.

4. Add scallions, mushrooms, bamboo shoots, and zucchini. Stir-fry until vegetables are warm, about 1 minute. Add soy sauce, oyster sauce, reserved mushroom water, and noodles. Stir-fry, tossing to mix, until noodles are hot, 2 to 3 minutes. Drizzle with sesame oil and serve.

242   SHRIMP LO MEIN

Prep: 30 minutes   Cook: 10½ to 12½ minutes   Serves: 4 to 6

1 pound fresh wheat flour
   noodles or thin spaghetti
   (spaghettini)
3 tablespoons vegetable oil
½ teaspoon minced fresh
   ginger
1 scallion, minced
1 celery rib, cut into 2-inch-
   long matchsticks

1 pound medium shrimp,
   shelled and deveined
½ cup bean sprouts
1 tablespoon soy sauce
½ cup chicken broth
   Salt and pepper
2 teaspoons Asian sesame oil

1. In a large pot of boiling water, cook noodles until just tender, 5 to 7 minutes. Drain and rinse under cold running water; drain well. Toss in 1 tablespoon of vegetable oil.

2. In a wok, heat remaining 2 tablespoons vegetable oil until just smoking. Add ginger and scallion and stir-fry over high heat until aromatic, about 20 seconds. Add celery and shrimp and continue to stir-fry until shrimp just turn pink, about 3 minutes.

3. Add noodles, bean sprouts, soy sauce, and chicken broth. Cook, stirring to mix and heat through, 2 minutes.

4. Remove from the heat. Season with salt and pepper to taste and drizzle with sesame oil, tossing to blend well.

243   VEGETABLE LO MEIN

Prep: 30 minutes   Cook: 8½ to 10½ minutes   Serves: 4 to 6

6 dried Chinese mushrooms
1 pound fresh wheat flour
   noodles or thin spaghetti
   (spaghettini)
3 tablespoons vegetable oil
½ cup Vegetable Stock (page
   28) or canned broth
1 tablespoon oyster sauce
½ teaspoon sugar

½ teaspoon salt
3 celery ribs, cut into 2-inch-
   long thin shreds
½ cup sliced bamboo shoots,
   cut into thin shreds
1 cup fresh bean sprouts
2 scallions, cut into 2-inch
   pieces

1. In a small bowl, soak dried mushrooms in ½ cup warm water until soft, about 15 minutes. Drain, reserving liquid. Remove and discard stems. Cut caps into thin shreds.

2. In a large pot of boiling water, cook noodles until just tender, 5 to 7 minutes. Drain and rinse under cold running water; drain well. Toss in 1 tablespoon of oil.

3. In a small bowl, mix together reserved mushroom liquid, stock, oyster sauce, sugar, and salt. Set sauce aside.

4. In a wok, heat remaining 2 tablespoons of oil. Add shredded mushroom caps, celery, and bamboo shoots and stir-fry over high heat until hot, about 30 seconds. Add noodles and sauce. Cook, tossing, until mixed and heated through, about 3 minutes. Add bean sprouts and scallions, toss to mix well, and serve.

---

244   CHICKEN AND CELERY CHOW MEIN
Prep: 15 minutes   Stand: 10 minutes   Cook: 18½ to 21½ minutes
Serves: 4

1½ pounds skinless, boneless
  chicken breast, cut into
  thin shreds
2 tablespoons soy sauce
1 tablespoon dry sherry
2 tablespoons cornstarch
1 teaspoon pepper
¼ cup vegetable oil
1 pound fresh wheat flour
  noodles or thin spaghetti
  (spaghettini)

1 scallion, minced
½ teaspoon minced fresh
  ginger
2 celery ribs, cut into 2-inch
  matchsticks
½ cup chicken broth
2 teaspoons Asian sesame oil

1. In a bowl, toss chicken with 1 tablespoon soy sauce, sherry, 1 tablespoon of cornstarch, pepper, and 1 teaspoon of vegetable oil. Let stand 10 minutes.

2. Meanwhile, in a large pot of boiling water, cook noodles until just tender, about 5 minutes. Drain and rinse under cold running water; drain well. Toss with 1 tablespoon of vegetable oil.

3. In a wok, heat 2 tablespoons of vegetable oil. Add noodles and press to form a large pancake. Cook over moderate heat until brown on bottom, 3 to 5 minutes. Flip noodle pancake over and brown second side, about 3 minutes. Remove to a serving platter and cover with foil to keep warm.

4. Return wok to heat, add remaining 2 teaspoons vegetable oil, and heat until just smoking. Add scallion and ginger and stir-fry over high heat until aromatic, about 20 seconds. Add chicken and stir-fry until meat turns white and opaque, tossing frequently to prevent sticking and browning, about 5 minutes. Chicken should remain white. Add celery and continue stir-frying until just soft, about 1 minute.

5. In a small bowl, whisk together broth, remaining 1 tablespoon soy sauce, remaining 1 tablespoon cornstarch, and sesame oil. Add to wok, return to a boil, and cook, stirring, until sauce thickens and coats chicken, 1 to 2 minutes. Pour over noodle pancake. Cut noodle pancake into wedges with kitchen shears to serve.

245   BEEF AND GREEN PEPPER CHOW MEIN

Prep: 15 minutes   Stand: 10 minutes   Cook: 16½ to 21½ minutes
Serves: 4 to 6

½ pound flank steak
1 tablespoon plus 2 teaspoons
  cornstarch
4 teaspoons soy sauce
1 tablespoon dry sherry
1 pound fresh wheat flour
  noodles or thin spaghetti
  (spaghettini)
¼ cup vegetable oil

1 scallion, minced
1 teaspoon minced fresh
  ginger
1 garlic clove, minced
1 green bell pepper, cut into
  thin strips
½ cup chicken broth
1 tablespoon oyster sauce
1 tablespoon ketchup

1. Cut flank steak lengthwise into 2-inch-wide strips; then cut crosswise into ¼-inch-thick slices. In a bowl, combine beef with 2 teaspoons cornstarch, 2 teaspoons soy sauce, and sherry. Toss to coat well. Let stand 10 minutes.

2. In a large pot of boiling water, cook noodles until just tender, about 5 minutes. Drain and rinse under cold running water. Toss in 1 tablespoon of oil.

3. In a wok, heat 2 tablespoons of oil. Add noodles and shape into a large pancake. Cook over moderate heat until brown and crisp on bottom, 3 to 5 minutes. Flip noodle pancake over and brown second side, about 3 minutes longer. Noodle pancake should be crisp outside and soft inside. Remove to a serving platter and cover to keep warm.

4. Return wok to heat, add remaining 1 tablespoon oil, and bring to a smoking point over high heat. Add scallion, ginger, and garlic and stir-fry until aromatic, about 20 seconds. Add beef and stir-fry until browned around edges but pink inside, 3 to 5 minutes. Add green pepper and cook until softened, about 1 minute.

5. In a small bowl, blend broth, oyster sauce, and ketchup with remaining soy sauce and cornstarch. Pour into wok, bring to a boil, and cook, stirring and tossing to coat meat and green pepper until thickened, 1 to 2 minutes. Remove from heat and pour over noodle pancake. To serve chow mein, cut pancake into wedges using kitchen shears.

246   PORK CHOW MEIN WITH BOK CHOY STEMS

Prep: 25 minutes   Cook: 18 to 25 minutes   Serves: 4 to 6

1 pound fresh wheat flour noodles or thin spaghetti (spaghettini)
¼ cup vegetable oil
½ pound bok choy
½ pound boneless lean pork, cut into ½ x 2-inch strips
1 tablespoon plus 1 teaspoon soy sauce
1 tablespoon dry sherry
1 tablespoon cornstarch
1½ teaspoons sugar

¼ teaspoon Chinese five-spice powder
½ teaspoon minced fresh ginger
1 garlic clove, minced
½ cup chicken broth
1 tablespoon oyster sauce
2 teaspoons Asian sesame oil
2 scallions, cut into 2-inch pieces
Salt and pepper

1. In a large pot of boiling water, cook noodles until just tender, 5 to 7 minutes. Drain and rinse under cold running water; drain well. Toss in 1 tablespoon of vegetable oil and set aside.

2. Trim leaves from bok choy and cut leaves into thin ribbons. Cut stalks into matchstick-size pieces about 2 inches long and ¼ inch thick.

3. In a small bowl, toss pork strips with 1 tablespoon of soy sauce, sherry, cornstarch, ½ teaspoon sugar, and five-spice powder.

4. In a wok, heat 2 tablespoons of vegetable oil until just smoking. Add noodles and press into a large pancake. Cook over moderate heat until bottom is brown and crisp, 3 to 5 minutes. Turn over and brown other side, 3 to 5 minutes longer. Remove to a serving platter and cover to keep warm.

5. Return wok to heat. Add remaining 1 tablespoon vegetable oil and heat until just smoking, about 30 seconds. Add ginger and garlic. Stir-fry over high heat until aromatic, about 20 seconds. Add pork and stir-fry until meat loses its pink color, about 3 minutes. Add bok choy stems and toss until tender, about 1 minute.

6. In a small bowl, combine broth, oyster sauce, remaining 1 teaspoon sugar and 1 teaspoon soy sauce, and sesame oil. Add to wok and bring to a boil. Cook, stirring until slightly thickened, 1 to 2 minutes. Stir in bok choy leaves and scallions. Stir-fry to warm 1 minute. Season with salt and pepper to taste and pour over noodle pancake. To serve, cut noodle pancake into wedges with kitchen shears.

247   TEMPURA SHRIMP NOODLES
Prep: 15 minutes   Cook: 15 to 18 minutes   Serves: 4

½ cup flour
½ cup cornstarch
½ teaspoon salt
½ teaspoon pepper
8 jumbo shrimp, shelled and
  deveined
1 cup vegetable oil
1 pound fresh or dried angel
  hair pasta

6 cups Chinese Chicken Stock
  (page 27) or reduced-
  sodium canned broth
2 teaspoons soy sauce
3 scallions, cut into 2-inch
  pieces
2 teaspoons Asian sesame oil

1. In a bowl, combine flour, cornstarch, salt, and pepper. Stir in enough ice water to make a batter with consistency of heavy cream. Place shrimp in batter.

2. In a wok, heat vegetable oil over high heat until smoking. With tongs, remove shrimp one at a time from batter. Gently place in oil and fry in 2 batches until crisp, about 5 minutes per batch. Remove to paper towels to drain.

3. In a large pot of boiling salted water, cook angel hair pasta until just tender, 2 to 3 minutes for fresh, 3 to 5 minutes for dried. Drain and place in 4 large soup bowls.

4. Meanwhile, in a medium saucepan, bring broth to a boil. Add soy sauce, reduce heat, and simmer 3 minutes. Ladle soup over noodles, add scallions, and drizzle sesame oil on top. Top each bowl with 2 tempura shrimp.

248   SOUPY NOODLES WITH FISH AND SPINACH WON TONS
Prep: 10 minutes   Cook: 6 minutes   Serves: 4

12 Fish and Spinach Won Tons
   (recipe follows)
½ pound Chinese wheat flour
   noodles or thin spaghetti
   (spaghettini)
3 cups Chinese Chicken Stock
   (page 27) or reduced-
   sodium canned broth

Salt and pepper
½ pound flounder fillets, cut
   into 2-inch pieces
2 scallions, cut into 2-inch
   pieces
2 teaspoons Asian sesame oil

1. Bring a large pot of water to a boil. Add won tons and cook until they float to surface, about 2 minutes. Remove with a slotted spoon and drain.

2. Return water to a boil, add noodles, and cook until just tender; drain. Divide among 4 soup bowls.

3. Meanwhile, in a large saucepan, bring stock to a boil. Season with salt and pepper to taste. Add fish fillets, reduce heat, and simmer until fish turns white and opaque, about 3 minutes. Remove with a slotted spoon. Add won tons to stock and heat through, about 1 minute.

4. To serve, top noodles with pieces of fish and scallions. Gently spoon hot soup and won tons over noodles. Drizzle with sesame oil.

---

249 FISH AND SPINACH WON TONS
Prep: 30 minutes   Cook: none   Makes: about 48

½ **(10-ounce) package frozen spinach, thawed**
½ **pound fish fillets, such as flounder or cod**
1 **scallion, minced**
1 **slice of fresh ginger, minced**
2 **teaspoons soy sauce**
½ **teaspoon salt**
½ **teaspoon pepper**
1 **tablespoon dry sherry**
1 **tablespoon Asian sesame oil**
1 **teaspoon cornstarch**
1 **egg, beaten**
1 **(1-pound) package won ton wrappers**

1. Squeeze spinach very dry. Make sure fish fillets are entirely free of bones.

2. In a food processor, combine spinach, fish, scallion, ginger, soy sauce, salt, pepper, sherry, sesame oil, and cornstarch. Process until ingredients are very finely chopped and well blended. In a small bowl, beat egg with 1 tablespoon water.

3. Lay a won ton wrapper on a flat work surface. Place 1 teaspoon filling in center of wrapper. Do not overfill won ton. Brush egg mixture around edges of wrapper; fold over corner to corner to form a triangle. Moisten 1 corner of triangle and squeeze onto opposite corner to form a peak-shaped won ton. Repeat until all won tons are formed. Cook as directed in recipe before eating.

250   BEAN CURD, MUSHROOMS, AND BOK CHOY ON SOUPY NOODLES

Prep: 20 minutes   Cook: 13 minutes   Serves: 4

1 pound rice stick noodles	½ cup sliced bamboo shoots
6 dried Chinese mushrooms	2 tablespoons soy sauce
1 pound bok choy	1 tablespoon miso
1 tablespoon vegetable oil	1 teaspoon sugar
1 teaspoon minced fresh ginger	6 cups Chinese Chicken Stock (page 27) or reduced-sodium canned broth
1 pound firm bean curd, cut into ½-inch dice	1 teaspoon pepper

1. In a large bowl, soak rice sticks in warm water until soft, about 15 minutes; drain. Meanwhile, in a small bowl, soak mushrooms in warm water until soft, about 15 minutes. Drain, reserving liquid. Remove and discard stems. Cut mushroom caps into quarters.

2. Clean bok choy and separate stems from leaves. Cut stems into matchsticks and shred leaves.

3. In a large saucepan, heat oil until just smoking. Add ginger and cook 1 minute. Add mushrooms, bok choy stems, bean curd, bamboo shoots, soy sauce, miso, sugar, stock, and pepper. Bring to a boil, reduce heat, and simmer 10 minutes.

4. Add rice sticks and bok choy leaves. Stir to mix well. Cook until noodles are hot and leaves are wilted, about 2 minutes. Serve hot.

251   PORK CUTLET WITH BUCKWHEAT NOODLES

Prep: 20 minutes   Cook: 19 to 22 minutes   Serves: 4

½ cup flour	6 cups Chinese Chicken Stock (page 27) or reduced-sodium canned broth
½ teaspoon salt	
1 teaspoon pepper	
4 boneless pork chops	2 tablespoons soy sauce
2 eggs, beaten	2 tablespoons vegetable oil
1 cup coarse bread crumbs	1 pound buckwheat noodles
¼ cup ketchup	2 scallions, minced
2 tablespoons Worcestershire sauce	

1. On a plate, combine flour, salt, and pepper. Dredge chops in seasoned flour, then dip in beaten eggs, and coat with bread crumbs. Press crumbs in with palms. In a small bowl, blend ketchup with Worcestershire to make sauce.

2. In a medium saucepan, bring stock to a boil. Reduce heat, add soy sauce, and simmer until hot, about 10 minutes.

3. In a large skillet, heat oil until just smoking. Over medium heat, cook pork chops until golden brown on underside, about 3 minutes. Turn and brown other side, 1 to 2 minutes longer. Remove to paper towels. Cut lengthwise into 1-inch-wide strips.

4. In a large pot of boiling water, cook buckwheat noodles until tender, about 5 to 7 minutes. Drain and divide into 4 deep soup bowls. Ladle hot broth into bowls, top with pork strips, and spoon a little sauce over meat. Sprinkle with scallions and serve.

252 SOUPY NOODLES WITH PORK WON TONS AND CHINESE ROAST PORK

Prep: 15 minutes   Cook: 12 minutes   Serves: 4

12 won tons, as prepared on page 195 but not deep-fried
½ pound Chinese wheat flour noodles or thin spaghetti (spaghettini)
3 cups reduced-sodium chicken broth

¼ pound snow peas, stringed
Salt and pepper
⅓ pound Red Roast Pork (page 146) or strips of ham
2 tablespoons minced scallion

1. Bring a large pot of water to a boil. Add won tons and cook until they rise to surface, about 2 minutes. Remove with a slotted spoon. Keep warm.

2. Add noodles to boiling water and cook until just done, about 5 minutes. Drain and divide into individual serving bowls.

3. Meanwhile, in a large saucepan, bring broth to a boil, reduce heat, and simmer 5 minutes. Add snow peas and cook until they turn a bright green, about 5 seconds. Season with salt and pepper to taste.

4. To serve, top noodles with won tons and sliced roast pork. Ladle hot broth with snow peas over noodles. Sprinkle with minced scallion.

253 DRY-FRIED SPICY BEEF AND WIDE RICE NOODLES

Prep: 15 minutes   Cook: 8 to 11 minutes   Serves: 4

1 pound beef flank steak, cut into thin strips, about 2 x ¼ inch
¼ cup soy sauce
2 teaspoons cornstarch
¼ cup plus 2½ tablespoons vegetable oil
1 pound fresh rice noodle sheets *(ho fun)*
1 tablespoon fermented black beans

1 teaspoon chile paste
1 teaspoon minced fresh ginger
2 garlic cloves, minced
3 or 4 fresh hot chile peppers, seeded and sliced
1 medium green bell pepper, cut into thin strips

1. In a bowl, toss steak strips with 1 tablespoon soy sauce, cornstarch, and 1½ teaspoons of oil. Let stand 10 minutes. Roll up rice noodle sheets and cut into ½-inch-wide pieces. Toss with 2 tablespoons of oil. Rinse black beans to remove excess salt. In a small bowl, mash black beans slightly with chile paste, ginger, and garlic.

2. In a wok, heat remaining ¼ cup oil until just smoking. Add beef and stir-fry over high heat until meat loses its pink color, about 3 minutes. Reduce heat to medium, add black bean mixture, and stir-fry until aromatic, about 30 seconds. Add hot chiles and green pepper and stir-fry until peppers are slightly softened, 1 to 2 minutes. Add noodles and cook, tossing, until warm and well blended, about 3 to 5 minutes.

254 SOUPY NOODLES WITH HAM AND CHICKEN

Prep: 10 minutes   Cook: 12 to 14 minutes   Serves: 4

½ pound fresh wheat flour noodles or angel hair pasta
3 cups Chinese Chicken Stock (page 27) or reduced-sodium canned broth
3 slices of fresh ginger
2 teaspoons soy sauce

1 cup shredded cooked chicken
½ cup shredded ham
2 scallions, cut into 2-inch pieces
Salt
2 teaspoons Asian sesame oil

1. In a large pot of boiling water, cook noodles until just tender, 3 to 5 minutes. Drain and rinse under cold running water; drain well.

2. In a large saucepan, combine stock and ginger. Bring to a boil, reduce heat to low, and simmer 5 minutes. Remove and discard ginger.

3. Add soy sauce and noodles to pan. Return to a simmer and cook 2 minutes. Add chicken, ham, and scallions. Simmer until just warm, about 2 minutes. Season with salt to taste. Add sesame oil and spoon into bowls to serve.

255 HOT AND COLD NORTHERN NOODLES
Prep: 20 minutes   Cook: 4 minutes   Serves: 4 to 6

This unusual dish is very popular in northern China, particularly in summer. The noodles are served cold topped by a hot meat mixture; hence, its name. The flat rice noodles *(ho fun)* available in Asian markets are best for this dish, but you can use lo mein noodles or even spaghetti.

1 pound fresh rice noodle
    sheets * *(ho fun)* or cooked
    substitute
1 teaspoon Asian sesame oil
2 cucumbers, peeled, seeded,
    and shredded
1 tablespoon vegetable oil

3 garlic cloves, minced
½ pound lean ground pork
2 tablespoons yellow bean
    sauce
¼ cup chicken broth
½ teaspoon pepper
½ teaspoon sugar

1. Cut fresh rice noodle sheets into wide noodle shape. Toss with sesame oil and mound on serving platter. Arrange shredded cucumbers around noodles.

2. In a wok, heat oil until just smoking. Add garlic and stir-fry over high heat 5 seconds. Add pork and stir-fry until meat loses its pink color, about 3 minutes. Stir to break up pork as it cooks. Add bean sauce, chicken broth, pepper, and sugar. Cook, stirring, 1 minute.

3. Spoon hot pork mixture on top of cold noodles and serve.

* *Fresh rice noodle sheets may be bought ready to eat from bean curd stores or Oriental markets. They are very white in color and soft. If they have been refrigerated and have hardened, soak them for a few minutes in tepid water.*

256 FUKIEN RICE STICKS

Prep: 20 minutes   Cook: 8½ to 9½ minutes   Serves: 4 to 6

1 pound rice stick noodles (*mei fun*)	2 Chinese sausages (*lop cheung*), diced
6 dried Chinese mushrooms	2 tablespoons soy sauce
3 tablespoons vegetable oil	1 teaspoon salt
1 scallion, minced	½ teaspoon pepper
1 garlic clove, minced	1 cup shredded Chinese (Napa) cabbage
½ pound pork, finely shredded	
1 cup sliced bamboo shoots, coarsely chopped	

1. In a medium bowl, soak rice stick noodles in warm water until soft, about 15 minutes; drain. At same time, in a small bowl, soak mushrooms in ½ cup warm water until soft, about 15 minutes. Drain, reserving liquid. Remove and discard stems. Cut caps into thin shreds.

2. In a wok, heat oil until just smoking. Add scallion and garlic and stir-fry over medium heat until aromatic, about 30 seconds. Add pork and stir-fry until meat loses its pink color, about 3 minutes.

3. Add mushrooms, bamboo shoots, and sausages. Stir-fry, tossing, 2 minutes. Add rice sticks, mushroom water, soy sauce, salt, and pepper. Cook over medium heat, stirring to mix well, until noodles are soft, 2 to 3 minutes.

4. Add shredded cabbage and stir-fry until cabbage wilts slightly, about 1 minute. Remove from heat and serve.

257 SOUPY SEAFOOD RICE STICK NOODLES WITH FRESH BASIL AND LIME

Prep: 15 minutes   Cook: 8 minutes   Serves: 6

1 pound rice stick noodles	½ pound snapper fillets, cut into 2-inch pieces
1 tablespoon vegetable oil	½ pound medium shrimp, shelled and deveined
1 slice of fresh ginger, shredded	½ pound scallops
1 cup dry white wine	4 scallions, cut into 2-inch pieces
2 cups Vegetable Stock (page 28) or canned broth	1 tablespoon fresh lime juice
2 small dried hot red peppers,	Salt and pepper
6 fresh basil leaves	
1 bay leaf	

1. In a bowl, soak rice sticks in warm water until soft, about 15 minutes. Drain.

2. In a saucepan, heat oil over medium heat. Add ginger and cook until aromatic, about 20 seconds. Add wine, stock, hot red peppers, basil leaves, and bay leaf. Bring to a boil, reduce heat to low, and simmer 5 minutes.

3. Add fish, shrimp, scallops, and rice stick noodles. Cook over low heat until fish and scallops turn white and shrimp pink, about 2 minutes. Add scallions and lime juice. Season with salt and pepper to taste and serve.

---

258 RICE STICKS WITH SINGAPORE-STYLE SHRIMP

Prep: 30 minutes   Cook: 17 to 20 minutes   Serves: 4 to 6

1 **pound rice stick noodles**
  (mei fun)
2 **tablespoons vegetable oil**
2 **garlic cloves, minced**
1 **cup minced onion**
2 **tablespoons curry powder**
1 **cup unsweetened coconut**
  milk

½ **to 1 teaspoon cayenne**
  Pinch of sugar
  Salt and pepper
1 **pound medium shrimp,**
  shelled and deveined

1. Soak rice stick noodles in a bowl of warm water until soft and pliable, about 15 minutes. Drain and set aside.

2. In a wok or large saucepan, heat oil over medium heat. Add garlic and onion and cook until golden, about 5 minutes. Add curry powder and continue cooking until aromatic, about 2 minutes. Add coconut milk, 1 cup water, cayenne, and sugar. Reduce heat to low and simmer sauce until thick, 7 to 10 minutes. Season with salt and pepper to taste.

3. Add shrimp to thickened sauce and cook, stirring, until shrimp just turn pink, about 3 minutes.

4. Add rice stick noodles and toss to blend and heat through.

259 YANG CHOW FRIED RICE

Prep: 25 minutes   Cook: 6 to 9 minutes   Serves: 8

6 dried black mushrooms
3 tablespoons vegetable oil
1 slice of fresh ginger
¼ cup coarsely chopped
　 cooked shrimp
¼ cup diced ham
6 water chestnuts, coarsely
　 chopped
¼ cup peas, fresh or frozen

4 cups cold cooked rice
2 tablespoons soy sauce
1 teaspoon salt
½ teaspoon pepper
6 Egg Crepes (page 22), cut
　 into thin ribbons
¼ cup minced scallions
1 cup shredded romaine
　 lettuce

1. Soak dried mushrooms in ¼ cup warm water until soft, about 10 minutes. Drain, reserving mushroom water. Cut off and discard stems. Slice caps into narrow strips.

2. In a wok, heat oil until just smoking. Add ginger and cook over high heat until brown, 1 to 2 minutes; discard ginger. Add shrimp, ham, water chestnuts, peas, and mushrooms. Stir-fry 1 minute, tossing to mix well. Add rice and continue to stir-fry until rice is hot, 3 to 5 minutes.

3. Add soy sauce, salt, pepper, and reserved mushroom water. Stir-fry 1 minute. Add egg ribbons, scallions, and shredded lettuce. Remove from heat, stir to mix, and serve.

260 FRIED RICE WITH CHINESE SAUSAGE

Prep: 20 minutes   Cook: 7 to 9 minutes   Serves: 6

6 dried Chinese mushrooms
3 tablespoons vegetable oil
1 garlic clove, minced
2 scallions, minced
¼ pound small shrimp,
　 shelled and deveined
4 Chinese sausages (*lop
　 cheung*), diced

¼ cup coarsely chopped water
　 chestnuts
3 cups cold cooked rice
2 tablespoons soy sauce
½ teaspoon salt
1 teaspoon pepper

1. In a small bowl, soak mushrooms in ¼ cup warm water until soft, about 15 minutes. Drain, reserving water. Remove and discard stems. Dice caps.

2. In a wok, heat oil until just smoking. Add garlic, scallions, and shrimp and cook over medium heat until shrimp just turn pink, about 3 minutes.

3. Add sausages, water chestnuts, and mushrooms. Cook 1 minute. Add rice, soy sauce, mushroom liquid, salt, and pepper. Stir-fry until mixture is hot, 3 to 5 minutes.

261 THAI-STYLE RICE NOODLES WITH SHRIMP AND CHICKEN

Prep: 20 minutes   Cook: 11½ minutes   Serves: 6

1 pound flat rice stick noodles
4 eggs
¼ cup fish sauce *(nuoc nam)*
3 tablespoons ketchup
1 teaspoon black pepper
¼ cup plus 2 tablespoons vegetable oil
¼ cup chopped cilantro plus ¼ cup leaves
8 garlic cloves, minced
½ pound skinless, boneless chicken breast, cut into ½-inch cubes

½ pound medium shrimp, shelled and deveined
4 scallions, cut into 1-inch pieces
3 cups fresh bean sprouts
1 tablespoon lime juice
¼ cup coarsely chopped dry-roasted peanuts
2 or 3 small dried hot red peppers, crumbled
4 limes, thinly sliced

1. Soak rice stick noodles in a bowl of warm water until pliable, about 20 minutes; drain. In a medium bowl, beat eggs until blended. Mix in fish sauce, ketchup, and black pepper.

2. In a wok, heat oil until just smoking. Over medium heat, stir-fry chopped cilantro and garlic until aromatic, about 30 seconds. Add chicken and stir-fry until meat turns white and opaque, 3 minutes. Add shrimp and continue to stir-fry until shrimp turn pink, about 2 minutes.

3. Add noodles and cook, stirring, until noodles are soft, about 5 minutes. Add egg mixture and continue cooking, tossing while eggs cook to blend with noodles. Add scallions and 2 cups bean sprouts. Stir-fry to wilt vegetables, about 1 minute. Sprinkle with lime juice. Toss to mix well.

4. Remove from heat. Mound noodles on a serving platter. Sprinkle with remaining bean sprouts, peanuts, crumbled hot red peppers, and ¼ cup cilantro leaves. Surround with lime slices. Serve warm or at room temperature.

262 FRIED RICE WITH PEAS AND HAM

Prep: 10 minutes   Cook: 6 to 9 minutes   Serves: 4

3 tablespoons vegetable oil
2 slices of fresh ginger
2 scallions, minced
1 cup peas, fresh or frozen

4 ounces ham, diced
3 cups cold cooked rice
1 teaspoon salt
½ teaspoon pepper

1. In a wok or skillet, heat oil until just smoking. Add ginger and cook until golden, 1 to 2 minutes. Remove and discard. Add minced scallions, peas, and ham. Stir-fry over medium heat until warm, about 2 minutes.

2. Add rice and continue to stir-fry until hot, 3 to 5 minutes. Season with salt and pepper. Toss to blend well and serve.

263   FRIED RICE WITH ROAST PORK

Prep: 15 minutes   Cook: 5 to 7 minutes   Serves: 8

3 tablespoons vegetable oil	½ cup minced scallions
1 teaspoon minced fresh ginger	2 tablespoons soy sauce
	1 teaspoon salt
4 cups cold cooked rice	½ teaspoon pepper
1 cup diced Red Roast Pork (page 146)	1 cup bean sprouts

1. In a wok, heat oil until just smoking. Add minced ginger and stir-fry over high heat until aromatic, about 10 seconds. Add rice and continue stir-frying until rice is hot, 3 to 5 minutes.

2. Add roast pork, scallions, soy sauce, salt, and pepper. Cook, tossing to mix and heat well, about 2 minutes.

3. Remove from heat, stir in bean sprouts, and serve.

264   SHRIMP FRIED RICE

Prep: 20 minutes   Cook: 6½ to 8½ minutes   Serves: 6 to 8

3 tablespoons vegetable oil	¼ cup coarsely chopped water chestnuts
2 scallions, minced	
1 garlic clove, minced	4 cups cold cooked rice
1 teaspoon minced fresh ginger	2 tablespoons soy sauce
	1 tablespoon ketchup
½ pound medium shrimp, shelled, deveined, and cut into ½-inch pieces	1 tablespoon dry white wine
	¼ teaspoon cayenne
	Salt and pepper

1. In a wok, heat oil until just smoking. Add scallions, garlic, and ginger. Stir-fry over high heat until aromatic, about 30 seconds. Add shrimp and water chestnuts. Stir-fry until shrimp turn pink, about 3 minutes.

2. Add rice and continue stir-frying until rice is hot, 3 to 5 minutes.

3. In a small bowl, combine soy sauce, ketchup, wine, and cayenne. Pour over rice and stir to mix well. Season to taste with salt and pepper. Remove from heat and serve.

265 CONFETTI RICE WITH PINE NUTS
Prep: 15 minutes   Cook: 7 to 8 minutes   Serves: 8

3 tablespoons vegetable oil
2 garlic cloves, lightly crushed
½ cup pine nuts
¼ cup diced red bell pepper
¼ cup diced yellow bell pepper
¼ cup green peas, fresh or frozen
¼ cup coarsely chopped water chestnuts
¼ cup corn kernels
4 cups cold cooked rice
2 tablespoons soy sauce
2 tablespoons dry white wine
1 teaspoon pepper
4 scallions, minced

1. In a wok or skillet, heat oil over medium heat until just smoking. Add garlic and cook until golden. Remove and discard. Add pine nuts and stir-fry until light brown, being careful not to burn, about 2 minutes. Remove with a slotted spoon to a plate.

2. Add red pepper, yellow pepper, peas, water chestnuts, and corn to wok. Stir-fry 1 to 2 minutes, tossing to mix well. Add rice, soy sauce, wine, and pepper. Stir-fry over medium heat until rice is hot, about 3 minutes. Add pine nuts and scallions, toss to mix well, and serve.

266 SAMPAN RICE
Prep: 10 minutes   Cook: 2 minutes   Serves: 4

This is a type of seafood congee, which is very popular in southern China. You can make your basic congee without chicken, but here we are using a richer version from our "Banquet Dishes" chapter as a base. The retained heat in the congee cooks the seafood as it stands.

½ pound flounder fillets
2 tablespoons dry white wine
2 tablespoons soy sauce
1 garlic clove, minced
¼ pound shucked oysters
¼ pound small shelled and deveined shrimp
3 cups Chicken Congee (page 140)
2 tablespoons finely shredded fresh ginger
1 scallion, finely shredded
1 tablespoon Asian sesame oil

1. Cut fish into 2-inch squares. In a bowl, combine wine, soy sauce, and garlic. Add fish, oysters, and shrimp and toss gently to coat. Let stand 10 minutes.

2. In a medium saucepan, heat congee to boiling point. Add seafood with sauce and simmer 2 minutes. Ladle into 4 deep soup bowls. Top with shredded ginger and scallions. Drizzle sesame oil over rice and serve.

267 SIMPLE RICE AND VEGETABLES
Prep: 10 minutes   Cook: 33 minutes   Serves: 4 to 6

This easy rice cooked with shredded vegetables is a nice change. The rice absorbs the flavors of the kind of vegetable you use. It can be eaten plain, perhaps with some pickled radish or bean curd as a side dish. Otherwise, it can be served as a side dish instead of white rice. I have substituted butter for the traditional lard.

1 tablespoon vegetable oil	1½ cups long-grain rice
3 cups (about 1 pound) finely shredded leafy vegetable, such as bok choy or Napa cabbage	1 cup Chinese Chicken Stock (page 27) or reduced-sodium canned broth
1 teaspoon salt	1 tablespoon butter

1. In a large saucepan or flameproof casserole, heat oil until just smoking. Add vegetable and stir-fry over medium heat until slightly wilted, about 3 minutes. Sprinkle with salt.

2. Add rice and stir to mix well. Add chicken stock and 2 cups water. Bring to a boil, reduce heat to low, cover, and cook until rice is tender and liquid is absorbed, about 30 minutes.

3. Remove from heat. Stir in butter and serve.

268 INDIVIDUAL STEAMED RICE WITH POACHED EGG
Prep: 10 minutes   Cook: 33 to 45 minutes   Serves: 2

Chinese rice bowls and a bamboo steamer with lid are best for this dish.

½ cup long-grain white rice	1 scallion, minced
2 eggs	2 teaspoons Asian sesame oil
2 teaspoons soy sauce	

1. Rinse rice in cold water. Drain and divide between 2 heatproof bowls. Fill bowls with boiling water to measure ¾ inch over rice. Place bowls in a bamboo steamer, cover, and place steamer in a wok. Fill wok one-third full of water, bring to a boil, reduce heat, and steam until rice is tender, 30 to 40 minutes. Replenish water in wok as needed.

2. With a spoon, make a hollow in center of rice in each bowl. Carefully break an egg into each hollow. Sprinkle each with half of soy sauce, scallion, and sesame oil. Cover steamer and return water to a boil. Steam until egg is set but yolk is still runny, about 3 to 5 minutes.

3. Remove from steamer and serve directly from bowls.

269 INDONESIAN-STYLE RICE WITH CHICKEN AND SHRIMP

Prep: 20 minutes   Cook: 31 to 33 minutes   Serves: 6

I remember eating this rice dish as a young girl in my Indonesian friend's house. This dish is typical of the multicultural influences that you find in Hong Kong food. I think it makes a great buffet dish.

2 cups rice	6 ounces medium shrimp,
3 cups Chinese Chicken Stock	shelled and deveined
(page 27) or reduced-	½ teaspoon ground coriander
sodium canned broth	½ teaspoon ground cumin
3 tablespoons vegetable oil	4 small dried hot red peppers,
2 medium onions, minced	crumbled
2 garlic cloves, minced	¼ teaspoon mace
1 teaspoon turmeric	¼ cup peanut butter
1 skinless, boneless chicken	
breast half (about	
5 ounces), diced	

1. In a medium saucepan, combine rice with chicken stock. Bring to a boil, reduce heat, and simmer until rice is cooked, about 20 minutes.

2. In a wok or large flameproof casserole, heat oil over medium heat. Add onions, garlic, and turmeric. Cook until onions are golden, 5 to 7 minutes. Add chicken and shrimp and cook until chicken turns white and shrimp turn pink, about 5 minutes. Add rice and stir to blend.

3. In a small bowl, blend together coriander, cumin, dried hot peppers, mace, peanut butter, and 2 to 3 tablespoons water to make a thin paste. Add to rice mixture. Stir well and cook until rice is hot, about 1 minute.

270 FRIED RICE WITH EGGS AND SCALLIONS

Prep: 10 minutes   Cook: 5 to 7 minutes   Serves: 6 to 8

¼ cup vegetable oil	2 scallions, minced
4 cups cold cooked rice	2 tablespoons soy sauce
4 eggs, beaten	Salt and pepper

1. In a wok, heat oil until just smoking. Add cold rice and stir-fry over high heat until hot, 3 to 5 minutes.

2. Reduce heat to medium, pour in beaten eggs, and stir constantly so eggs coat rice grains as they set. Add scallions and soy sauce and stir-fry 2 minutes. Season with salt and pepper to taste. Remove from heat and serve.

271   SCRAMBLED EGGS AND BACON RICE
Prep: 15 minutes   Cook: 9 to 12 minutes   Serves: 4

We make this rice when we have no Chinese ingredients but still want fried rice. It's quick, easy, and good.

1 tablespoon vegetable oil	3 eggs, beaten
1 medium onion, minced	2 cups cold cooked rice
4 strips of bacon, cut crosswise into ¼-inch strips	2 scallions, minced
	Salt and pepper

1. In a wok or large nonstick skillet, heat oil over medium heat. Add onion and stir-fry until softened, 3 to 5 minutes. Add bacon pieces and cook until crisp, about 3 minutes longer.

2. Add rice and stir-fry to mix and heat through, 2 to 3 minutes. Make a well in center of rice and pour beaten eggs into wok. Quickly break up eggs to scramble as they set, tossing to mix with rice. Add scallions and stir-fry 1 minute.

3. Remove from heat, season to taste with salt and pepper, and serve.

272   YELLOW RICE WITH CHERRY TOMATOES
Prep: 10 minutes   Cook: 25 minutes   Serves: 4 to 6

This rice goes very well with the Super Spicy Spareribs on page 93.

2 tablespoons vegetable oil	1 teaspoon salt
1 medium onion, minced	½ teaspoon pepper
2 garlic cloves, minced	1 pint basket of cherry tomatoes
1 teaspoon minced fresh ginger	2 scallions, minced
1 teaspoon turmeric	
2 cups long-grain white rice	
3½ cups Chinese Chicken Stock (page 27) or reduced-sodium canned broth	

1. In a wok or skillet, heat oil. Add onion, garlic, ginger, and turmeric and cook over medium heat until onion is softened, about 3 minutes.

2. Add rice, chicken stock, salt, and pepper. Bring to a boil, reduce heat, cover, and cook until rice is tender and liquid is absorbed, about 20 minutes.

3. Add cherry tomatoes and scallions. Cook, stirring to mix in, until tomatoes begin to burst, about 2 minutes. Remove from heat and serve.

273   CHICKEN RICE CASSEROLE
Prep: 15 minutes   Cook: 30 to 35 minutes   Serves: 4 to 6

1 tablespoon vegetable oil
1 (3-pound) chicken, cut into
    16 pieces*
1 teaspoon minced fresh
    ginger
1 garlic clove, minced
2 scallions, minced
3 tablespoons soy sauce
3 tablespoons dry sherry

1 teaspoon pepper
2 cups long-grain white rice
4¼ cups Chinese Chicken Stock
    (page 27) or reduced-
    sodium canned broth
4 Chinese sausages *(lop
    cheung)*, cut into ½-inch
    pieces
5 sprigs of cilantro

1. In a large flameproof casserole, heat oil until just smoking. Add chicken and cook, turning, until browned, about 10 minutes. With a slotted spoon, remove to a plate.

2. Add ginger, garlic, and scallions. Cook over medium heat, stirring, until aromatic, about 30 seconds. Add soy sauce, sherry, pepper, and rice. Stir to coat rice and mix well. Add chicken broth, bring to a boil, and reduce heat. Arrange chicken pieces over rice, pushing down slightly. Cover and cook over medium heat until liquid is almost all absorbed, about 15 minutes.

3. Reduce heat to low, add sausage pieces, pushing down into rice. Cover and steam 5 to 10 minutes. Remove from heat. Garnish with cilantro.

4. To serve, bring casserole to table and spoon out rice, chicken, and sausage.

* *Ask your butcher to do this for you.*

274   CANTONESE ROAST PORK RICE
Prep: 10 minutes   Cook: none   Serves: 1

This is the most common one-dish meal served in Chinatown rice shops. It is quick and easy if you have some roast pork on hand. It can also be made with roast duck. The pork and/or duck is usually served at room temperature and the hot rice warms it just enough to taste good.

1 cup hot cooked rice
2 to 4 ounces Sweet Aromatic
    Roast Pork (page 145),
    sliced

2 broccoli spears, cooked
1 tablespoon soy sauce
½ teaspoon sugar

1. Spoon hot rice onto individual plate. Arrange pork slices over rice and broccoli spears around edge of plate.

2. Mix soy sauce with sugar, stirring to dissolve. Drizzle over pork and rice and serve.

275   SUNNYSIDE EGG BEEF RICE
Prep: 15 minutes   Cook: 15 minutes   Serves: 2

To eat this homey dish, each diner breaks up the yolk on top and mixes it with the rice before eating.

1 **pound lean ground beef**	1 **medium onion, minced**
2 **tablespoons soy sauce**	2 **scallions, minced**
½ **teaspoon pepper**	¼ **cup chicken broth**
1 **tablespoon plus 2 teaspoons**	1 **tablespoon ketchup**
vegetable oil	2 **cups hot cooked rice**
1 **garlic clove, minced**	2 **eggs**

1. In a small bowl, combine beef with soy sauce and pepper. Mix to blend well.

2. In a wok or large skillet, heat 1 tablespoon oil until just smoking. Add garlic, onion, and scallions. Stir-fry over high heat until aromatic, about 30 seconds. Add beef and cook, stirring to break up lumps, until meat loses its pink color, about 5 minutes. Add chicken broth and ketchup. Bring to a boil, reduce heat, and simmer 5 minutes.

3. Spoon cooked rice onto 2 individual plates or shallow bowls. Divide meat mixture in half and spoon over each serving of rice. Cover to keep warm.

4. Wipe out pan, return to medium heat, and add remaining 2 teaspoons of oil. Crack eggs into pan and cook sunnyside up until whites are set but yolks remain runny. Top each serving of beef and rice with an egg and serve.

276   BAKED PORK CHOPS IN VEGETABLE RICE CASSEROLE
Prep: 10 minutes   Cook: 29 to 34 minutes   Serves: 2

1 **tablespoon vegetable oil**	1 **carrot, peeled and diced**
4 **thin pork chops**	2 **eggs**
1 **medium onion, sliced**	½ **cup chicken broth**
2 **cups cold cooked rice**	1 **tablespoon tomato paste**
½ **cup tiny peas, fresh or**	1 **teaspoon salt**
frozen	1 **teaspoon pepper**

1. Preheat oven to 375°F. In a large skillet, heat oil until just smoking over high heat. Add pork chops and cook, turning, until browned, about 8 minutes. Remove to a plate.

2. Add onion to skillet and cook over medium heat, stirring occasionally, until soft, about 5 minutes. With a slotted spoon, remove onions to a plate. Add rice, peas, and carrots. Cook, stirring to mix, 1 minute. Make a well in center of rice. Break eggs into well and quickly break up as eggs cook. Do not overmix; there should be streaks of white. Transfer to a shallow casserole.

3. In a bowl, mix chicken broth, tomato paste, salt, and pepper. Place chops and onions on top of rice. Pour sauce over all. Place casserole in oven and bake until chops brown slightly and rice is hot, about 15 to 20 minutes. Serve from casserole at table.

---

277   PORK, ONION, AND TOMATO ON RICE
Prep: 15 minutes   Cook: 18 to 20 minutes   Serves: 2

4 thin pork chops, cut into
   thin strips
½ teaspoon salt
½ teaspoon pepper
2 tablespoons ketchup
2 tablespoons soy sauce
2 tablespoons chicken broth
2 teaspoons cornstarch

1 tablespoon vegetable oil
1 medium onion, sliced
2 small tomatoes, peeled,
   seeded, and cut into strips
2 cups cold cooked rice
2 cups bean sprouts
1 scallion, minced

1. In a bowl, toss pork strips with salt and pepper to season. In a small bowl, blend ketchup, soy sauce, chicken broth, and cornstarch to make a sauce.

2. In a flat skillet, heat oil until just smoking over medium heat. Add pork strips and stir-fry until lightly browned, about 5 minutes. Remove to a plate. Add onion and cook until soft and lightly browned, 3 to 5 minutes. Add tomato strips and cook another minute. Return chops to skillet, add sauce, reduce heat to low, and simmer until sauce thickens, about 5 minutes. Remove meat and most of sauce.

3. Add rice to skillet and cook over medium heat, stirring, until hot, about 3 minutes. Add bean sprouts and scallion, stirring to mix and wilt sprouts. Remove to individual plates. Spoon pork, vegetables, and sauce over rice and serve.

278   SOY LAMB CHOPS WITH ONION ON RICE
Prep: 10 minutes   Stand: 10 minutes
Cook: 10 to 17 minutes   Serves: 2

2 shoulder lamb chops
1 tablespoon soy sauce
2 teaspoons dry sherry
1 tablespoon vegetable oil
1 medium onion, sliced

¼ cup chicken, beef, or
    vegetable stock
1 teaspoon cornstarch
¼ teaspoon sugar
2 cups hot cooked rice

1. In a bowl, combine lamb chops, soy sauce, and sherry. Rub to coat well and let stand 10 minutes.

2. In a large skillet, heat oil over medium heat. Add onion and cook until softened, 3 to 5 minutes. Remove to a plate. Add lamb chops and cook, turning once, until browned outside and medium-rare to medium inside, about 3 to 5 minutes each side.

3. In a small bowl, blend stock with cornstarch and sugar. Add to skillet, return onion to pan, and bring to a boil. Cook until sauce thickens, 1 to 2 minutes. Serve over white rice on individual plates.

279   SPICY HALIBUT STEAKS ON RICE
Prep: 10 minutes   Stand: 20 minutes
Cook: 11 to 14 minutes   Serves: 4

2 tablespoons curry powder
½ teaspoon cayenne
1⅓ pounds halibut steak
¼ cup vegetable oil
2 garlic cloves, sliced
¼ cup sliced shallots

½ cup chicken broth
2 teaspoons cornstarch mixed
    with 2 tablespoons water
Salt and pepper
4 cups hot cooked rice

1. In a small bowl, combine curry powder and cayenne. Cut halibut into 4 equal pieces, removing center bone. Rub half of curry mixture on fish pieces. Let stand 20 minutes.

2. In a wok or large nonstick skillet, heat oil until just smoking over medium-high heat. Add fish and cook, turning once, until white and opaque in center, 5 to 7 minutes. Remove to a plate. Pour off all but 2 tablespoons of oil.

3. Return wok to heat. Add garlic and shallots and cook over medium heat until aromatic, about 30 seconds. Add remaining curry mixture and cook 1 minute. Add chicken broth and cornstarch mixture. Bring to a boil and cook, stirring, until sauce thickens, 1 to 2 minutes. Return fish to sauce and simmer until heated, about 3 minutes. Add salt and pepper to taste.

4. To serve, divide rice among 4 individual plates. Spoon one piece of fish and some sauce over each serving.

Chapter 9

Chinese Light

This chapter explores two special Chinese cooking techniques: steaming and poaching

A bamboo steamer basket with lid set over a wok is an ideal implement for steaming. If you don't have a Chinese steamer, improvise a rack and place a damp towel on the inside of the pot lid to absorb condensation and prevent it from dripping onto your dish and diluting the flavors. Bamboo steamer baskets are inexpensive and are sold in markets all over Chinatown and in the equipment sections of many regular department stores and cooking shops.

Besides steaming foods in the conventional manner where they are placed directly on the steaming rack, Chinese also steam foods on plates or in bowls. To differentiate, I usually call this "wet steaming" as all the juices and flavors are retained on the plate and served as part of the dish.

All the dishes in this chapter are "wet steamed." When we use this method of cooking, we are able to present light, low-fat foods artfully arranged, or in pretty bowls and plates. As the steam is a gentle, indirect heat, the food remains succulent, moist, and tender. Fish done in this way is superb, and I have included eight fish or seafood recipes in this chapter. All the recipes require little preparation, and as they are served directly from the plates they are steamed in, cleanup is minimized.

In this chapter, I have included poached dishes as well, because this gentle cooking in liquid is another low-fat way to prepare wonderful, light Chinese food. Remember never to let the poaching liquid boil rapidly; always keep it at a gentle simmer, or the food will toughen.

280 WHITE POACHED CHICKEN WITH SCALLION OIL

Prep: 5 minutes   Cook: 25 minutes   Stand: 45 to 60 minutes
Serves: 4

I like to call this "No-Cook Chicken" because of the very short cooking time required for delectable, juicy chicken—perfect for eating cold or using in salads. It is great for the dog days of summer when you don't want to heat up yourself or your kitchen. To serve in the Chinese tradition, arrange the pieces of white poached chicken into a stylized chicken shape and garnish with greens and carved vegetable flowers.

1 **(3-pound) whole chicken**	1 **slice of ginger**
1 **scallion**	1 **cup Scallion Oil (page 24)**

1. Remove giblets from chicken and reserve for another use or discard. Rinse chicken well inside and out under cold running water.

2. In a large pot, bring 8 cups (2 quarts) of water to a boil. Add scallion and ginger, cover, and simmer 15 minutes to flavor water.

3. Submerge chicken in flavored water, bring just to boiling point (212°F) and simmer, uncovered, 10 minutes. Remove from heat. Cover pot and let chicken stand in hot liquid 45 to 60 minutes. Chicken will finish cooking in retained heat of the water. Remove chicken and let cool completely.

4. Cut chicken into bite-size pieces. Serve at room temperature with small side dishes of scallion oil for dipping.

281 POACHED BROWN CHICKEN

Prep: 10 minutes   Cook: 30 minutes   Stand: 1 hour   Serves: 4

1 **(3-pound) whole chicken**	3 **slices of fresh ginger**
1 **cup dark soy sauce**	1 **tablespoon Asian sesame oil**
2 **scallions**	

1. Remove any excess fat from chicken. Rinse well inside and out under cold running water. Discard giblets or reserve for another use.

2. In a large stockpot, bring soy sauce and 10 cups water to a boil. Add scallions and ginger, reduce heat, and simmer 10 minutes.

3. Add chicken, pushing down to submerge chicken under liquid. Return to a boil and immediately reduce heat to a low simmer. Cook chicken 20 minutes. Turn off heat and cover pot. Let stand 1 hour. Retained heat will finish cooking chicken.

4. When cool, remove chicken from liquid. Paint with sesame oil and cut into bite-size pieces to serve.

282 CHICKEN WITH CHINESE SAUSAGE
Prep: 10 minutes   Cook: 15 minutes   Serves: 4

1 skinless, boneless chicken breast (10 to 12 ounces)	½ teaspoon pepper
1 tablespoon soy sauce	2 scallions, minced
1 tablespoon yellow bean sauce	1 tablespoon Asian sesame oil
1 teaspoon oyster sauce	2 Chinese pork sausages (*lop cheung*), sliced

1. Cut chicken into thin strips. In a medium bowl, combine soy sauce, bean sauce, oyster sauce, pepper, scallions, and 2 teaspoons of sesame oil. Blend well. Add chicken and sausage slices and toss to coat well.

2. Oil a shallow heatproof bowl with remaining 1 teaspoon sesame oil. Pour chicken mixture into bowl and gently pat down. Place bowl in a bamboo steamer basket and cover with lid.

3. Fill a wok one-third full of water. Place bamboo steamer in wok. Bring water to a boil, reduce heat to medium, and steam until chicken is white and cooked through, about 15 minutes.

283 HOISIN CHICKEN STRIPS WITH CILANTRO
Prep: 15 minutes   Cook: 15 to 20 minutes   Serves: 2

1 whole skinless, boneless chicken breast (10 to 12 ounces)	2 teaspoons dry sherry
2 tablespoons hoisin sauce	2 tablespoons Asian sesame oil
1 tablespoon soy sauce	2 tablespoons minced cilantro leaves
1 tablespoon cornstarch	1 garlic clove, minced

1. Cut chicken into thin strips. In a small bowl, combine hoisin sauce, soy sauce, cornstarch, sherry, 1 tablespoon of sesame oil, cilantro, and garlic. Add chicken strips and toss until well mixed.

2. Coat a shallow heatproof bowl with remaining 1 tablespoon oil. Fill with chicken mixture and gently pat smooth.

3. Place bowl in a bamboo steamer basket and cover with lid. Fill a wok one-third full of water. Bring water to a boil and place bamboo steamer in wok. Steam chicken over medium heat until chicken is white and opaque throughout, 15 to 20 minutes.

284 BEEF BALLS WITH OYSTER SAUCE
Prep: 20 minutes   Cook: 20 minutes   Serves: 6

1½ pounds lean ground beef
2 tablespoons sliced bamboo shoots
4 water chestnuts
1 scallion
2 teaspoons minced fresh ginger
1 tablespoon cornstarch
1½ teaspoons salt
½ teaspoon pepper
1 egg
2 tablespoons oyster sauce
2 tablespoons dry sherry
1 tablespoon soy sauce
2 teaspoons Asian sesame oil

1. In a food processor, combine beef, bamboo shoots, water chestnuts, scallion, ginger, cornstarch, salt, pepper, and egg. Process until mixture is smooth and well combined.

2. With wet hands, form into meatballs about 1½ inches in diameter. Place in a 9-inch heatproof glass pie plate. Place plate in bamboo steamer basket. In a small bowl, stir together oyster sauce, sherry, soy sauce, and sesame oil. Drizzle over meatballs.

3. Fill a wok one-third full of water. Bring water to a boil and place steamer basket in wok. Reduce heat to medium-low and steam until meatballs are cooked through, about 20 minutes.

285 PEARL MEATBALLS
Prep: 20 minutes   Stand: 1 hour   Cook: 20 minutes   Serves: 4

½ cup glutinous rice
2 teaspoons salt
5 water chestnuts
1 scallion
½ pound ground pork
1 tablespoon soy sauce
2 teaspoons dry sherry
1 tablespoon cornstarch
¼ teaspoon pepper
1 teaspoon sugar
1 egg
Lettuce leaves
2 teaspoons Asian sesame oil

1. Soak glutinous rice in cold water for 1 hour. Drain and mix with salt. Spread out on a large plate.

2. In a food processor, coarsely chop water chestnuts and scallion. Add ground pork, soy sauce, sherry, cornstarch, pepper, sugar, and egg. Process until finely ground and blended. With wet hands, form pork mixture into 1-inch balls. Roll balls in rice to coat.

3. Line a heatproof plate with lettuce leaves. Place meatballs on leaves and drizzle sesame oil over meatballs. Place plate in a bamboo steamer basket and cover with lid. Fill a wok one-third full of water. Bring water to a boil, place steamer in wok, reduce heat to medium, and steam meatballs until cooked through, about 20 minutes. Serve pearl meatballs directly from plate.

286   STEAMED PORK CAKE
Prep: 10 minutes   Cook: 30 minutes   Serves: 6

1 **pound ground pork**	½ **teaspoon salt**
4 **water chestnuts, minced**	½ **teaspoon pepper**
1 **tablespoon soy sauce**	½ **teaspoon sugar**
1 **tablespoon cornstarch**	1 **teaspoon Asian sesame oil**

1. In a bowl, combine pork, water chestnuts, soy sauce, cornstarch, salt, pepper, and sugar. Mix well.

2. Oil a 7-inch shallow heatproof bowl with sesame oil and lightly pat pork mixture into bowl.

3. Set bowl in a bamboo steamer basket and cover. Fill a wok one-third full of water, bring water to a simmer, and set bamboo basket in wok. Steam over medium heat until juices run clear when pork cake is pricked with a knife, about 30 minutes.

287   RED-POACHED LAMB STRIPS WITH NOODLES AND CABBAGE BROTH
Prep: 20 minutes   Cook: 28 to 30 minutes   Serves: 4

2 **pounds boneless leg of lamb, well trimmed**	2 **scallions, minced**
	1 **star anise**
4 **cups Rich Meat Stock (page 28)**	4 **ounces bean thread noodles**
3 **tablespoons dark soy sauce**	1 **small Chinese (Napa) cabbage, about 1 pound**
2 **tablespoons dry sherry**	**Salt and freshly ground pepper**
2 **slices of fresh ginger, shredded**	

1. Cut lamb into thin strips about 2 inches long and ¼ inch thick.

2. In a medium saucepan, combine stock, soy sauce, sherry, ginger, scallions, and star anise. Bring to a boil, reduce heat, cover, and simmer 15 minutes.

3. Meanwhile, soak bean threads in warm water until soft, about 10 minutes. Drain and cut into 8-inch lengths.

4. Using a slotted spoon, gently poach lamb strips in 3 or 4 batches until just done, about 2 minutes per batch. Remove to a plate. Add noodles and cabbage to stock. Bring to a boil and cook 5 minutes, or until cabbage is wilted. Season with salt and pepper to taste. Return lamb strips to pan, setting them on top of noodles and vegetables, and simmer 2 minutes to reheat. Serve while hot.

288 STEAMED WHOLE CATFISH WITH BLACK BEANS
Prep: 10 minutes   Cook: 15 to 20 minutes   Serves: 4

2 tablespoons fermented
  black beans
1 tablespoon vegetable oil
1 whole catfish, about 1½
  pounds, with head on

1 scallion, cut into 2-inch
  pieces
1 tablespoon shredded fresh
  ginger
1 tablespoon soy sauce

1. Rinse black beans and soak in warm water for 5 minutes. Drain and coarsely mash with oil.

2. Rinse catfish inside and out under cold running water. Pat dry and makes 3 evenly spaced slashes on one side.

3. Place fish, slashed side up, on a 9-inch heatproof plate. Spread black beans into cavity and slashes. Sprinkle scallion, ginger, and soy sauce over fish.

4. Fill a wok one-third full of water and bring water to a simmer. Place plate in a bamboo steamer basket, cover, and steam over medium heat until fish is opaque throughout, about 15 to 20 minutes. Serve directly from steamer basket.

289 STEAMED BLACK SEA BASS
Prep: 10 minutes   Cook: 15 to 20 minutes   Serves: 4

For this dish it is best to use a heatproof plate that fits into a 10-inch bamboo steamer with a lid. The bamboo cover absorbs any condensation and prevents the sauce from being diluted. And the fish can be served directly from the basket. If you do not have a bamboo steamer, you can improvise a steamer system by using a rack that fits into a wok and lining the inside of the metal wok lid with a damp kitchen towel, which will absorb condensation.

1 whole black sea bass with
  head on, about 2 pounds
1 scallion, cut into 2-inch
  pieces
1 tablespoon finely shredded
  fresh ginger

1 tablespoon soy sauce
1 tablespoon dry sherry
2 teaspoons Asian sesame oil

1. Rinse fish inside and out under cold running water and pat dry. Make 3 evenly spaced slashes on top side of fish and place on a 9-inch plate. Fill cavity of fish with half the scallion and ginger. Sprinkle remaining scallion and ginger over fish. Drizzle soy sauce, sherry, and sesame oil over fish.

2. Place plate in a bamboo steamer basket and cover with lid.

3. Fill a wok one-third full of water. Bring water to a simmer and place bamboo basket over water. Steam over medium heat until fish is opaque throughout, 15 to 20 minutes.

290   FLOWER SHRIMP
Prep: 10 minutes   Cook: 6 minutes   Serves: 4

12 **jumbo shrimp**	1 **pound broccoli**
2 **teaspoons salt**	3 **tablespoons vegetable oil**
1 **tablespoon dry white wine**	2 **cups Chinese Chicken Stock**
1 **scallion, minced**	**(page 27) or reduced-**
2 **tablespoons minced fresh**	**sodium canned broth**
ginger	**Freshly ground pepper**

1. Shell shrimp, but leave tail shell on. Cut along backs of shrimp lengthwise, devein, and lay flat. Make a small slit in the middle of each shrimp and push tail through to form a flower shape.

2. In a medium bowl, combine salt, wine, scallion, and ginger. Add shrimp and toss to coat well. Cut florets from broccoli. Discard stems.

3. Grease a deep 9-inch heatproof plate with 1 tablespoon of oil. Arrange shrimp on plate, plate in bamboo steamer, cover, and steam over medium heat until shrimp turn pink and are just done, about 5 minutes. Remove from heat. In a saucepan, bring 1 cup chicken stock to a boil. Season with pepper and additional salt to taste and gently pour over shrimp. Keep warm.

4. In a wok, heat remaining 2 tablespoons oil over medium heat, add broccoli florets, and stir-fry 1 minute. Add remaining 1 cup chicken stock, bring to a boil, cover, and cook until broccoli is crisp-tender. Remove with a slotted spoon and arrange in a ring around shrimp.

291   STEAMED SEA SCALLOPS
Prep: 10 minutes   Cook: 3 to 5 minutes   Serves: 4 to 6

1 **pound sea scallops**	1 **tablespoon finely shredded**
2 **tablespoons oyster sauce**	**fresh ginger**
2 **scallions, cut into 2-inch**	2 **tablespoons vegetable oil**
pieces	

1. Clean sea scallops, removing and discarding any muscles on the sides. Place scallops on a heatproof plate that will fit into a bamboo steamer basket. Drizzle with oyster sauce and steam scallops until they turn opaque and are just done, about 3 to 5 minutes.

2. Remove from heat. Sprinkle with shredded scallions and ginger.

3. In a small saucepan, heat oil until smoking. Drizzle over scallops and serve.

292   POACHED COD FILLETS IN SOUR SAUCE
Prep: 10 minutes   Cook: 6 to 7 minutes   Serves: 6

The sauce in this dish is an elegant change from everyday sweet and sour sauce. If you have Chinese black vinegar on hand, do use it instead of cider vinegar. The distinctive flavor of black vinegar will enhance the sauce even more.

2 pounds cod fillets
2 scallions, cut into 2-inch-
   long shreds
1 tablespoon shredded fresh
   ginger
1 teaspoon pepper
3 tablespoons vegetable oil
2 cups Chinese Chicken Stock
   (page 27) or reduced-
   sodium canned broth

¼ cup dry white wine
2 tablespoons soy sauce
2 tablespoons cider vinegar
1 tablespoon Asian sesame oil
½ teaspoon sugar
1 tablespoon cornstarch

1. Make sure fish fillets are completely free of bones. Cut into 2 x 3-inch pieces.

2. Fill a wok or skillet with water and bring to a boil; reduce heat to a gentle simmer. Add fish and poach until fillets turn white and opaque, about 5 minutes. With a slotted spoon, remove fish to a serving platter. Sprinkle shredded scallions, ginger, and pepper over fish.

3. In a small saucepan, heat vegetable oil until smoking and pour over fish.

4. In a small nonreactive saucepan, combine stock, wine, soy sauce, vinegar, sesame oil, sugar, and cornstarch. Bring to a boil, stirring constantly, until sauce thickens, 1 to 2 minutes. Pour over fish and serve at once.

293   STEAMED CUCUMBERS STUFFED WITH FLOUNDER
Prep: 15 minutes   Cook: 15 to 20 minutes   Serves: 6

½ pound flounder fillets
1 slice of fresh ginger
1 garlic clove
1 scallion, minced
1 tablespoon cilantro leaves

2 teaspoons soy sauce
1 tablespoon Asian sesame oil
3 cucumbers
   White Cream Sauce (recipe
   follows)

1. In a food processor, coarsely chop fish, ginger, garlic, scallion, and cilantro leaves. Add soy sauce and 1 teaspoon of sesame oil. Puree until smooth.

2. Peel cucumbers and cut into 2-inch lengths. With a teaspoon, scoop out and discard seeds in center, leaving enough flesh to hold filling. Stuff cucumber rings with fish filling.

3. Oil a 9-inch heatproof plate with remaining sesame oil and arrange cucumbers on a plate. Place plate in a bamboo steamer basket, cover, and set in a wok one-third full of water. Bring water to a boil, reduce heat, and steam until cucumbers are tender and filling is cooked through, 15 to 20 minutes.

4. Spoon cream sauce over cucumbers and serve.

---

294   WHITE CREAM SAUCE
Prep: 5 minutes   Cook: 1 to 2 minutes   Makes: 1 cup

1 cup Chinese Chicken Stock
     (page 27) or reduced-
     sodium canned broth
1 tablespoon cornstarch

¼ teaspoon pepper
2 tablespoons heavy cream
   Salt

In a small saucepan, stir together chicken stock, cornstarch, and pepper. Bring to a boil, reduce heat to low, and cook, stirring, until thickened and smooth, 1 to 2 minutes. Stir in heavy cream. Season with salt to taste.

---

295   STEAMED FISH BALLS ON A BED OF WATERCRESS
Prep: 25 minutes   Cook: 15 to 20 minutes   Serves: 6

1½ pounds flounder or sole
      fillets
2 slices of fresh ginger
2 scallions
1 egg white
1 tablespoon cornstarch
1 teaspoon soy sauce
½ teaspoon pepper

½ teaspoon salt
½ pound watercress
6 sprigs of cilantro
2 teaspoons Asian sesame oil
1 tablespoon dry white wine
1 tablespoon chicken broth or
   water

1. Pick over fish fillets to make sure there are no tiny bones. In a food processor, combine fish, ginger, and scallions. Process to a smooth puree. Add egg white, cornstarch, soy sauce, pepper, and salt. Process to blend well. Remove to a bowl.

2. With wet hands, form fish mixture into 1-inch balls.

3. Remove tough stems from watercress. Lay watercress on a plate large enough to hold fish balls. Arrange fish balls on top of watercress. Lay sprigs of cilantro over fish balls, reserving 2 tablespoons leaves for garnish. In a small bowl, combine sesame oil, wine, and chicken broth. Drizzle over fish balls. Place plate in a bamboo steamer basket. Cover.

4. Fill a wok one-third full of water. Bring water to a boil and set steamer basket in a wok. Over low heat, steam until fish balls are cooked, about 15 to 20 minutes. Serve directly from basket.

296   OYSTER-FLAVORED BEAN CURD
Prep: 5 minutes   Cook: 5 to 10 minutes   Serves: 4

2 teaspoons Scallion Oil
  (page 24)
1 pound soft bean curd
2 scallions, cut into 2-inch
  pieces

1 slice of fresh ginger, finely
  shredded
2 tablespoons oyster sauce
2 teaspoons soy sauce

1. Oil a 9-inch heatproof plate with 1 teaspoon of scallion oil. Drain bean curd and cut into 2-inch cubes. Lay on plate. Sprinkle scallions and ginger over bean curd. In a small bowl, blend oyster sauce with soy sauce. Drizzle over bean curd squares.

2. Place plate in a 10-inch bamboo steamer basket; cover with lid. Fill a wok one-third full of water, bring to a boil, and place steamer basket in wok. Steam over medium heat 5 to 10 minutes, until bean curd is hot.

3. Drizzle remaining 1 teaspoon scallion oil over bean curd and serve.

297   SAVORY EGG CUSTARD
Prep: 5 minutes   Cook: 15 minutes   Serves: 2

To attain the smooth velvety textures of custard, cook over very low heat and watch carefully so as not to overcook. You can vary this dish by adding bits of cooked ham, chicken, pork, or shrimp.

4 eggs
2 teaspoons light soy sauce
½ teaspoon pepper

2 teaspoons Asian sesame oil
1 scallion, minced

1. With one chopstick, gently beat eggs to mix, trying not to form too much foam. With chopsticks, mix in soy sauce, pepper, and ¼ cup water.

2. Lightly oil a shallow heatproof bowl with 1 teaspoon of sesame oil. Gently pour in egg mixture. Sprinkle scallion on top. Place bowl in bamboo steamer; cover.

3. Fill a wok one-third full of water. Bring water to a boil and reduce heat to low. Place bamboo steamer in wok and very gently steam custard until set, about 15 minutes. Do not overcook. Remove from wok immediately. Drizzle remaining 1 teaspoon sesame oil on top and serve at once.

298   BEAN CURD POCKETS
Prep: 10 minutes   Cook: 10 minutes   Serves: 4 or 8

¼ pound shrimp, shelled and
    deveined
½ pound flounder fillet
½ teaspoon minced fresh
    ginger
1 scallion, minced
1 teaspoon minced cilantro
2 teaspoons soy sauce
1 teaspoon dry sherry

1 teaspoon Asian sesame oil
¼ teaspoon sugar
    Pinch of salt
1 egg white
8 squares of firm bean curd
2 teaspoons vegetable oil
1 tablespoon oyster sauce
1 tablespoon chicken or meat
    stock or water

1. In a food processor, coarsely chop shrimp and fish. Add ginger, scallion, cilantro, 1 teaspoon soy sauce, sherry, sesame oil, sugar, salt, and egg white. Pulse to combine well.

2. Cut bean curd squares diagonally to form triangles. Scoop out a small pocket in each triangle. Fill with 1 tablespoon seafood filling.

3. Oil a 9-inch plate with vegetable oil and arrange bean curd triangles on plate. Mix oyster sauce with remaining 1 teaspoon soy sauce and 1 tablespoon stock. Drizzle over bean curd. Place plate in a bamboo steamer basket, cover, and steam in a wok until filling is cooked and bean curd is hot, about 10 minutes.

Chapter 10

Little Packages, Big Packages

In Chinese cooking, we love to wrap things. Sometimes this is done by cooks in the kitchen and sometimes by the diners themselves, just before they pop the packages into their mouths. Here you will find recipes using all types of wrappers, won ton skins, lettuce leaves, dried lotus leaves, and pancakes. Ants Climbing a Tree, Mu Shu Pork Packages, and Ginger Duck Roll-Ups are just a few of our many recipes that will set your mouth watering.

This chapter includes all those recipes we know as *dim sum*, the little packages, dumplings, and other bite-size foods we all love. Some of the recipes such as Siu Mei Flower Dumplings, Shrimp and Pork Dumplings, and of course, Fried Won Tons, are quick and easy and use store-bought wrappers. But for those of you who are more adventurous, I have included recipes for special dumplings, where making your own wrappers is essential. Potsticker Dumplings are never just right unless the dough is homemade. And it is impossible to buy the translucent dough made from wheat starch for making Shrimp Dumplings *(Har Kow)*. Fortunately, both these doughs are very easy to make, so I urge you to try them.

This chapter also includes main dishes that are wrapped and cooked in dough or edible leaves. Try these popular "big packages," especially the unusually flavored Malaysian-style Fish Custard in Banana Leaves, and for a special dinner, the fabled Beggar's Chicken. You'll be surprised at just how easy this is and of course, presenting the food in its "packaging" makes for an exotic presentation!

Lotus leaves impart a fragrant subtle flavor to the food wrapped in them. They are available dry and keep almost forever, so make a trip to Chinatown and stock up on some. Once you try the easy recipes for Eight Jewel Rice in Lotus Package, Pungent Pork in Lotus Leaf, or Chicken in Sticky Rice Bundles, you will add them to your repertoire. As a bonus, use the "tea" from soaking lotus leaves to make the unusual sorbet in the "Chinese Sweets" chapter at the end of the book.

299 MINCED CORNISH GAME HEN IN LETTUCE LEAVES

Prep: 20 minutes   Cook: 10 minutes   Serves: 4

5 dried Chinese mushrooms	2 tablespoons chicken broth
1 tablespoon dried black tree ears	1 teaspoon sugar
1 cup water chestnuts	¼ cup vegetable oil
2 (1-pound) Cornish game hens	2 scallions, minced
¾ pound lean pork loin	4 slices of fresh ginger, minced
¼ cup soy sauce	2 teaspoons cornstarch
3 tablespoons dry white wine	2 heads of Boston lettuce, rinsed and dried
2 tablespoons Asian sesame oil	

1. In a small bowl, soak mushrooms in ½ cup warm water until soft, about 15 minutes. Remove mushrooms, reserving soaking water; cut off and discard stems. Cut caps into thin strips. In another bowl, soak tree ears in warm water until soft, about 15 minutes. Remove and trim off stems, if necessary; mince tree ears coarsely. Coarsely chop water chestnuts.

2. Bone game hens and remove skin from meat. In a food processor, coarsely chop game hen meat and pork. Remove to a medium bowl. Add 2 tablespoons soy sauce, 2 tablespoons wine, 1 tablespoon sesame oil, and chicken broth. Mix well.

3. In a small bowl, combine reserved mushroom water, remaining 2 tablespoons soy sauce, 1 tablespoon wine, 1 tablespoon sesame oil, and sugar. Set sauce aside.

4. In a wok, heat vegetable oil over medium heat until just smoking. Add scallions and ginger and stir-fry until fragrant and scallions are soft, about 30 seconds. Add meat and stir-fry until it just loses its pink color, about 5 minutes. Add mushrooms, tree ears, and water chestnuts. Stir-fry 2 minutes, tossing to combine. Add liquid mixture and simmer 1 minute.

5. Dissolve cornstarch in ¼ cup cold water and add to wok. Bring to a boil and cook, stirring, until thickened, about 1 minute. To eat, spoon meat mixture into lettuce leaves, roll up to form packages, and serve.

300   FRIED WON TONS
Prep: 45 minutes   Cook: 10 minutes   Makes: about 48

Won tons are the original "little packages," and this chapter would be incomplete without a recipe for them. They may be boiled in soup or deep-fried and served with a dip or sweet and sour sauce. They make wonderful hors d'oeuvres, but are equally loved as a main dish. In this recipe, we deep-fry them. Won ton wrappers are readily available in the refrigerator or freezer section in most supermarkets, or they can be bought at Asian markets.

3 cups finely shredded Chinese (Napa) cabbage	2 teaspoons dry sherry
½ pound ground pork	1 tablespoon chicken broth or water
1 scallion, minced	1 egg
1 teaspoon minced fresh ginger	1 (1-pound) package won ton wrappers
1 teaspoon soy sauce	2 cups vegetable oil
1 teaspoon salt	Easy Sweet and Sour Sauce (recipe follows)
½ teaspoon pepper	

1. Place shredded cabbage in a medium bowl and pour boiling water over it to wilt. Drain, run under cold water, and squeeze dry. In bowl, combine cabbage, pork, scallion, ginger, soy sauce, salt, pepper, sherry, and broth. Mix well. In a small bowl, beat egg with 1 tablespoon cold water.

2. Lay a won ton wrapper on a flat work surface. Place 1 scant teaspoon filling in center of won ton wrapper. Do not overfill won ton, or it will break when cooked. Brush egg around edges of won ton and fold over, corner to corner, to form a triangle. Moisten one corner of triangle and squeeze onto opposite corner to form a peaked-shaped won ton. Repeat with remaining wrappers, until all filling is used up. Set out won tons on a well-floured cookie sheet, standing them so they do not touch.

3. In a wok, heat oil to 375°F, or until a cube of bread browns in 1 minute. Deep-fry won tons in batches without crowding, until they are crisp and golden, about 1 minute per batch. Drain on paper towels. Serve with Easy Sweet and Sour Sauce.

301   EASY SWEET AND SOUR SAUCE
Prep: 2 minutes   Cook: none   Makes: about 1 cup

1 cup Chinese plum sauce	1½ tablespoons rice vinegar

In a small bowl, stir together plum sauce and vinegar until blended.

302   ANTS CLIMBING A TREE
Prep: 20 minutes   Cook: 11 minutes   Serves: 4

Children love this dish with its quaint name. Ground beef provides the "ants"; noodles are the twigs or branches of the tree.

2 ounces bean threads (cellophane noodles)	2 tablespoons dry sherry
3 tablespoons vegetable oil	1½ tablespoons dark soy sauce
3 scallions, minced	2 teaspoons chile paste
1 tablespoon minced fresh ginger	Salt
1 pound ground beef	2 teaspoons Asian sesame oil
¾ cup Chinese Chicken Stock (page 27) or reduced-sodium canned broth	Boston lettuce leaves

1. Soak bean threads in warm water until soft, about 15 minutes. Cut into 4-inch lengths.

2. In a wok, heat vegetable oil over high heat, add scallions and ginger, and stir-fry until aromatic, about 30 seconds. Add ground beef and stir-fry until beef loses its pink color, about 5 minutes.

3. Add chicken stock, sherry, soy sauce, and chile paste. Bring to a boil, stirring to blend; reduce heat and simmer until liquid is almost all absorbed, about 5 minutes. Stir in bean threads and cook 30 seconds. Season with salt to taste and drizzle with sesame oil. Spoon beef onto lettuce leaves, fold over to form a package, and serve, or serve beef on the side with lettuce leaves and let diners fold up their own packages.

303   CONFETTI BEEF IN LETTUCE CUPS
Prep: 15 minutes   Cook: 6 minutes   Serves: 4

1 pound beef fillet	¼ cup finely diced carrots
2 tablespoons dry sherry	¼ cup finely diced green bell pepper
1 tablespoon soy sauce	¼ cup finely diced red bell pepper
½ cup plus 2 teaspoons hoisin sauce	1 scallion, minced
1 tablespoon cornstarch	8 Boston lettuce leaves
2 tablespoons vegetable oil	
2 ounces sliced bamboo shoots, diced	

1. Slice beef into 2½-inch slivers. In a bowl, combine sherry, soy sauce, 2 teaspoons hoisin sauce, cornstarch, and 1 tablespoon water. Add meat and toss to mix well.

2. In a wok, heat 1 tablespoon oil over high heat until just smoking. Add beef and stir-fry until lightly browned, about 2 minutes. Remove to a plate.

3. Heat remaining 1 tablespoon oil in wok, Add bamboo shoots, carrots, green pepper, and red pepper. Stir-fry 2 minutes. Return meat to wok and stir-fry to mix and heat through, about 2 minutes. Mix in minced scallion.

4. To serve, spoon beef into lettuce cups. Diners fold over cups and dip in remaining hoisin sauce.

304   SHRIMP AND PORK DUMPLINGS
Prep: 45 minutes   Cook: 20 to 30 minutes   Makes: 36

The ingredients for these dumplings are simple and easy to find, and they are delicious. A bamboo steamer with a lid is the best way to steam them, as the bamboo lid absorbs the condensation and the dumplings will not become too wet. I often make a double or triple batch and freeze them. They keep wonderfully well and can be reheated while still frozen.

½ **cup cilantro leaves**
½ **pound shrimp, shelled and**
    deveined
½ **pound ground pork**
1 **tablespoon sugar**
1½ **teaspoons salt**
¼ **teaspoon pepper**

1 **teaspoon Asian sesame oil**
2 **teaspoons cornstarch**
1 **(1-pound) package round**
    won ton skins
3 **tablespoons vegetable oil**
    Soy Vinegar Dip (page 18)

1. In a food processor, chop cilantro; remove and set aside. Place shrimp in processor bowl and coarsely chop. Add ground pork, sugar, salt, pepper, sesame oil, cornstarch, and chopped cilantro leaves. Pulse to blend well.

2. Lay several round won ton skins on work surface. Spoon a scant teaspoon of filling in the center of each skin. Wet edges with water, then fold over, making 3 pleats on one side of semicircle. Press edges together to seal, forming a half-moon-shaped dumpling. Repeat until you have formed 36 dumplings and all filling is used up.

3. Pour vegetable oil into a pie plate. Stand dumplings in oil to grease bottoms. Remove half to a bamboo steamer basket, arranging them in a single layer without touching. Cover and steam until dumplings are firm, about 10 to 15 minutes. Repeat with remaining dumplings. Serve with Soy Vinegar Dip.

305   BEAN CURD AND SPINACH DUMPLINGS
Prep: 30 minutes   Cook: 5 to 10 minutes   Makes: 3 to 4 dozen

1 (10-ounce) package frozen spinach, thawed	1 tablespoon soy sauce
½ cup cilantro leaves	½ teaspoon pepper
2 scallions	1 teaspoon Asian sesame oil
1 slice of fresh ginger	1 tablespoon cornstarch
4 water chestnuts	1 egg white

½ pound firm bean curd, cut
      into ¼-inch dice
	1 (1-pound) package round
	      won ton skins

	1 tablespoon vegetable oil

1. Squeeze spinach very dry. In a food processor, coarsely chop spinach, cilantro, scallions, ginger, and water chestnuts. Remove to a bowl. Add bean curd, soy sauce, pepper, sesame oil, cornstarch, and egg white. Mix well.

2. On a work surface, lay out won ton skins. Spoon 1 teaspoon of filling in center of each skin. Wet edges with water. Pleat and fold over to form dumpling. Repeat until all dumplings are formed. Pour vegetable oil into a pie plate. Stand dumplings in oil to grease bottoms. Arrange dumplings in bamboo steamer baskets.

3. Fill a wok one-third full of water and bring to a boil over medium heat. Place steamer baskets in wok, cover, and steam dumplings until filling is set and skins are cooked through, 5 to 10 minutes.

306   POTSTICKER DUMPLINGS
Prep: 35 minutes   Chill: 30 minutes   Cook: 9 to 10 minutes
Makes: 48

Here is a great recipe for these popular dumplings. Homemade dough produces a chewy, earthy dumpling, but you can substitute gyoza skins, which are available in many supermarkets as well as in Asian markets.

1 pound Chinese (Napa) cabbage, shredded	1 tablespoon Asian sesame oil
½ pound ground pork	½ teaspoon salt
2 scallions, minced	1 recipe Potsticker Dough
3 slices of fresh ginger, minced	(recipe follows)
1 teaspoon dry sherry	½ cup vegetable oil
1 tablespoon soy sauce	Spicy Dipping Sauce (page 199)

1. Bring a large saucepan of water to a boil. Add cabbage and cook until just wilted, about 1 minute. Drain, rinse under cold water, and squeeze dry.

2. In a food processor, combine cabbage, pork, scallions, ginger, sherry, soy sauce, sesame oil, and salt. Pulse to chop and mix well. Remove to a bowl, cover, and refrigerate 30 minutes.

3. On a work surface, divide dough into 4 parts. Roll each part into a long thin sausage about ½ inch in diameter. Cut each dough sausage into 12 pieces. Roll each piece between palms to form a smooth ball. Sprinkle with flour and roll each into a 3-inch round pancake. Place 1 teaspoon of filling on each pancake. Pleat half of pancake, fold over, and seal with water. Or pleat and seal edges together to form beggars' purses. Repeat until all dumplings are formed.

4. In a large nonstick skillet, heat 3 tablespoons vegetable oil over medium-high heat. Add as many dumplings as will fit in skillet without touching. Cook until bottoms of dumplings are lightly browned, 1 to 2 minutes. All at once add enough cold water to cover dumplings. Cover pan and bring to a boil over high heat. Cook until tops of dumplings are waxy and cooked through, about 5 minutes. Drain off water, return skillet to heat, and crisp bottoms, about 2 minutes. Repeat until all dumplings are cooked. Serve with Spicy Dipping Sauce.

307 POTSTICKER DOUGH
Prep: 20 minutes   Stand: 15 minutes   Cook: none
Makes: enough for 48

This flour and water mixture is characteristic of many Chinese doughs. The result is a sticky dough, so do not be afraid to add more flour as you work with it, especially in humid weather.

2½ cups flour
½ cup cold water

¾ cup boiling water

1. In 2 separate bowls, place 1¼ cups flour.

2. Add cold water to one bowl and stir to form a soft dough. Add boiling water to second bowl and stir to form a dough. Combine two doughs and knead until smooth, about 15 minutes. Cover with a damp towel and let stand 15 minutes.

3. Dough can be made ahead and stored well wrapped in refrigerator overnight.

308 SPICY DIPPING SAUCE
Prep: 5 minutes   Cook: none   Makes: ½ cup

½ cup soy sauce
1 teaspoon chile oil or hot pepper sauce

1 tablespoon Asian sesame oil
1 tablespoon minced scallion
1 teaspoon minced garlic

In small bowl, combine soy sauce, chile oil, sesame oil, scallion, and garlic. Whisk to blend well.

309   SIU MEI FLOWER DUMPLINGS

Prep: 1 hour   Cook: 50 minutes   Makes: about 75

These dumplings freeze very well, so making a large batch is well worth the time. With a little practice, they will shape up in no time at all, and they are so easy that children can help. *Siu mei* do not need to be thawed before reheating, which can be done in a steamer or microwave. A dozen or so make a great lunch.

3 dried Chinese mushrooms	1½ teaspoons Asian sesame oil
2 slices of fresh ginger	½ teaspoon sugar
¼ cup water chestnuts	⅛ teaspoon pepper
¼ cup loosely packed cilantro leaves	1 (1-pound) package thin won ton skins (about 80 to 100 sheets per package)
1 pound ground pork	1 tablespoon vegetable oil
¼ cup cornstarch	Spicy Dipping Sauce (page 199)
1½ teaspoons soy sauce	

1. In a small saucepan, bring 1 cup water, mushrooms, and ginger slices to a boil. Reduce heat and simmer until mushrooms are soft and water is reduced by half, about 20 minutes. Remove mushrooms and cut off stems; reserve caps. Remove ginger slices from liquid and reserve liquid.

2. In a food processor, coarsely chop mushroom caps, ginger slices, water chestnuts, and cilantro. Add ground pork, cornstarch, soy sauce, sesame oil, sugar, pepper, and reserved mushroom liquid. Blend well. Remove to a bowl. Filling may be made up to a day ahead and refrigerated, well covered.

3. With a 3½-inch round cookie cutter, cut won ton skins into circles. Lay 24 skins on work surface. Place 1 scant teaspoon of filling in center of each circle. Gather won ton skins up around filling, but do not enclose top. Squeeze lightly in center to form a "waist." Pat down filling to flatten top. Dumplings should resemble a flower. Repeat in batches of 24.

4. Grease a flat plate with vegetable oil and place finished dumplings on plate to oil bottoms. Remove about one-third to each of 3 steamer baskets, arranging dumplings in a single layer without touching. Stack steamer baskets and steam dumplings until firm, about 10 minutes. Serve with Spicy Dipping Sauce.

310   GARLIC CHIVE DUMPLINGS
Prep: 35 minutes   Chill: 20 minutes   Cook: 10 minutes
Makes: 48

Garlic chives, sometimes called Chinese chives, have a stronger flavor than regular chives and give these dumplings a special flavor. You can recognize them in Chinatown and greengrocers by their long, flat, grasslike leaves and deep green color. I store them for a day or two in a brown paper bag in the vegetable bin of the refrigerator. Their smell becomes too strong if kept much longer, and they deteriorate rapidly, so it is best to use them when they are fresh. If you have an herb garden, they can be grown quite easily.

½ cup plus 1 tablespoon
   vegetable oil
2 scallions, minced
1½ tablespoons minced fresh
   ginger
½ pound Chinese (Napa)
   cabbage, finely shredded
½ pound garlic chives,* cut
   into 1-inch lengths
1 teaspoon dry sherry

1 tablespoon soy sauce
2 tablespoons Asian sesame
   oil
½ teaspoon pepper
2 teaspoons cornstarch
1 recipe Potsticker Dough
   (page 199) or 1 (12-ounce)
   package gyoza skins
¾ cup flour
   Soy Vinegar Dip (page 18)

1. In a wok or large skillet, heat 1 tablespoon of vegetable oil over medium heat. Add scallions and ginger and stir-fry until aromatic, about 30 seconds. Add shredded cabbage and garlic chives. Cook, stirring, until vegetables are wilted, about 2 minutes. Add sherry, soy sauce, 1 tablespoon of sesame oil, pepper, and cornstarch. Cook, stirring, until cornstarch thickens and binds vegetables lightly. Remove filling to a bowl and let cool, then cover and refrigerate about 20 minutes to cool completely.

2. On a floured work surface, divide dough into 4 parts. Roll each part into a long thin sausage about ½ inch thick. Cut each dough sausage into 12 pieces. Roll each piece between your palms to form a smooth ball. Sprinkle with flour and roll out each ball into a 3-inch round pancake.

3. Place 1 teaspoon of filling in center of each pancake. Moisten edges of pancake with water, pull up to enclose filling, and press and pleat to seal. Crimp to form beggars' purses. Repeat until all dumplings are formed.

4. In a large pot of boiling water, cook dumplings over high heat until dough becomes waxy, about 5 minutes; drain. Transfer to a serving platter and drizzle remaining 1 tablespoon sesame oil over dumplings. Serve with Soy Vinegar Dip.

* *Available in Asian markets*

311   SHRIMP DUMPLINGS *(HAR KOW)*
Prep: 45 minutes   Cook: 8 to 10 minutes   Makes: 36

1 pound shrimp, shelled and
   deveined
¼ cup water chestnuts
1 scallion, minced
2 teaspoons soy sauce
½ teaspoon salt
½ teaspoon Asian sesame oil

Vegetable oil, to grease
   hands, work surface,
   and steamer basket
   (about ¼ cup)
1 recipe Wheat Starch Dough
   (recipe follows)
Soy Vinegar Dip (page 18)

1. In a food processor, combine shrimp, water chestnuts, scallion, soy sauce, salt, and sesame oil. Pulse to chop coarsely and blend. Remove to a bowl.

2. Oil hands and work surface lightly. Divide dough into 4 equal parts. Roll each piece with hands into a sausage about 1 inch in diameter. Cut each sausage crosswise into 1-inch pieces. Roll each piece between palms to a smooth ball.

3. Roll out a ball of wheat starch dough into a 3-inch circle. Place 1 teaspoon filling in center of circle. Lift up one side of dough and pleat half of dough; press to join to remaining half. Repeat with remaining dough and filling.

4. Lightly oil steamer basket with a pastry brush. Place dumplings in basket, cover, and steam until dumpling becomes translucent, about 8 to 10 minutes. Do not overcook, or wrapper will fall apart. Serve hot with Soy Vinegar Dip.

312   WHEAT STARCH DOUGH
Prep: 10 minutes   Cook: none   Makes: 36 wrappers

This is one dumpling wrapper that cannot be bought, so I have included the recipe. It is quite simple and when made in a small batch, does not become overwhelming. The combination of two flours—wheat and tapioca—is the secret to the translucent dough that is essential to these *har kow,* shrimp dumplings.

1 cup wheat starch *
½ cup tapioca flour **

1 cup boiling water
2 tablespoons vegetable oil

1. In a bowl, combine wheat starch and tapioca flour. Whisk together to mix well. Make a well and pour in boiling water, stirring with a fork to form a dough. Let cool 5 minutes.

2. Grease hands and work surface with oil. Transfer dough to work surface and knead until smooth, about 3 minutes. Cover with a clean kitchen towel and let rest 10 minutes before using.

* *Available in Asian markets*
** *Available in health food stores and specialty food shops*

313   LOTUS LEAF RICE PACKAGES WITH PEANUTS AND SCALLIONS

Prep: 15 minutes   Stand: 1 hour   Cook: 1 hour   Serves: 4

1 cup glutinous (sweet) rice	1 tablespoon soy sauce
2 lotus leaves	2 teaspoons salt
½ cup peanuts, raw or dry-roasted	1 teaspoon freshly ground pepper
8 scallions, minced	1 tablespoon Asian sesame oil
2 slices of fresh ginger, minced	

1. Rinse rice and soak in cold water for 1 hour. Meanwhile, soak lotus leaves in warm water until pliable, about 15 minutes; drain.

2. Drain rice well. In a medium bowl, mix rice with peanuts, scallions, ginger, soy sauce, salt, pepper, and sesame oil.

3. Lay lotus leaves on work surface. Divide rice mixture in half and mound in center of each leaf. Fold into 2 packages; lay seam side-down in steamer basket. Cover and steam until rice is cooked, about 1 hour.

4. To serve, cut a cross on top of each lotus leaf package, open, and spoon out rice.

314   CHICKEN IN PARCHMENT PACKAGES

Prep: 30 minutes   Cook: 15 minutes   Makes: 36

These little packets are messy to unwrap, but delicious to eat. To make them, you'll need parchment cooking paper. It is sold in specialty cookware shops.

1 pound skinless, boneless chicken breast	1 scallion, minced
2 tablespoons hoisin sauce	1 tablespoon Asian sesame oil
2 teaspoons soy sauce	¼ teaspoon pepper
2 garlic cloves, minced	1 tablespoon cornstarch
	2 cups vegetable oil

1. Cut chicken into thin strips no more than ¼ inch thick. In a small bowl, combine hoisin sauce, soy sauce, garlic, scallion, sesame oil, pepper, and cornstarch. Stir until blended. Add chicken pieces and toss to coat well.

2. Lay out 36 (5-inch) parchment squares on work surface. Place 1 teaspoon chicken mixture on a corner. Fold over twice, fold sides, then fold and tuck in last corner to form a 2 x 1-inch packet. Repeat with remaining chicken.

3. In a wok, heat vegetable oil over high heat to 375°F, or until a cube of bread browns in 1 minute. Add chicken packets in batches without crowding and fry, turning frequently, until packets are lightly browned, about 3 minutes per batch. Remove to paper towels, drain, and cool slightly before serving. Chicken packets are unwrapped by diners.

315 BEGGAR'S CHICKEN

Prep: 30 minutes   Stand: 15 minutes   Cook: 2½ hours   Serves: 4

One of the many versions of how this unique dish came to be is that a beggar, having stolen a chicken, was faced with the problem of how to cook it undetected. He built a fire by a lotus pond where he was camped, and struck on the solution of wrapping the chicken in mud and burying it in the coals. To protect the chicken from getting muddy, he wrapped it in a few lotus leaves. The aromatic result told him he had created a gourmet's delight! Pond mud being something hard to come by today, we have included a recipe for a wrapping made of flour paste as a substitute. The flour crust is for cooking only; it is discarded before eating.

1 (3½-pound) whole chicken	1 teaspoon sugar
1 tablespoon vegetable oil	1 tablespoon dark soy sauce
½ pound ground pork	1 tablespoon dry sherry
1 teaspoon minced fresh	1 teaspoon Asian sesame oil
ginger	4 lotus leaves
2 tablespoons minced pickled	1 recipe Dough Wrapper
mustard greens	(recipe follows)

1. Trim chicken and remove excess fat. Pat dry with paper towels.

2. In a wok, heat vegetable oil over high heat until just smoking. Add pork and stir-fry until no longer pink, about 2 minutes. Add ginger, mustard greens, and sugar. Stir-fry 1 minute, tossing to mix well. Remove from heat and cool.

3. In a small bowl, combine dark soy sauce, sherry, and sesame oil. Rub all over chicken, inside and out. Set aside to dry 15 minutes.

4. Meanwhile, in a large bowl, soak lotus leaves in hot water until soft and pliable, about 10 minutes. Drain and pat dry. Lay on work surface. Stuff chicken loosely with pork and mustard green mixture. Wrap in lotus leaves.

5. Preheat oven to 550°F. Roll out dough about ¼ inch thick. Cut into a circle large enough to enfold chicken. Wrap dough around chicken package, sealing edges well with water. Line a baking sheet with foil and place chicken on it, seam side down.

6. Bake chicken until crust hardens and turns brown, about 1 hour. Reduce oven temperature to 350° and continue cooking chicken 1½ hours longer.

7. To serve, present wrapped chicken, crack dough at table, and remove and discard dough. Cut lotus leaves with scissors and serve chicken by tearing apart with fork or chopsticks. (Traditionally, guests use chopsticks to pick apart chicken.) Chicken should be falling apart. Spoon out stuffing. Be sure everyone is served some chicken and some stuffing.

DOUGH WRAPPER FOR BEGGAR'S CHICKEN
Makes: wrap for 1 chicken

6 cups all-purpose flour
2 cups coarse kosher salt

2½ cups water

1. In a large bowl, combine flour and salt. Make a well in center and pour in water. Stir to form dough. Knead to a smooth ball.

2. Roll dough out between 2 sheets of parchment or wax paper.

---

316 GARLIC CHIVE ROLLS
Prep: 25 minutes   Chill: 15 minutes
Cook: 10 to 14 minutes   Makes: 20

These rolls are unusual and delicious. As garlic chives are seasonal, you might like to substitute regular chives in this recipe.

2 tablespoons plus
    2 teaspoons vegetable oil
2 ounces garlic chives,*
    minced (1½ to 2 cups)
½ cup shredded Chinese
    (Napa) cabbage

2 teaspoons soy sauce
¼ teaspoon pepper
1 teaspoon cornstarch
1 package (10 sheets) spring
    roll wrappers

1. In a medium skillet, heat 2 teaspoons oil over medium heat. Add garlic chives and cabbage and cook, stirring often, until wilted, about 1 minute. Add soy sauce and pepper and stir to blend. Mix cornstarch with 1 tablespoon cold water and add to skillet. Cook, stirring, until thickened, about 1 minute. Remove to a bowl, cover, and refrigerate until cold, about 15 minutes.

2. Cut spring roll wrappers in half diagonally to form 20 triangles. Spoon 1 teaspoon filling onto middle of wrapper and pat into sausage shape. Fold long side of triangle over filling, fold in sides, and roll up to form a small spring roll about 2 x 1 inch. Seal corner with cold water. Repeat until all rolls are formed.

3. In a large skillet, heat 1 tablespoon oil over high heat. Reduce heat to medium. Add 10 rolls and cook, turning once, until light brown, 2 to 3 minutes per side. Repeat with remaining oil and rolls. Serve warm.

* *Available in Asian markets*

317 CURRY TRIANGLES

Prep: 35 minutes   Cook: 9 to 11 minutes plus 3 minutes per batch
Makes: 80

2 cups plus 1 tablespoon
    vegetable oil
¼ cup minced onion
½ pound ground round
1 tablespoon Madras curry
    powder

1 scallion, minced
1 tablespoon bread crumbs
½ teaspoon salt
1 package won ton skins
1 egg, beaten with
    1 tablespoon water

1. In a medium skillet, heat 1 tablespoon oil over medium-high heat. Add onion and cook until golden, 3 to 5 minutes. Add beef and cook, breaking up lumps of meat until beef loses its pink color, about 5 minutes. Add curry powder and cook, stirring constantly, until aromatic, about 1 minute. Add scallion and bread crumbs; mix well. Remove from heat. Season with salt to taste.

2. Cut won ton skins in half to form 2 strips. Place ½ teaspoon filling at one end and fold over repeatedly to form a little triangle. Brush with egg wash to seal. Place on a well-floured cookie sheet, setting triangles apart. Repeat until all triangles are formed.

3. In a wok, heat 2 cups oil to 375°F, or until a bread cube browns in 1 minute. Fry triangles, in batches without crowding, until crisp and golden, about 3 minutes. Drain on paper towels. Serve hot.

318 EGG CREPE ROLLS

Prep: 10 minutes   Cook: 9 to 13 minutes   Serves: 2

1 tablespoon vegetable oil
¼ cup minced onion
1 pound ground beef
2 tablespoons plus 1 teaspoon
    minced scallion

1 tablespoon dark soy sauce
2 teaspoons hoisin sauce
3 tablespoons Ginger Oil
    (page 24)
Egg Crepes (page 22)

1. In a large skillet or wok, heat vegetable oil. Add onion and cook over medium-high heat until golden, 2 to 3 minutes. Add beef and cook, stirring, until meat loses its pink color, about 5 minutes. Add 2 tablespoons minced scallion, soy sauce, and hoisin sauce. Stir to mix well. Remove from heat and let cool slightly.

2. Grease a 9-inch plate with 1 teaspoon of ginger oil. On a work surface, lay out egg sheets. Divide meat into equal portions and spoon onto sheets, a little off center. Roll up to form a cannellonilike shape. Place on oiled plate and repeat with remaining sheets. (Recipe can be made ahead and refrigerated.)

3. Shortly before serving, warm rolls in a microwave on High 2 to 3 minutes until heated through or steam about 5 minutes. Drizzle remaining ginger oil over rolls, sprinkle with 1 teaspoon minced green scallion, and serve.

319 GINGER DUCK ROLL-UPS
Prep: 15 minutes   Cook: 6 minutes   Serves: 4

1 skinless, boneless duck breast (about 1½ pounds)	1 tablespoon dry sherry
2 teaspoons soy sauce	1 tablespoon dry white wine
1 teaspoon cornstarch	1 teaspoon sugar
¼ pound fresh ginger, preferably young	¼ teaspoon pepper
1 tablespoon vegetable oil	8 Mu Shu Pancakes (page 210)
1 tablespoon yellow bean sauce	

1. Slice duck meat into 1 x ½-inch strips. Toss with soy sauce and cornstarch. Cut ginger into ¼-inch dice.

2. In a wok, heat oil until just smoking. Add ginger and stir-fry 1 minute. Add duck and stir-fry until duck loses its pink color, about 3 minutes. Add bean sauce, sherry, wine, sugar, and pepper. Stir-fry 2 minutes.

3. To serve, divide duck into 8 portions and place on pancakes. Roll up to form spring roll shapes and serve.

320 CHICKEN IN STICKY RICE BUNDLES
Prep: 20 minutes   Stand: 1 hour   Cook: 1 hour   Serves: 4

2 cups glutinous rice	2 tablespoons mushroom soy sauce
6 large dried Chinese mushrooms	2 tablespoons dry sherry
2 lotus leaves	1 scallion, minced
1 (3-pound) chicken, cut into bite-size pieces	1 tablespoon minced fresh ginger

1. Soak glutinous rice in cold water 1 hour. Meanwhile, soak mushrooms in warm water until soft, about 15 minutes. Drain and remove and discard stems; cut caps into quarters. Soak lotus leaves in hot water until soft and pliable, about 15 minutes.

2. In a large bowl, combine chicken pieces with mushroom soy sauce, sherry, scallion,and ginger.Toss to mix well. Let stand 20 minutes.

3. Remove lotus leaves from water and lay on a flat work surface. Drain rice and divide into 4 parts. Pour one part rice on each lotus leaf and flatten into a circle. Place chicken pieces on top of rice. Drizzle with any remaining marinade. Top each mound with remaining rice so that chicken is covered. Fold leaves over to form a rounded package.

4. Place lotus bundles, seam side down, in a steamer basket, cover, and steam until rice is completely cooked, about 1 hour.

5. To serve, cut a cross at top of lotus leaf bundle, open, and spoon out rice and chicken.

321   DUCK IN LOTUS LEAVES

Prep: 20 minutes   Chill: 30 minutes   Cook: 30 minutes   Makes: 12

Lotus leaves are available in dried bundles in Asian markets. I have found them all over the country, even in little towns in the Midwest. They keep indefinitely and are great for wrapping food, as they impart a subtle aroma to the dish. While the leaves are not edible, the bundles are always served wrapped, and they make an intriguing presentation. If you cannot find lotus leaves, aluminum foil is an acceptable substitute.

2 **pounds duck breast, boned with skin on**	2 **teaspoons sugar**
2 **scallions, minced**	1 **tablespoon yellow bean sauce**
2 **tablespoons minced fresh ginger**	1 **tablespoon Asian sesame oil**
2 **tablespoons dry sherry**	3 **lotus leaves**
2 **tablespoons soy sauce**	1 **cup Aromatic Rice (recipe follows)**

1. Cut duck into bite-size pieces, about 1 inch square.

2. In a medium bowl, combine scallions, ginger, sherry, soy sauce, sugar, bean sauce, and sesame oil. Add duck and toss to coat well. Cover and refrigerate 30 minutes.

3. Meanwhile, in a large bowl, soak lotus leaves in hot water until soft and pliable, about 15 minutes. Cut each leaf into quarters.

4. Roll duck pieces in aromatic rice to coat. Place a few pieces on a lotus leaf quarter and roll up to form a spring roll-like bundle. Repeat until all duck is wrapped. Place bundles in steamer basket, cover, and steam until duck is tender and cooked through, about 30 minutes. Duck can be prepared ahead and refrigerated, or frozen in the lotus leaves. They are simply reheated by steaming.

322   AROMATIC RICE

Prep: 1 minute   Cook: 5 minutes   Makes: 1 cup

As we Chinese do not have bread crumbs, aromatic rice serves this purpose. Small packages of this rice, generally flavored with five-spice powder, are available in Asian markets, but it is so easy to make that I never bother to buy them.

1 **cup long-grain raw rice**	¼ **teaspoon Chinese five-spice powder or ½ teaspoon Szechuan pepper mixed with ¼ teaspoon ground star anise**

1. In a dry wok, roast rice over high heat, tossing constantly, until slightly browned and nutty, about 5 minutes. Be careful not to let rice burn.

2. Transfer rice to a blender or spice grinder, add five-spice powder, and grind to a coarse crumb. Aromatic rice may be stored in a covered jar after it is completely cool.

---

323   EIGHT JEWEL RICE IN LOTUS PACKAGE

Prep: 30 minutes   Cook: 34 to 39 minutes   Serves: 4

1   cup glutinous rice
6   dried Chinese mushrooms
2   lotus leaves
1½ cups Chinese Chicken Stock (page 27) or reduced-sodium canned broth
¼   cup dry sherry
2   teaspoons soy sauce
1   teaspoon pepper
2   tablespoons vegetable oil

2   scallions, minced
2   garlic cloves, minced
2   Chinese sausages *(lop cheung)*, diced
2   ounces Smithfield or country ham, finely diced (about ½ cup)
½   cup sliced bamboo shoots
½   cup pine nuts
    Salt

1. Rinse and drain glutinous rice. Soak mushrooms in ½ cup warm water until soft, about 10 minutes. Drain, reserving soaking water. Remove and discard stems. Cut caps into thin strips. In a large bowl, soak lotus leaves in warm water until soft and pliable, about 10 minutes.

2. In a medium saucepan, combine rice, mushroom water, chicken stock, sherry, soy sauce, and pepper. Bring to a boil, reduce heat to low, and simmer, covered, until rice is just tender and liquid is absorbed, about 20 minutes. Remove from heat.

3. In a wok, heat oil over high heat until just smoking. Add scallions and garlic and stir-fry until fragrant, about 30 seconds. Add mushrooms, sausages, ham, and bamboo shoots and stir-fry 2 minutes, tossing to mix well. Add pine nuts and stir-fry 1 minute longer. Remove to a large mixing bowl. Add rice and mix with a large fork, tossing gently so as not to mash rice. Season with salt to taste.

4. Lay out lotus leaves on work surface. Divide rice mixture in half and mound in center of each leaf. Fold over to form a package. Before serving, place packages in a steamer basket, cover, and steam until heated, about 10 to 15 minutes. Rice may be prepared a day ahead and reheated.

324   MU SHU PORK PACKAGES
Prep: 20 minutes   Cook: 8 to 11 minutes   Serves: 4

Mu shu pork should be served wrapped in pancakes. These are fun to make, but require extra time. If you are in a hurry, substitute flour tortillas, which can be brushed with a little sesame oil before they are warmed in a microwave oven.

4 dried Chinese mushrooms	4 eggs, beaten
6 water chestnuts	Salt
¾ pound well-trimmed boneless pork loin	4 scallions, minced
	4 slices of fresh ginger, minced
2 tablespoons cornstarch	
2 tablespoons dark soy sauce	10 Mu Shu Pancakes (recipe follows) or 6-inch flour tortillas
1 tablespoon dry white wine	
1 teaspoon sugar	
¼ cup plus 2 tablespoons vegetable oil	Hoisin sauce

1. Soak mushrooms in ½ cup warm water until soft, about 15 minutes. Remove mushrooms, reserving soaking water. Cut off and discard stems. Cut caps into thin strips. Coarsely chop water chestnuts. Cut pork into 1 x ¼-inch strips. In a medium bowl, toss pork strips with cornstarch, soy sauce, white wine, and sugar to coat evenly.

2. In a wok, warm 3 tablespoons oil over medium heat. Add beaten eggs and cook, stirring, until eggs are just set, about 2 minutes. Remove to a plate and drain off excess oil.

3. Return wok to heat. Add remaining 3 tablespoons oil and stir-fry pork until meat is no longer pink, 2 to 3 minutes. Add mushrooms and water chestnuts; stir-fry 1 minute. Add eggs and reserved mushroom water and cook until liquid is almost all absorbed, 3 to 5 minutes. Season with salt to taste. Remove from heat and immediately stir in scallions and ginger.

4. Serve pork rolled in pancake packages with hoisin sauce on the side.

325   MU SHU PANCAKES
Prep: 30 minutes   Stand: 30 minutes   Cook: 10 minutes   Makes: 10

These classic pancakes take time, but are really fun to make. I always try to include them in children's cooking classes. They can be prepared ahead of time and stored, well wrapped, in the refrigerator or freezer.

1½ cups unsifted flour	2 tablespoons Asian sesame oil
½ cup boiling water	
2 tablespoons cold water	

1. In a medium bowl, stir together flour and boiling water. Add cold water and stir until dough forms. Turn out dough onto a lightly floured surface and knead until smooth, about 10 minutes. Cover with plastic wrap and let rest 30 minutes.

2. Divide dough in half. Roll each piece with your hands into a thin rope about ½ inch in diameter. Cut each rope into 5 pieces and roll pieces between your palms into even-sized balls.

3. On a floured surface, roll each ball into a thin, 3-inch pancake. Brush 5 pancakes with sesame oil and cover with remaining 5 pancakes. Place double pancake rounds on a floured surface and roll each into a larger thin circle about 8 inches in diameter.

4. Heat a dry heavy skillet, preferably cast-iron, over medium heat. Add one pancake and cook without browning until pancake is blistered with one or more air pockets. Turn and cook other side until dry but not brown, about 1 minute total. If pancakes begin to brown, lower heat.

5. Transfer pancake to a plate and let cool slightly. Repeat with remaining dough. While still warm, carefully pull pancakes apart, being careful not to burn hands with escaping steam. Stack to cool. To serve, warm pancakes in a steamer basket or in a microwave oven.

326 SALMON-CABBAGE PILLOWS
Prep: 15 minutes   Cook: 10 to 12 minutes   Serves: 4

8 large leaves Chinese (Napa)
   cabbage
4 salmon steaks, cut ¾ inch
   thick (about 6 ounces
   each)
2 teaspoons soy sauce
1 tablespoon dry white wine
1 scallion, minced

1 tablespoon minced fresh
   ginger
8 sprigs of fresh thyme or
   ¼ teaspoon dried thyme
   leaves
1 teaspoon cornstarch
   Salt and pepper

1. Bring a pot of water to a boil. Add cabbage leaves and cook until softened, about 10 *seconds.* Rinse under cold running water to cool; drain. Skin salmon steaks and remove bone. Wrap thin tails around to form each steak into a circle.

2. In a small bowl, combine soy sauce and wine. Sprinkle over salmon. On a work surface, overlap 2 cabbage leaves. Lay 1 salmon steak on each pair of leaves. Top each with one-fourth of scallion, ginger, and thyme. Fold leaves around fish to form a package.

3. Place packages on a plate that fits into a bamboo steamer basket, cover, and steam until fish is firm to touch and just cooked to the center, 10 to 12 minutes.

4. Remove fish to a serving platter. Pour off juices that have accumulated on plate into a small saucepan. Stir in cornstarch and bring to a boil, stirring until lightly thickened. Season with salt and pepper to taste and pour over fish packages.

327   PUNGENT PORK IN LOTUS LEAF
Prep: 20 minutes   Cook: 30 minutes   Makes: 12 bundles

2 pounds pork butt (with
    some fat)
2 tablespoons hoisin sauce
1 tablespoon fermented red
    bean curd cheese *(nam yue)*

2 tablespoons soy sauce
1 teaspoon sugar
3 lotus leaves
1 cup Aromatic Rice (page
    208)

1. Cut pork into thin slices 2 x 1-inch. In a medium bowl, combine hoisin sauce, red bean curd cheese, soy sauce, and sugar. Add pork strips and toss to coat well.

2. In a large bowl, soak lotus leaves in hot water until soft and pliable, about 15 minutes. Drain and cut each leaf into quarters.

3. Separate pork strips into 12 parts and roll each part in aromatic rice. Place on lotus leaf quarter and roll up tightly to form a spring roll-like bundle.

4. Place pork bundles in a steamer basket, cover, and steam until pork is tender and cooked through, about 30 minutes. Lotus bundles are served wrapped; each person unwraps the packet and discards the leaf.

328   FISH CUSTARD IN BANANA LEAVES
Prep: 15 minutes   Cook: 8 minutes   Serves: 4

This is a Malaysian-inspired dish that makes a lovely presentation. It is often cooked around the edges of a barbecue grill, or can be steamed in bamboo baskets. I serve these packages as appetizers or a side dish with rice. Banana leaves can be found in frozen packets in Asian markets, but you can substitute aluminum foil for a wrapper.

½ pound flounder fillets
1 small fresh hot chile pepper
1 garlic clove, crushed
5 whole blanched almonds
1 teaspoon turmeric
1 piece of lemon peel, about
    1 x ½ inch
¼ cup minced onion

1 slice of fresh ginger
1 egg
½ cup unsweetened coconut
    milk
½ teaspoon salt
1 stalk of lemongrass, cut into
    1-inch pieces
Banana leaves

1. In a food processor, combine fish with chile, garlic, almonds, turmeric, lemon peel, onion, ginger, egg, coconut milk, and salt. Process to a smooth paste. Remove fish custard to a bowl and fold in lemongrass.

2. Rinse banana leaves with warm water. Cut into pieces 4 inches wide. Place 1 tablespoon of fish custard on end of leaf and fold over to form a flat package about 3 x 4 inches. Secure end with toothpick. Do not worry about open sides. Repeat until all packages are formed. Grill on edges of a barbecue or steam in bamboo baskets until fish custard is set, about 8 minutes. Serve warm.

Chapter 11

Main-Course Salads and Other Cold Dishes

In America, we love salads; as starters, side dishes, main dishes, as a special course, and a buffet dish. Salad-style dishes are also much loved in Chinese cuisine. Traditionally, many cold dishes such as Drunken Shrimp, Tea-Smoked Fish, or Tea-Smoked Chicken are served as first courses in formal dinners or banquets.

In this chapter, I played with ideas for food and ingredients to come up with salads that are not necessarily traditional in the Chinese sense, but that combine flavors to make easy-to-put-together dishes that everyone will enjoy. Chicken salads are personal favorites because they are perfect for sweltering summer days when no one wants to be in the kitchen and a main-dish salad is all we want to eat. I use poached chicken, which remains juicy and succulent. Duck salads, beef salads, seafood salads, and even pasta salads are also featured here. These main-dish salads fit in so well in our busy lives that I know you will be using the recipes in this chapter over and over.

329   LEMON-FLAVORED CHICKEN AND BEAN SPROUT SALAD

Prep: 15 minutes   Stand: overnight   Cook: 20 minutes   Serves: 4

2 skinless, boneless chicken breast halves (about 5 ounces each)	2 teaspoons freshly ground pepper
3 garlic cloves, minced	1 tablespoon soy sauce
1 tablespoon minced fresh ginger	6 tablespoons lemon juice
1 teaspoon lemon zest	2 tablespoons dry white wine
½ teaspoon salt	2 tablespoons vegetable oil
	2 tablespoons olive oil
	4 cups bean sprouts

1. Cut chicken breasts in half crosswise to make 4 pieces and place in a small nonreactive dish. Combine garlic, ginger, lemon zest, salt, and pepper. Rub all over chicken breasts. In a small bowl, combine soy sauce, half of lemon juice, white wine, and vegetable oil. Pour over chicken breasts; turn to coat well. Cover and refrigerate overnight.

2. Preheat oven to 425°F. Remove chicken from marinade; reserve marinade. Lay chicken breasts on a baking sheet and bake 10 minutes. Turn and continue cooking until chicken is white in center, about 5 minutes longer. Remove to a plate; reserve pan juices.

3. In a small saucepan, bring marinade to a boil. Cook 5 minutes. Remove to a small heatproof bowl and stir in reserved pan juices. Whisk in olive oil and remaining 3 tablespoons lemon juice.

4. Toss bean sprouts with half of dressing. Arrange on a serving plate. Slice chicken and arrange over bean sprouts. Drizzle remaining dressing over chicken.

330   SESAME CHICKEN SALAD

Prep: 15 minutes   Cook: 8 minutes   Serves: 4

1 pound asparagus	1 tablespoon vegetable oil
2 tablespoons sesame seeds	1 teaspoon minced fresh ginger
3 cups diced White Poached Chicken with Scallion Oil (page 182)	1 teaspoon Dijon mustard
2 tablespoons Chile Oil (page 23)	2 tablespoons soy sauce
	½ teaspoon pepper
3 tablespoons Asian sesame oil	3 tablespoons rice vinegar
	1 scallion, minced

1. Trim asparagus and cut diagonally into 2-inch pieces. Bring a large saucepan of salted water to a boil. Add asparagus and cook until bright green and crisp-tender, about 3 minutes. Drain and rinse under cold running water until cool; drain well.

2. In a small dry skillet, cook sesame seeds over low heat until toasted, about 5 minutes.

3. Combine chicken and asparagus in a mixing bowl. In a measuring cup, combine chile oil, sesame oil, and vegetable oil. In a small bowl, whisk together minced ginger, mustard, soy sauce, pepper, and rice vinegar. Gradually whisk in oils until sauce is well blended.

4. Pour dressing over chicken and asparagus. Add 1 tablespoon sesame seeds and toss to mix. Transfer to a serving platter. Sprinkle remaining sesame seeds and minced scallion over salad and serve.

---

331 CHICKEN SALAD WITH HOISIN DRESSING
Prep: 15 minutes   Cook: 20 minutes   Serves: 6

2 scallions—1 whole, 1 minced	1 tablespoon vegetable oil
1 slice of fresh ginger plus 2 tablespoons minced	1 garlic clove, minced
2 pounds chicken breasts with skin and bones	1 tablespoon Asian sesame oil
2 teaspoons Szechuan peppercorns	1 tablespoon hoisin sauce
1 small dried hot red pepper	1 tablespoon soy sauce
	2 teaspoons brown sugar
	1 head of romaine lettuce, shredded

1. In a large saucepan, combine 6 cups water, whole scallion, and ginger slice. Bring to a boil, reduce heat to low, cover, and simmer 5 minutes. Add chicken breasts and poach uncovered 15 minutes, or until white in center but still juicy. Remove from heat and let chicken cool in liquid. Skin and bone cooled chicken breasts. With your fingers, shred chicken in thin strips.

2. In a spice grinder or blender, crush Szechuan peppercorns with dried hot red pepper. Heat 1 teaspoon vegetable oil in a small saucepan over medium heat. Add garlic, minced ginger and scallion, and crushed peppercorns and chile. Stir-fry 2 seconds, or until aromatic. Set aside to cool.

3. In a small bowl, mix together remaining 2 teaspoons vegetable oil with sesame oil, hoisin sauce, soy sauce, brown sugar, and cooled aromatic mix. Set dressing aside.

4. Make a bed of shredded lettuce on a platter. Toss chicken with all but 1 tablespoon of dressing. Arrange on shredded lettuce and drizzle reserved dressing over top. Serve at room temperature or slightly chilled.

332   TEA-SMOKED CHICKEN
Prep: 10 minutes   Chill: overnight   Cook: 53 to 63 minutes
Serves: 4

This chicken should be prepared at least one day in advance, as the flavor improves upon standing. It will keep up to a week, refrigerated.

2 tablespoons Szechuan
   peppercorns
2 tablespoons coarse salt
1 (3-pound) whole chicken or
   chicken breasts, with skin
   and bones
1 cup dark soy sauce
2 slices of fresh ginger

2 scallions
1 cinnamon stick
2 whole star anise
¾ cup sugar
¾ cup rice
¾ cup lapsang souchong tea
   leaves
1 tablespoon Asian sesame oil

1. In a small dry skillet, toast Szechuan peppercorns and salt over medium heat until aromatic, about 3 minutes. In a spice grinder or blender, grind mixture coarsely. Rub seasoning over chicken inside and out. Place chicken in plastic bag, seal, and refrigerate overnight.

2. In a large pot, combine soy sauce, ginger, scallions, cinnamon stick, star anise, and 10 cups water. Bring to a boil, reduce heat, and simmer 10 minutes. Add chicken and simmer over medium heat until chicken is tender and cooked through, 20 to 25 minutes. Remove chicken and let cool to room temperature.

3. Line a wok with aluminum foil. Layer sugar evenly over bottom of wok, then layer rice over sugar and tea leaves over rice. Place a metal rack over the smoking mixture. Place cooled chicken on rack. Line wok lid with enough foil to form an overlap. Cover, crimp foil to seal well, and smoke chicken over medium heat 20 to 25 minutes. Turn off heat but do not uncover wok for 10 minutes to allow smoke to dissipate. Remove chicken and let cool, then wrap and refrigerate overnight.

4. Before serving chicken, rub all over with sesame oil. Cut into bite-size pieces and arrange neatly on a serving platter. Garnish as desired.

333   SMOKED CHICKEN-NOODLE SALAD

Prep: 10 minutes   Cook: 3 to 5 minutes   Serves: 6

½ pound angel hair pasta
1 tablespoon vegetable oil
1 whole Tea-Smoked Chicken
   breast (page 216) or
   ½ pound smoked chicken
½ cup dry-roasted cashew nuts
6 scallions, cut into ½-inch
   pieces

1 teaspoon minced fresh
   ginger
2 teaspoons salt
½ teaspoon pepper
¼ cup cider vinegar
¾ cup Chile, Black Bean, and
   Garlic Oil (page 23)

1. In a large pot of boiling water, cook pasta until tender but still firm, 3 to 5 minutes; drain. Toss with vegetable oil. Remove chicken from bone and thinly slice.

2. In a large bowl, toss together chicken, cashew nuts, and scallions. In a small bowl, combine minced ginger, salt, pepper, vinegar, and oil. Whisk to blend well.

3. Add pasta to chicken mixture, pour dressing over salad, toss, and serve.

334   COLD POACHED DUCK

*Prep: 10 minutes   Cook: 1 hour 40 minutes to 2 hours 10 minutes
Serves: 6*

Here is a succulent way to cook duck that is to be served cold. The poaching removes most of the fat. Remaining poaching liquid can be strained, degreased, and used again within 2 days if refrigerated.

1 (4- to 5-pound) whole duck
1 tablespoon vegetable oil
2 cups dark soy sauce
¾ cup dry sherry
¼ cup brown sugar
1 cinnamon stick

2 star anise
2 pieces of dried tangerine
   peel
5 slices of fresh ginger
3 scallions

1. Trim duck of excess fat. Bring a large pot of water to a boil and plunge duck into water for a few seconds. Remove and pat dry inside and out.

2. In a wok, heat oil over medium heat until just smoking. Add duck and cook, turning, until browned all over, about 10 minutes. Remove duck.

3. In a large flameproof casserole, combine soy sauce, sherry, sugar, cinnamon stick, star anise, tangerine peel, ginger, and scallions. Add duck. Bring to a boil, reduce heat, and simmer, turning duck 2 or 3 times, 1½ to 2 hours, until duck is very tender and well done.

4. Remove duck and let cool. Cut through skin and bones into bite-size pieces to serve.

335　ROAST DUCK WITH TROPICAL FRUIT SALAD

Prep: 20 minutes　　Cook: 63 minutes　　Stand: overnight
Serves: 6 to 8

This recipe looks long, and it needs to stand overnight, but I guarantee the results will win raves.

¼　cup pine nuts
1　Cantonese Crispy Roast Duck (page 141)
¼　cup candied ginger
¼　cup shredded fresh ginger
2　cups dry white wine
½　cup orange juice

Juice of 3 limes
¼　cup Asian sesame oil
½　cup safflower oil
Salt and pepper
3　ripe papayas
2　small heads of Boston lettuce

1. In a dry medium skillet, toast pine nuts over medium-low heat, shaking pan occasionally, until nuts are fragrant and lightly browned, about 3 minutes.

2. Remove skin from duck and reserve. Bone duck and cut meat into thin shreds. Reserve meat and bones separately. Soak candied ginger in ½ cup warm water for 10 minutes. Drain, reserving water.

3. In a large pot, combine duck bones, candied ginger water, shredded ginger, wine, orange juice, and 2 cups water. Bring to a boil, reduce heat, and simmer 1 hour. Strain stock into a bowl. Skim off fat and pour stock into a clean saucepan. Boil rapidly to reduce liquid to ¼ cup.

4. In a bowl, whisk together reduced stock, lime juice, sesame oil, and safflower oil. Season with salt and pepper to taste. Toss shredded duck with dressing and let stand overnight. Most of dressing will be absorbed.

5. Peel papayas, remove seeds, and cut into 1-inch chunks. Combine with duck, add pine nuts, and toss to mix well. Line a platter with outer leaves of lettuce. Mound duck salad on leaves. Shred lettuce hearts and toss over salad.

336   THAI-STYLE BEEF SALAD

Prep: 20 minutes   Stand: 2 hours   Cook: 10 to 14 minutes
Serves: 6

1 large flank steak
  (about 2½ pounds)
2 tablespoons dark soy sauce
1 tablespoon honey
6 garlic cloves, minced
½ teaspoon salt
½ teaspoon freshly ground
  pepper
1 large head of Boston lettuce
1 pound fresh bean sprouts
1 long seedless cucumber, cut
  into thin matchstick strips
2 red onions, thinly sliced
1 red bell pepper, thinly
  sliced

¼ cup lightly packed mint
  leaves
¼ cup lightly packed cilantro
  leaves
2 teaspoons crushed hot red
  pepper
2 limes
2 tablespoons fish sauce
  (nuoc nam)
3 jalapeño peppers, seeded
  and finely minced
1 tablespoon light brown
  sugar

1. Trim flank steak and prick all over on both sides. In a baking dish, combine soy sauce, honey, 1½ teaspoons minced garlic, salt, and pepper. Add steak and turn to coat. Marinate at room temperature for 2 hours.

2. Preheat broiler or prepare a hot fire in a barbecue grill. Add steak and broil or grill, turning once, until browned outside but still rare inside, about 5 to 7 minutes per side. Remove and thinly slice.

3. Line a serving platter with lettuce leaves. Layer bean sprouts, cucumber, onion slices, and red pepper over lettuce. Arrange beef slices on top. Garnish with mint leaves, 2 tablespoons cilantro leaves, and crushed hot pepper. Slice 1 lime and arrange around platter.

4. Coarsely chop remaining 2 tablespoons cilantro leaves. In a small bowl, combine remaining garlic, jalapeño peppers, chopped cilantro, fish sauce, and brown sugar. Squeeze juice from remaining lime into bowl and stir to mix. Pour over salad and serve.

337   HOISIN BEEF SALAD
Prep: 10 minutes   Cook: 20 to 25 minutes   Serves: 4

Use a mild olive oil here, so it does not overpower the other flavors.

8 small red potatoes	2 tablespoons fresh lime juice
2 pounds Hoisin-Flavored	2 tablespoons soy sauce
Roast Filet of Beef (recipe	2 tablespoons Asian sesame
follows)	oil
2 heads of red leaf lettuce	⅓ cup olive oil
1 teaspoon Dijon mustard	1 small red onion, thinly
1 teaspoon freshly ground	sliced
pepper	

1. In a medium saucepan of cold water, cook unpeeled potatoes over medium heat until tender but not breaking apart, 20 to 25 minutes. Drain and let cool. Cut potatoes into 1-inch dice. Slice beef ¼ inch thick.

2. Rinse and dry lettuce. Remove and reserve large outer leaves. Cut remaining lettuce into shreds.

3. In a small bowl, whisk together mustard, pepper, lime juice, and soy sauce. Slowly whisk in sesame oil and then olive oil until well blended. In a medium bowl, toss potatoes with ¼ cup dressing. In another bowl, toss shredded lettuce with 2 tablespoons dressing.

4. Line a serving platter with outer leaves of lettuce. Mound potatoes in center of platter. Arrange sliced beef over potatoes. Arrange shredded lettuce around potatoes and beef. Scatter onion rings over beef and pour remaining dressing over salad.

338   HOISIN-FLAVORED ROAST FILET OF BEEF
Prep: 10 minutes   Stand: 2 to 3 hours   Cook: 30 minutes   Serves: 8

This roast is great in Hoisin Beef Salad, but also is delicious when used with Thai-Style Beef Salad for a change. I also like to offer this roast by itself, either warm or at room temperature. It serves well at a Western or Eastern-style meal or buffet.

¼ cup hoisin sauce	1 teaspoon freshly ground
2 tablespoons soy sauce	pepper
2 tablespoons dry sherry	2 tablespoons vegetable oil
1 tablespoon minced garlic	1 whole filet mignon (about
1 tablespoon minced fresh	3 pounds), trimmed and
ginger	tied

1. In a small bowl, combine hoisin sauce, soy sauce, sherry, garlic, ginger, pepper, and oil. Mix to blend well. Pour over filet and turn to coat well. Let stand at room temperature 2 to 3 hours.

2. Preheat oven to 450°F. Remove filet from marinade and place on a roasting rack; reserve marinade. Roast filet 10 minutes, until lightly browned.

3. Reduce oven temperature to 350°. Baste filet with marinade and return to oven. Continue roasting, basting often, until meat is rare, about 20 minutes longer. Remove from oven. Let stand 10 minutes, carve, and serve.

---

339 GRILLED LAMB SALAD
Prep: 15 minutes   Stand: 2 to 3 hours
Cook: 28 to 30 minutes   Serves: 8

1 leg of lamb, boned
   and butterflied
   (about 3 pounds)
½ cup soy sauce
2 tablespoons honey
¼ cup white vermouth
1 teaspoon Chinese five-spice
   powder

1 tablespoon minced fresh
   ginger
3 garlic cloves, minced
1 teaspoon Tabasco sauce
¼ cup vegetable oil
2 pounds green beans
¼ cup fresh lemon juice
3 medium tomatoes, sliced

1. Trim lamb of all fat and gristle. In a nonreactive baking dish, combine soy sauce, honey, vermouth, five-spice powder, ginger, garlic, Tabasco, and vegetable oil. Add lamb and turn to coat well. Cover and let stand 2 to 3 hours.

2. In a large saucepan of boiling salted water, cook green beans until crisp-tender, 3 to 5 minutes. Drain and rinse under cold running water to cool. Drain well.

3. Preheat broiler or outdoor barbecue grill. Remove lamb from marinade; reserve marinade. Grill lamb, turning once, until browned outside and pink inside, about 10 minutes per side. Remove to a carving board and let stand 15 minutes. Pour marinade into a small nonreactive saucepan, bring to a boil, and cook 5 minutes. Remove to a bowl and whisk in lemon juice.

4. To serve, arrange sliced tomatoes in a ring around serving platter. Mound green beans in the middle and arrange carved slices of lamb over green beans. Pour dressing over salad. Serve warm or at room temperature.

340 ANGEL HAIR PASTA, TOMATO, AND SHRIMP SALAD

Prep: 15 minutes   Cook: 8 to 10 minutes   Serves: 6

1 cup dry white wine	3 tablespoons cider vinegar
1 slice of fresh ginger plus 2 teaspoons minced	1 teaspoon soy sauce
	½ teaspoon salt
1 scallion	1 teaspoon pepper
1 pound medium shrimp, shelled and deveined	1 pint cherry tomatoes
	1 tablespoon black sesame seeds
1 pound angel hair pasta	
½ cup Asian sesame oil	

1. In a large saucepan, combine wine, ginger slice, scallion, and 3 cups cold water. Bring to a boil, reduce heat to low, and add shrimp. Poach until shrimp are pink and loosely curled, about 5 minutes. With a skimmer or slotted spoon, remove shrimp and let cool. Reserve poaching liquid.

2. In a large pot of boiling salted water, cook pasta until tender but still firm, 3 to 5 minutes. Drain and rinse under cold water; drain well. In a large bowl, toss pasta with 2 teaspoons sesame oil.

3. In a small bowl, whisk together remaining sesame oil with cider vinegar, soy sauce, salt, and pepper. Add 2 tablespoons reserved poaching liquid and blend.

4. Add shrimp and cherry tomatoes to pasta. Pour on dressing, sprinkle with black sesame seeds, and toss to mix.

341 MARINATED BAY SCALLOPS WITH CILANTRO

Prep: 15 minutes   Chill: 2 hours   Cook: none   Serves: 6

The lime juice in this recipe "cooks" the scallops without heat, making this a perfect dish for a hot day.

2 pounds bay scallops	½ cup chopped cilantro leaves
1 small onion, minced	2 tablespoons sour cream
1 teaspoon minced fresh ginger	1 head of Boston lettuce
	1 long seedless cucumber, peeled and cut into ½-inch dice
1 scallion, finely minced	
1 cup fresh lime juice	

1. In a bowl, combine scallops, onion, ginger, scallion, and lime juice. Toss to mix, cover, and refrigerate 2 hours. Add cilantro and sour cream and toss again to blend.

2. Remove outer leaves from lettuce and use to line a serving platter. Cut remaining lettuce into fine ribbons. Mound in center of platter. Layer cucumber over lettuce and pour scallops over vegetables. Serve at once.

342   SHREDDED CUCUMBER AND BEAN THREADS WITH DRUNKEN SHRIMP

Prep: 20 minutes   Cook: 1 minute   Serves: 6

4 ounces bean threads
2 long seedless cucumbers
1 recipe Drunken Shrimp
   (recipe follows)
¼ teaspoon prepared white
   horseradish
¼ teaspoon powdered mustard

½ teaspoon pepper
1 garlic clove, minced
2 tablespoons soy sauce
¼ cup olive oil
¼ cup vegetable oil
1 tablespoon minced chives

1. In a bowl of warm water, soak bean threads until soft, about 15 minutes. Cut into 6-inch pieces. Bring a small saucepan of water to a boil, reduce heat, and simmer bean threads 1 minute; drain.

2. Peel cucumbers and cut into very thin matchstick pieces. In a large bowl, toss bean threads, cucumbers, and shrimp to mix well.

3. In a small bowl, combine horseradish, mustard, pepper, garlic, and soy sauce. Whisk in olive oil and vegetable oil. Pour dressing over salad mixture and toss to mix well. Sprinkle with minced chives and serve.

343   DRUNKEN SHRIMP

Prep: 15 minutes   Cook: 3 to 5 minutes
Stand: 2 to 3 hours   Serves: 4

2 pounds medium shrimp in
   the shell
2 cups dry sherry
¼ cup brandy
1 tablespoon minced fresh
   ginger
1 tablespoon minced scallion

2 tablespoons rice vinegar
2 tablespoons soy sauce
¼ teaspoon sugar
   Ginger Oil (page 24) or Soy
   Vinegar Dip (page 18)

1. Rinse shrimp and drain. In a medium nonreactive saucepan, combine sherry and brandy. Bring to a boil. Add shrimp and cook over medium heat until shrimp just turn pink, 3 to 5 minutes. Drain immediately and let cool.

2. In a medium bowl, combine ginger, scallion, vinegar, soy sauce, and sugar. Stir to dissolve sugar. Add shrimp and toss to coat. Let stand, tossing occasionally, 2 to 3 hours. Peel shrimp and serve with Ginger Oil or Soy Vinegar Dip.

344   CRABMEAT AND CUCUMBER SALAD
Prep: 20 minutes   Cook: none   Serves: 4 to 6

1 **pound fresh crabmeat**	1 **tablespoon dry white wine**
¼ **cup rice vinegar**	1 **teaspoon sugar**
3 **tablespoons safflower oil**	½ **teaspoon salt**
1 **teaspoon soy sauce**	½ **teaspoon pepper**

1. Pick over crabmeat carefully to remove any shell or cartilage.

2. In a small bowl, combine vinegar, oil, soy sauce, wine, sugar, salt, and pepper. Stir to dissolve sugar.

3. Mound shredded cucumber on a serving platter. Drizzle one-third of dressing over cucumber. Toss crabmeat with remaining dressing and arrange over cucumber. Serve at room temperature or slightly chilled.

345   TEA-SMOKED FISH
Prep: 20 minutes   Stand: 30 minutes   Cook: 26 minutes   Serves: 4

This smoked fish is served at room temperature, often as the first course in a banquet. Yellowtail, bass, tilefish, or trout are excellent choices for this dish.

1 **whole fish, about 2 pounds, with head and tail on**	1 **tablespoon dark soy sauce**
2 **scallions, minced**	4 **cups vegetable oil**
2 **slices of fresh ginger, minced**	½ **cup sugar**
	½ **cup flour**
¼ **cup dry white wine**	½ **cup black tea leaves**
	1 **tablespoon Asian sesame oil**

1. With a small knife, make 2 or 3 diagonal slits on top side of fish. In a small bowl, combine scallions, ginger, wine, and soy sauce. Rub all over fish, inside and out. Let stand 30 minutes.

2. In a wok, heat vegetable oil to 375°F, or until a bread cube browns in 1 minute. Add fish and deep-fry 1 minute. Remove with 2 wide spatulas and drain on paper towels. Discard oil and clean and dry wok.

3. Line wok with foil. Scatter sugar in an even layer over bottom of wok. Cover sugar with a layer of flour and then a layer of tea leaves. Line wok cover with enough foil to form an overlap.

4. Place a metal rack in wok and heat over medium heat until smoking begins, then place fish on rack. Cover and crimp foil to seal well. Smoke fish for 15 minutes. Turn off heat. Let rest for 10 minutes to dissipate smoke. Uncover.

5. Remove fish to a serving platter and brush with sesame oil. Garnish platter with leafy greens to serve.

346 GRILLED TUNA SALAD
Prep: 10 minutes   Stand: 10 minutes
Cook: 6 to 10 minutes   Serves: 6

This untraditional salad is Asian in flavor, delicious, and ve particularly with sushi lovers.

1 tablespoon soy sauce	2 pounds fresh tuna steak, cut
1 tablespoon mirin*	1 inch thick
¼ teaspoon wasabi*	2 large red onions, thinly
1 teaspoon minced fresh	sliced
ginger	Wasabi Dressing
1 tablespoon vegetable oil	(recipe follows)

1. In a shallow dish, combine soy sauce, mirin, wasabi, ginger, and oil. Add tuna steak and turn to coat well. Let stand 10 minutes.

2. Preheat broiler or heavy cast-iron grill pan. Add tuna and cook until browned outside but rare to medium inside, 3 to 5 minutes per side. Remove from heat and let cool, then cut into 1-inch cubes.

3. In a bowl, toss tuna, sliced red onions, and Wasabi Dressing. Serve at room temperature or chilled.

* *Available in Asian markets*

347 WASABI DRESSING
Prep: 5 minutes   Cook: none   Makes: 1 cup

¼ cup vegetable oil	1 teaspoon salt
¼ cup olive oil	¼ cup rice vinegar
2¼ teaspoons powdered	¾ teaspoon sugar
wasabi*	1½ teaspoons minced fresh
½ teaspoon soy sauce	ginger

In a measuring cup, combine vegetable oil and olive oil. In a small bowl, combine wasabi, soy sauce, salt, and vinegar. Slowly drizzle oil into bowl, whisking constantly. Add sugar and minced ginger and whisk to blend.

* *Japanese powdered green horseradish, available in Asian markets*

48 SMOKED TROUT SALAD

Prep: 20 minutes   Cook: none   Serves: 4

2 (1½-pound) tea-smoked trout (see Tea-Smoked Fish, page 224) or store-bought smoked trout

2 apples, peeled and cut into 1-inch chunks

2 tablespoons fresh lemon juice

½ cup walnut pieces

2 scallions, minced

1 teaspoon grainy mustard

1 teaspoon soy sauce

¼ teaspoon salt

½ teaspoon pepper

½ teaspoon sugar

1 tablespoon rice vinegar

½ cup Ginger Oil (page 24)

2 tablespoons sour cream

Lettuce leaves

1. Skin and bone trout. Break fish up into chunks. In a bowl, toss apple pieces with 1 tablespoon lemon juice. Add trout pieces, walnuts, and scallions. Toss to mix well.

2. In a small bowl, whisk together mustard, soy sauce, salt, pepper, sugar, vinegar, and remaining 1 tablespoon lemon juice. Slowly whisk in Ginger Oil. Add sour cream and blend well. Gently toss trout mixture with dressing and serve on a bed of lettuce.

Chapter 12

Chinese Sweets

Chinese *do* eat sweets, but seldom at the end of a meal. Sweets are eaten as snacks, in between meals, for special festivals, and during New Year festivities. However, in this chapter I have included sweets, such as Almond Float with Raspberries, Honeyed Bananas, and Toffee Apples, that work well as desserts, even after a Western-style meal.

After spicy food or a big meal, light refreshing sorbets are especially welcome. Two unusual ones are offered here. The idea for Lotus Leaf Sorbet was developed during a cooking class, when I asked students to taste the subtle "tea" that resulted from steeping lotus leaves in water to soften them for wrapping other foods. The sorbet is very gentle and a little bit tannic, which makes it a perfect ending for a rich Chinese meal. The more familiar Lichee Sorbet is a quick and easy dessert made with canned lichees, which can always be on hand.

The two recipes for cookies are also quick and easy to make, and the cookies keep very well in an airtight tin. I often make the Almond Cookies for gifts at Christmas. They go well with the sorbets or a cup of tea, and even a glass of wine.

A couple of the other desserts are quite unusual: Sweet Red Bean Soup is traditionally served hot at the end of formal dinners. We also often had it as a snack after school or sometimes late in the evenings. Gummy Cake, which is more like a chewy coconut bar than a cake, is typical of many Asian sweets.

349   ALMOND FLOAT WITH RASPBERRIES

Prep: 10 minutes   Cook: 10 minutes   Stand: 1 hour
Chill: 4 hours   Makes: 4 cups

This jelly can be made with agar-agar, a seaweed gelatin that sets up at room temperature.

2 (¼-ounce) envelopes unflavored gelatin	1 tablespoon almond extract
3 cups milk	2 pint baskets of raspberries
1 cup heavy cream	1 tablespoon raspberry or orange liqueur
½ cup plus 2 tablespoons sugar	

1. In a small bowl, dissolve gelatin in ½ cup cold water. In a saucepan, combine milk, cream, and ½ cup sugar. Bring to a simmer, stirring to dissolve sugar. Remove from heat. Add almond extract and dissolved gelatin. Stir to blend.

2. Rinse a 9 x 11-inch glass dish or individual serving bowls with cold water and pour in gelatin mixture. Refrigerate until set, 4 hours or overnight.

3. Pick over raspberries. In a bowl, combine raspberries, remaining 2 tablespoons sugar, and liqueur. Toss gently. Let stand 1 hour at room temperature.

4. To serve, cut almond jelly into diamond shapes and spoon into serving dishes. Top with raspberries.

350   GINGER MOUSSE

Prep: 25 minutes   Cook: 5 to 8 minutes   Chill: 2 hours
Serves: 4

My friend, Richard Simpson, suggested this delicious ginger mousse as a good dessert to end a Chinese meal.

3 egg yolks	2 cups heavy cream
2 tablespoons white rum	½ cup confectioners' sugar
2 tablespoons very finely minced fresh ginger	

1. In a stainless steel bowl, combine egg yolks, white rum, and minced ginger. Whisk until slightly foamy, then place bowl over a saucepan of simmering water and whisk constantly until warm, 5 to 8 minutes. Remove from heat and whisk until cool and thickened.

2. In another bowl, with a whisk or electric mixer, beat cream with confectioners' sugar until stiff. Stir one-fourth of whipped cream into egg mixture to lighten. Fold remaining whipped cream into egg mixture with a rubber spatula. Spoon mousse into individual dessert dishes, cover, and refrigerate until cold, about 2 hours.

351 SWEET CRESCENTS

Prep: 25 minutes   Cook: 15 minutes   Makes: 50

2 teaspoons sesame seeds
1 cup chopped dates
½ cup currants
¼ cup chopped dried apricots
¼ cup crunchy peanut butter
2 teaspoons brown sugar

Pinch of salt
1 (1-pound) package won ton skins
Flour
2 cups vegetable oil
Confectioners' sugar

1. In a small dry skillet, toast sesame seeds over medium heat, shaking pan often, until fragrant and lightly browned, about 3 minutes. Immediately pour into a medium bowl. Add dates, currants, apricots, peanut butter, brown sugar, and salt. Mix well.

2. Using a 3-inch round biscuit cutter, cut won ton skins into circles. Place 1 scant teaspoon of filling on each circle. Fold over in half and moisten edges with water to seal. Stand crescents on a well-floured baking sheet, making sure they do not touch. Repeat until all crescents are formed.

3. In a wok, heat oil to 350°F over medium-high heat until a bread cube browns in 1 minute. In batches without crowding, deep-fry crescents to a golden brown, about 3 minutes per batch. With a slotted spoon, remove to paper towels and drain.

4. Dust with confectioners' sugar before serving.

352 GINGERED ORANGES

Prep: 10 minutes   Cook: 15 minutes   Chill: overnight   Serves: 6

This simple, refreshing dessert is best prepared one day in advance and chilled thoroughly. The oranges may be served by themselves, or for real ginger lovers, with a little Ginger Custard Cream (page 232).

6 navel oranges
1½ cups sugar

⅓ cup finely shredded fresh ginger

1. With a citrus zester or vegetable peeler, cut zest from 1 orange. Finely shred and reserve. Peel oranges and cut into sections, removing all membrane between sections. Reserve in a heatproof bowl.

2. In a medium saucepan, dissolve sugar in 3 cups water. Add ginger and bring to a simmer. Cook over low heat until syrup tastes of ginger, about 15 minutes. Let cool slightly. Strain syrup over orange sections. Add reserved zest. Let cool completely, cover, and refrigerate overnight.

3. Serve orange sections cold with a little syrup and zest.

353   HONEYED BANANAS
Prep: 15 minutes   Cook: 27 to 28 minutes   Serves: 4

Traditionally, this dessert is served warm. A bowl of ice water is set on the table, and diners plunge honeyed bananas in the water to harden syrup. You can skip this step and still have a nice dessert.

4 **ripe bananas**	1 **cup sugar**
2 **tablespoons flour**	¾ **cup light corn syrup**
2 **tablespoons cornstarch**	**Few drops of lemon juice**
2 **egg whites**	⅓ **cup vegetable oil**

1. Peel bananas and halve lengthwise. Cut halves crosswise into thirds.

2. In a bowl, blend flour, cornstarch, egg whites, and enough water to make a stiff batter. Add bananas and turn gently to coat with batter.

3. In a small saucepan, combine sugar, corn syrup, lemon juice, and 1 tablespoon water. Cover and cook over low heat until syrup turns golden, about 25 minutes. Remove from heat and set bottom of saucepan in a bowl of cold water a few minutes to stop cooking. Remove from water and cover to keep syrup warm.

4. Heat oil in a wok over medium heat. Add bananas and cook, turning once, until light golden, 2 to 3 minutes. Remove to paper towels. Place in serving dish and pour syrup over bananas.

354   STAR ANISE RICE PUDDING
Prep: 10 minutes   Cook: 45 minutes   Serves: 4 to 6

This pudding would be very nice served warm with fresh ripe peaches.

½ **cup milk**	¾ **cup long-grain white rice**
½ **cup heavy cream**	¾ **cup sugar**
4 **whole star anise**	3 **egg yolks**
1 **cinnamon stick**	

1. In a small saucepan, combine milk, cream, star anise, and cinnamon stick. Bring just to a boil, reduce heat, and simmer 10 minutes.

2. In another saucepan, combine rice with 1½ cups cold water. Bring to a boil, reduce heat, cover, and simmer until water is almost completely absorbed but rice is not dry and is still crunchy, about 15 minutes. Add milk and cream with spices, stir, and cook over low heat 10 minutes. Stir in sugar and continue cooking until rice is soft and creamy, about 10 minutes longer. Remove and discard star anise and cinnamon stick.

3. Let pudding cool 5 to 10 minutes. Beat in egg yolks 1 at a time, beating in after each addition. Pour into serving bowl and serve warm or cold.

355 LICHEE SORBET
Prep: 10 minutes   Cook: none   Makes: 4 cups

2 (20-ounce) cans lichees
½ teaspoon ground cinnamon

⅛ teaspoon ground cloves
Grated zest of 1 lemon

1. Drain lichees, reserving liquid.

2. In a food processor, puree lichees. There should be 2 cups of pureed fruit. Add 2 cups reserved lichee liquid, cinnamon, cloves, and lemon zest. Blend well.

3. Transfer puree to an ice cream machine and freeze according to manufacturer's instructions until sorbet is set but still soft. Serve immediately, or remove to a storage container, cover, and freeze.

4. To serve frozen sorbet, remove from freezer and refrigerate until softened, about 15 minutes.

---

356 TOFFEE APPLES
Prep: 20 minutes   Cook: 31 to 35 minutes   Serves: 6

Serve these the traditional way, or skip the ice water. Either way, they are a wonderful sweet.

¼ cup plus 2 tablespoons flour
2 tablespoons cornstarch
2 egg whites
Pinch of salt
4 eating apples, such as
McIntosh

1 cup packed brown sugar
¼ cup light corn syrup
¼ teaspoon lemon juice
½ cup plus 1 tablespoon
vegetable oil
1 tablespoon sesame seeds

1. In a small bowl, mix 2 tablespoons of flour, cornstarch, egg whites, salt, and 1 to 2 tablespoons water, just enough to make a batter of coating consistency.

2. Peel apples, cut in half, and remove seeds. Cut each apple into 6 wedges. Dust apple wedges with remaining ¼ cup flour. Drop into batter to coat.

3. In a small saucepan, combine brown sugar, corn syrup, lemon juice, and 2 tablespoons of water. Cover and cook over low heat until syrup turns a light brown color, about 25 minutes. Add 1 teaspoon oil and stir in with a wooden spoon. Remove from heat and set bottom of pan in a bowl of cold water a few minutes to stop cooking. Remove from water and cover to keep syrup warm.

4. In a wok or large saucepan, heat ½ cup oil over medium heat to 350°F, or until a cube of bread browns in 1 minute. Add half of apple wedges and cook, turning once, until batter is golden and crisp and apples are tender, 3 to 5 minutes. Oil a serving plate with remaining 2 teaspoons oil. Mound apples on plate. Repeat with remaining apples. Sprinkle with sesame seeds and pour warm syrup over apples. Serve immediately with a bowl of ice water, so diners can dip hot apples in water to harden toffee.

357   SESAME PUFFS WITH HONEY
Prep: 10 minutes   Cook: 12 minutes   Makes: 48

2 cups flour	⅓ cup sesame seeds
½ teaspoon baking powder	2 cups vegetable oil
1 teaspoon butter	1 cup honey
¼ teaspoon salt	2 cinnamon sticks
5 eggs	

1. Sift together flour and baking powder. In a large saucepan, combine 2 cups water, butter, and salt. Bring to a boil over medium-high heat. Add flour mixture all at once and stir with a wooden spoon until dough balls together and pulls away from sides of saucepan. Reduce heat to low and cook, stirring constantly, 5 minutes. Remove from heat and let cool. With an electric hand beater or wire whisk, beat in eggs 1 at a time, making sure to whisk in each egg thoroughly before adding another.

2. With 2 wet teaspoons, form dough into balls. Gently roll in sesame seeds.

3. In a wok or large saucepan, heat oil over medium-high heat to 375°F, or until a bread cube browns in 1 minute. Drop dough into hot oil and cook, in batches without crowding, until balls are puffed and golden, about 2 minutes per batch. With a slotted spoon, remove to paper towels to drain.

4. In a small saucepan, heat honey with cinnamon sticks for 5 minutes. Remove cinnamon sticks, but keep honey warm. To serve, mound puffs on a serving platter and drizzle honey over sesame puffs.

358   GINGER CUSTARD CREAM
Prep: 10 minutes   Cook: 15 to 20 minutes   Chill: 1 hour
Makes: 1½ cups

1 cup milk	¼ cup sugar
1 tablespoon minced fresh	2 teaspoons orange liqueur
ginger	½ cup heavy cream
3 egg yolks	

1. In a small saucepan, combine milk and minced ginger. Steep over low heat 10 minutes. Strain and let cool slightly.

2. In a small bowl, whisk egg yolks and sugar until light and lemon-colored and a ribbon forms on surface when whisk is lifted from mixture, 2 to 3 minutes. Whisk in half of warm milk until well blended.

3. Pour egg mixture into a small saucepan and whisk in remaining milk. Cook over low heat, stirring constantly with whisk or wooden spoon, until custard thickens, 5 to 10 minutes. Do not let custard boil or it will curdle.

4. Immediately remove from heat and stir in orange liqueur. Let cool. With a wire whisk or electric beater, beat heavy cream until soft peaks form. Fold into custard mixture. Cover well and refrigerate until cold, at least 1 hour.

359   CINNAMON PINWHEELS
Prep: 5 minutes   Cook: 20 minutes   Makes: about 40

The trick to this simple dessert is how to form the pinwheels. You can make as few or as many as you wish. With a little practice, you will have no trouble whizzing through half a package of won ton skins, which will make about 40 pinwheels.

2 cups vegetable oil	1 cup confectioners' sugar
½ (1-pound) package won ton skins	1 teaspoon ground cinnamon

1. In a wok, heat oil to 350°F. Gently slide 1 won ton skin into oil. Immediately stick a wooden chopstick in the center of the skin and twirl chopstick between your palms. This motion will pleat soft won ton skin into a pinwheel. Hold chopstick a few seconds until won ton skin begins to crisp. Remove to paper towels. Repeat until all pinwheels are formed.

2. In a small bowl, mix confectioners' sugar with cinnamon. Dust pinwheels before serving.

360   ALMOND COOKIES
Prep: 20 minutes   Chill: 40 minutes   Cook: 12 to 15 minutes
Makes: about 60

Traditionally, these cookies are made with lard, which results in a light, crumbly cookie. You can substitute vegetable shortening, if you prefer.

2 cups flour	1 cup sugar
2 teaspoons baking powder	1 egg
½ teaspoon salt	2 teaspoons almond extract
1 cup lard, at room temperature	Slivered almonds

1. Sift together flour, baking powder, and salt.

2. In a large bowl, with an electric hand mixer, beat together lard and sugar until light and fluffy, about 10 minutes. Beat in egg. Add almond extract and stir to mix well. Gradually stir in dry ingredients and mix to form a stiff dough. Wrap well and refrigerate 30 minutes.

3. Preheat oven to 375°F. Pinch off 1-inch pieces of dough and roll into balls between palms. Set on ungreased cookie sheets 1 inch apart. Press a piece of slivered almond into center of each ball, pressing down very slightly. Chill cookies 10 minutes before baking.

4. Bake cookies until barely golden, about 12 to 15 minutes. They should remain very pale. Remove from oven, carefully transfer to a rack, and let cool. Cookies may be stored in an airtight container up to 2 weeks.

361 SESAME PEANUT COOKIES
Prep: 20 minutes   Chill: 30 minutes   Cook: 15 to 20 minutes
Makes: 50 to 60

Black sesame seeds, available in Asian markets, are a nice novelty, but if you can't find them, white sesame seeds can be used instead.

2 cups flour	¼ cup chunky peanut butter
1 tablespoon baking powder	1 cup sugar
1½ sticks (6 ounces) butter, at	1 egg
room temperature	¼ cup black sesame seeds

1. Sift together flour and baking powder.

2. In large bowl of an electric mixer, beat butter and peanut butter until smooth, about 5 minutes. Add sugar and beat until light and fluffy, about 10 minutes. Beat in egg until well blended. Gradually add flour mixture and blend to form dough. Wrap and refrigerate dough 30 minutes.

3. Preheat oven to 375°F. Spread sesame seeds on a plate. Divide dough into 4 pieces. Roll each piece into a log about 1½ inches in diameter. Roll cylinder in sesame seeds to coat. Cut log into ¼-inch-thick slices. Place about 1 inch apart on greased cookie sheets. Repeat until all cookies are formed.

4. Bake until cookies are light golden, 15 to 20 minutes. Remove from oven and let cool. Cookies may be stored in an airtight tin for 1 to 2 weeks, or frozen for longer storage.

362 SWEET RED BEAN SOUP
Prep: 10 minutes   Stand: 1 hour   Cook: 2 hours   Serves: 10

This is a traditional warm sweet soup that is served as dessert in formal Chinese dinners. It is very easy to make, and you might find it interesting. I have used brown sugar in this recipe, but you might like to try rock sugar, which is available in Asian markets.

8 ounces (1½ cups) dried	3 pieces of dried tangerine
Chinese red beans	peel
(*adzuki*) *	¾ cup brown sugar
1 tablespoon rice	

1. In a large pot, bring 10 cups water to a boil. Add red beans and remove from heat. Let soak 1 hour.

2. Add rice and tangerine peel to beans. Bring to a boil, reduce heat to low, cover, and simmer until beans break up, about 2 hours. Add sugar, stir to dissolve, and serve hot or cold.

* *Available in Asian markets*

363   LOTUS LEAF SORBET

Prep: 20 minutes   Cook: none   Stand: 10 minutes   Makes: 4 cups

4 lotus leaves	¾ cup sugar
4 cups boiling water	2 tablespoons lemon juice

1. Rinse lotus leaves and steep in 1 quart boiling water 10 minutes. Remove leaves and discard or reserve for another use. Add sugar to water while tea is still hot. Stir to dissolve. Add lemon juice. Let cool completely.

2. Pour cold tea into an ice cream machine and freeze according to manufacturers' instructions until sorbet is set. Serve immediately, or remove to a storage container, cover, and freeze.

3. Sorbet should be slightly softened in refrigerator about 10 minutes before serving.

364   RED PEACHES

*Prep: 30 minutes   Cook: 25 to 30 minutes
Chill: 3 to 4 hours   Serves: 6*

6 ripe peaches	1 cinnamon stick
1 quart red burgundy	½ teaspoon whole cloves
2 cups sugar	½ teaspoon coriander seeds
1 star anise	2 cardamom pods
2 slices of fresh ginger	

1. Bring a large pot of water to a boil. Add peaches and boil until skins loosen, about 10 seconds. Immediately plunge into ice water, cool, and peel peaches.

2. In a large nonreactive saucepan, combine wine, sugar, star anise, ginger, cinnamon stick, cloves, coriander seeds, and cardamom pods. Bring to a boil, stirring to dissolve sugar. Reduce heat, cover, and simmer 15 minutes. Strain and return syrup to saucepan.

3. Add peaches to syrup, return to a simmer, and poach gently until peaches can be pricked with a toothpick without resistance, 10 to 15 minutes. With a slotted spoon, remove peaches to a serving dish. Cover and refrigerate until cold, 3 to 4 hours.

4. Meanwhile, return poaching liquid to a boil and boil over high heat until thickened and syrupy. Let cool. Spoon a little syrup over peaches before serving.

365   GUMMY CAKE

Prep: 10 minutes   Cook: 1 hour   Serves: 10

My sister-in-law makes this cake for many family parties. It is easy and quick to put together. The sweet or sticky rice flour produces an unusual chewy texture that is very Asian.

2 sticks (8 ounces) unsalted	1½ cups milk
butter, at room	1½ cups water
temperature	1 pound sweet rice flour*
2 cups sugar	4 ounces flaked coconut
6 eggs	

1. Preheat oven to 325°F. Grease an 8 x 10 x 2-inch glass baking dish with 1 tablespoon of butter.

2. In a mixer bowl, beat remaining butter with sugar until light and fluffy. Add eggs, 1 at a time, beating well after each addition. In a large measuring cup, combine milk and water. Divide rice flour into 3 batches. Add one-third flour to batter; stir well. Add half of liquid and stir in before adding another one-third of flour. Stir to blend. Add remaining liquid, blend, and then add remaining flour. Stir until batter is smooth. Fold in 3 ounces of coconut.

3. Pour batter into baking dish and bake 10 minutes. Remove from oven. Sprinkle remaining coconut evenly over top. Return to oven and continue baking until top is light brown, about 50 minutes longer. Remove cake from oven and let cool completely. Cut into squares to serve.

* *Available in Asian markets*

Index

Abalone, in oyster sauce, 146
Agar-agar
about, 3
and daikon salad, 21
Almond
cookies, 233
float with raspberries, 228
Angel hair pasta, tomato, and shrimp salad, 222
Anise beef, pressed, 134
Ants climbing a tree, 196
Appetizers. See also *Dim sum;* Dip;
Pickles; Relish
about, 9
agar-agar and daikon salad, 21
chicken livers with oyster sauce, 11
chicken satay, 13
cold sesame noodles, 10
egg crepes, 22
eggplant salad, Chinese, 10
marinated cold tofu, 21
plum-flavored pork tenderloin, 16
shrimp balls, 12
shrimp toasts, 12
skewered pork cubes with fresh
pineapple, 15
soy-braised chicken wings, 15
spareribs, barbecued, 14
spareribs, steamed, 14
spring rolls, 18
stuffed mushrooms, savory, 11
sugared walnuts, 16
tea eggs, 17
vegetable pear rolls, 17
Apples, toffee, 231
Aromatic rice, 208
Arrowhead tubers, beef with, 50
Asparagus
chicken with, sliced, 44
five fragrant spice pork with, 57
spears, sesame, 110
spicy black bean beef with, 90

Bacon and scrambled eggs rice, 176
**Baked pork chops in vegetable rice
casserole,** 178
Baked vegetarian bean curd pockets,
126
Bamboo shoots
about, 3
duck braised with chestnuts,
mushrooms, and, 75
red-braised bean curd with
mushrooms and, 123
shredded pork, and green pepper in
black bean sauce, 60
spicy chicken with peanuts and, 87
with spinach greens, 109
Banana leaves, fish custard in, 212
Bananas, honeyed, 230

Banquet dishes, 129–52
abalone in oyster sauce, 146
about, 129–30
braised gizzards in oyster sauce, 140
Buddha's delight (*lo hon chai*), 152
Cantonese crispy roast duck, 141
chicken congee, 140
chrysanthemum squid, 149
congee sauce, 141
crispy squab, 143
drunken chicken, 137
duck soup, 134
firepot Hong Kong style, 144
firepot sauces, 145
garlic frog legs, 151
hoisin-glazed roast chicken with
sweet rice stuffing, 139
jellyfish salad, 135
long life noodles in egg sauce, 136
old and new eggs, 136
Peking duck, 142
pressed anise beef, 134
red roast pork (*char sui*), 146
salt-baked chicken, 138
savory pressed bean curd slivers, 138
shark fin soup, 133
shrimp in broth with sizzling rice, 131
sizzling rice, 131
sizzling rice soup, 130
squirrel fish, 147
steamed dried oysters, 148
sweet aromatic roast pork, 145
tea leaf shrimp, 148
vegetarian mock fish, 150
winter melon pond, 132
Barbecued spareribs, 14
**Basil, soupy seafood rice stick
noodles with lime and fresh,** 168
Bean curd. *See also* Tofu
about, 4
cheese, 4
dry, 4
and bean sprouts, cold, with chile oil
and cilantro, 106
casserole, 82
cheese, spinach with, 115
with ground pork, 58
with ground pork, spicy, 94
marinated pressed, 124
mushrooms, and bok choy on soupy
noodles, 164
oyster-flavored, 190
pockets, 191
baked vegetarian, 126
pressed, 125
red, pork, and taro, 80
red-braised, with mushrooms and
bamboo shoots, 123
with scrambled eggs, 123
slivers, savory pressed, 138
smoked, with oyster sauce and
vegetables, 127
soup, 29

Bean curd *(cont.)*
and spinach dumplings, 198
squares
in black bean sauce, crusty, 122
crunchy very spicy, 103
sticks with mushrooms, 125
stir-fried, 122
tea-smoked, 127
and vegetable kebabs, 124
watercress soup with, 38
Bean(s). *See* Black bean(s); Long beans
Bean sauce. *See also* Black bean sauce;
Yellow bean sauce
about, 4
Bean sprout(s)
and bean curd, cold, with chile oil
and cilantro, 106
and chicken salad, lemon-flavored,
214
chicken with celery and, 43
with chives, quick tossed, 109
quick hot, 103
salad, 108
Bean threads (glass noodles)
about, 4
braised pork, vegetables, and, 81
and cucumber salad, 121
shredded cucumber and, with
drunken shrimp, 223
zucchini soup, 38
Beef
with arrowhead tubers, 50
with asparagus, spicy black bean, 90
ball soup, 29
balls with oyster sauce, 184
with black bean sauce, 52
braised
on a bed of spinach, Hunan, 89
red-, 78
broccoli with, 48
confetti, in lettuce cups, 196
cubes, hoisin, 54
ginger, 51
and green pepper chow mein, 160
with green peppers, 49
ground, and peas, 54
hoisin-flavored roast filet of, 220
hot and spicy shredded, 90
long-simmered, 78
orange, 53
with oyster sauce, 49
pressed anise, 134
rice, sunnyside egg, 178
salad
hoisin, 220
Thai-style, 219
spicy dry-fried, and wide rice
noodles, 166
steak kew, 52
stir-fried, 55
Beggar's chicken, 204
Black bean(s)
about, 4

beef with asparagus, spicy, 90
chile, and garlic oil, 23
cod steak with hot chiles and, 102
steamed whole catfish with, 186
Black bean sauce
beef with, 52
clams with, 66
crusty bean curd squares in, 122
green beans with, 110
pork and eggplant with, 59
shredded pork, bamboo shoots, and
green pepper in, 60
shrimp in spicy, 96
shrimp with, 62
Black sea bass, steamed, 186
Blistered spicy green beans, 105
Bok choy
bean curd, and mushrooms on soupy
noodles, 164
stems, pork chow mein with, 161
**Braised bean threads, pork, and
vegetables,** 81
Braised Chinese mushrooms, 118
Braised duck with leeks, 76
Braised gizzards in oyster sauce, 140
Braised noodles with chicken, 154
Braised taro root, 117
Braised vegetable medley, 120
Braises. *See* Stews and braises
Broccoli
with beef, 48
and cauliflower tossed in hot and
sour sauce, 105
chicken, and water chestnuts in
oyster sauce, 42
oyster sauce, 111
Broth
cabbage, red-poached lamb strips
with noodles and, 185
coconut, chicken in, 30
lemongrass, shrimp in, 34
shrimp in, with sizzling rice, 131
Brown sauce, Chinese, 65
shrimp omelet with, 65
Buckwheat noodles, pork cutlet with,
164
Buddha's delight *(lo hon chai)*, 152
fresh vegetable, 108

Cabbage, Chinese. *See* Chinese
cabbage (Napa)
Cake, gummy, 236
Calves' liver with garlic chives, 55
Cantonese crispy roast duck, 141
Cantonese roast pork rice, 177
Carrot(s)
and daikon pickle, 20
ginger-braised, 112
slivered lamb with turnips and, 96
Cashews
chicken cubes with chiles and, 88
diced chicken with, 44
velvet shrimp with, 64

Casserole
  bean curd, 82
  chicken rice, 177
  vegetable rice, baked pork chops in, 178
Catfish, steamed whole, with black beans, 186
Cauliflower and broccoli tossed in hot and sour sauce, 105
Cayenne, about, 4
Celery
  and chicken chow mein, 159
  chicken with bean sprouts and, 43
Char sui **(red roast pork),** 146
Cherry tomato(es)
  jicama, and long beans salad, 112
  yellow rice with, 176
Chestnuts, duck braised with bamboo shoots, mushrooms, and, 75
Chicken
  with asparagus, sliced, 44
  balls, lichee, 46
  beggar's, 204
  braised noodles with, 154
  broccoli, and water chestnuts in oyster sauce, 42
  with celery and bean sprouts, 43
  and celery chow mein, 159
  with Chinese sausage, 183
  in coconut broth, 30
  congee, 140
  corn soup, 31
  cubes
    with cashews and chiles, 88
    in yellow bean sauce, 42
  curry, 72
  distilled, 74
  drumsticks, hot and spicy, 85
  drunken, 137
  empress, 72
  everyday velvet, 47
  gizzards, braised, in oyster sauce, 140
  with ham and snow peas, 45
  hoisin diced, 43
  hoisin-glazed roast, with sweet rice stuffing, 139
  Indonesian-style rice with shrimp and, 175
  Kung Pao, 46
  lemon, 73
  livers with oyster sauce, 11
  lo mein, 156
  ma la, 86
  in parchment packages, 203
  with peanuts and bamboo shoots, spicy, 87
  with pea sprouts, shredded, 48
  poached
    brown, 182
    white, with scallion oil, 182
  rice casserole, 177
  rice noodles with shrimp and, Thai-style, 171

  salad
    with hoisin dressing, 215
    lemon-flavored, bean sprout and, 214
    sesame, 214
    smoked, noodle, 217
  salt-baked, 138
  satay, 13
  shredded cold, with hot peanut dressing, 86
  soupy noodles with ham and, 166
  in sticky rice bundles, 207
  stock, Chinese, 27
  strips with cilantro, hoisin, 183
  with tangerine peel, spicy, 88
  tea-smoked, 216
  with tree ears and mushrooms, shredded, 45
  wings, soy-braised, 15
Chile paste, about, 4
Chile pepper(s)
  about, 4
  chicken cubes with cashews and, 88
  cod steak with black beans and hot, 102
  oil, 23
    black bean, garlic, and, 23
    cold bean curd and bean sprouts with cilantro and, 106
  sauce, velvet pork slices in, 93
  velvet scallops, peas, and, 102
Chinese brown sauce, 65
  shrimp omelet with, 65
Chinese cabbage (Napa)
  broth, red-poached lamb strips with noodles and, 185
  hot and sour, 104
  relish, sweet-spicy, 19
  -salmon pillows, 211
  slow-cooked, 113
  soup, 30
  sweet and sour, 111
Chinese five-spice powder
  about, 4
  in five fragrant spice pork with asparagus, 57
Chinese mushrooms, dried
  bean curd, and bok choy on soupy noodles, 164
  braised, 118
  red-braised bean curd with bamboo shoots and, 123
Chinese sausage (*lop cheung***)**
  about, 4
  chicken with, 183
  fried rice with, 170
Chive(s)
  garlic. *See* Garlic chive(s)
  quick tossed bean sprouts with, 109
Chowder, crab corn, 32
Chow mein
  beef and green pepper, 160
  chicken and celery, 159
  pork, with bok choy stems, 161

Chrysanthemum squid, 149
Cilantro
about, 5
cold bean curd and bean sprouts with chile oil and, 106
hoisin chicken strips with, 183
marinated bay scallops with, 222
Cinnamon pinwheels, 233
Clams
with black bean sauce, 66
spicy, 99
Clear soup with fish fillets and spinach, 32
Coconut broth, chicken in, 30
Coconut milk, about, 5
Cod
fillets, poached, in sour sauce, 188
steak with black beans and hot chiles, 102
Cold bean curd and bean sprouts with chile oil and cilantro, 106
Cold melon soup, 33
Cold noodles with peanut sauce and cucumbers, 154
Cold poached duck, 217
Cold sesame noodles, 10
Confetti beef in lettuce cups, 196
Confetti rice with pine nuts, 173
Congee
chicken, 140
sauce, 141
Cookies
almond, 233
sesame peanut, 234
Corn
chowder, crab, 32
soup
chicken, 31
velvet, 31
Cornish game hens, minced, in lettuce leaves, 194
Crab(meat)
in a cloud, 67
corn chowder, 32
and cucumber salad, 224
omelet, 67
Cream sauce, white, 189
Crepes, egg, 22
Crescents, sweet, 229
Crispy squab, 143
Crunchy very spicy bean curd squares, 103
Crusty bean curd squares in black bean sauce, 122
Cucumber(s)
and bean thread salad, 121
cold noodles with peanut sauce and, 154
and crabmeat salad, 224
pickle, 19
shredded, and bean threads with drunken shrimp, 223

spicy velvet shrimp with peas and, 97
stuffed with flounder, steamed, 188
Curry
chicken, 72
triangles, 206
Custard
cream, ginger, 232
fish, in banana leaves, 212
savory egg, 190

Daikon
and agar-agar salad, 21
and carrot pickle, 20
Deep-fried shrimp in shells, 63
Desserts. See Sweets and desserts
Diced chicken with cashews, 44
Dim sum, 193–212
about, 193
ants climbing a tree, 196
aromatic rice, 208
bean curd and spinach dumplings, 198
beggar's chicken, 204
chicken in parchment packages, 203
chicken in sticky rice bundles, 207
confetti beef in lettuce cups, 196
curry triangles, 206
duck in lotus leaves, 208
egg crepe rolls, 206
eight jewel rice in lotus package, 209
fish custard in banana leaves, 212
fried won tons, 195
garlic chive dumplings, 201
garlic chive rolls, 205
ginger duck roll-ups, 207
lotus leaf rice packages with peanuts and scallions, 203
minced Cornish game hens in lettuce leaves, 194
mu shu pancakes, 210
mu shu pork packages, 210
potsticker dumplings, 198
pungent pork in lotus leaf, 212
salmon-cabbage pillows, 211
shrimp and pork dumplings, 197
shrimp (Har Kow) dumplings, 202
siu mei flower dumplings, 200
Dip (dipping sauce)
herbed tofu, 22
peanut hoisin, 21
soy vinegar, 18
spicy, 199
Distilled chicken, 74
Double-cooked Szechuan pork, 91
Dough
mashed potato, 114
potsticker, 199
wheat starch, 202
wrapper for beggar's chicken, 205
Dressing. See also Salad dressing
hoisin, chicken salad with, 215
peanut, hot, shredded cold chicken with, 86
wasabi, 225

Drunken chicken, 137
Drunken shrimp, 223
  shredded cucumber and bean threads
    with, 223
Dry-fried spicy beef and wide rice
    noodles, 166
Duck
  braised, with leeks, 76
  braised with bamboo shoots,
    chestnuts, and mushrooms, 75
  cold poached, 217
  ginger roll-ups, 207
  in lotus leaves, 208
  Peking, 142
  pineapple, in ginger fruit sauce, 56
  red-braised, 76
  roast
    Cantonese crispy, 141
    with tropical fruit salad, 218
  soup, 134
Dumplings
  bean curd and spinach, 198
  garlic chive, 201
  potsticker, 198
  shrimp and pork, 197
  shrimp (Har Kow), 202
  siu mei flower, 200

Eggplant
  and pork with black bean sauce, 59
  salad, Chinese, 10
  in spicy garlic meat sauce, 106
Egg(s)
  beef rice, sunnyside, 178
  crepe rolls, 206
  crepes, 22
  custard, savory, 190
  flower soup, 33
  fried rice with scallions and, 175
  old and new, 136
  omelet
    crabmeat, 67
    shrimp, with Chinese brown sauce,
      65
  poached, individual steamed rice
    with, 174
  sauce, long life noodles in, 136
  scrambled
    and bacon rice, 176
    bean curd with, 123
  tea, 17
Eight jewel rice in lotus package, 209
Empress chicken, 72
Equipment, 8
Everyday velvet chicken, 47

Fast and easy dishes, 41–70
  beef
    with arrowhead tubers, 50
    with black bean sauce, 52
    broccoli with, 48
    cubes, hoisin, 54
    ginger, 51

    with green peppers, 49
    ground, and peas, 54
    orange, 53
    with oyster sauce, 49
    steak kew, 52
    stir-fried, 55
    with tomato and onion, sliced, 50
  chicken
    with asparagus, sliced, 44
    balls, lichee, 46
    broccoli, and water chestnuts in
      oyster sauce, 42
    with cashews, diced, 44
    with celery and bean sprouts, 43
    cubes in yellow bean sauce, 42
    everyday velvet, 47
    with ham and snow peas, 45
    hoisin diced, 43
    Kung Pao, 46
    with pea sprouts, shredded, 48
    with tree ears and mushrooms,
      shredded, 45
  clams with black bean sauce, 66
  crabmeat
    in a cloud, 67
    omelet, 67
  fish fillets in wine sauce, 69
  honeyed ham steak, 61
  lamb with scallions, 62
  liver with garlic chives, 55
  lobster with scallions and ginger, 68
  pineapple duck in ginger fruit sauce,
    56
  pork
    bean curd with ground, 58
    cubes in sweet sauce, 57
    and eggplant with black bean sauce,
      59
    five fragrant spice, with asparagus,
      57
    with green beans, sliced, 60
    with jicama, 59
    shredded, bamboo shoots, and
      green pepper in black bean sauce,
      60
    sweet and sour, 58
  sea scallops, sautéed, 68
  shrimp
    with black bean sauce, 62
    deep-fried, in shells, 63
    omelet with Chinese brown sauce,
      65
    red garlic, 63
    and scallops with peas, 66
    sherried, with snow peas and water
      chestnuts, 64
    velvet, with cashews, 64
  squid rings with pepper strips, 70
Firepot, Hong Kong style, 144
Fish
  balls on a bed of watercress, steamed,
    189
  black sea bass, steamed, 186

Fish *(cont.)*
catfish, steamed whole, with black
beans, 186
cod
fillets, poached, in sour sauce, 188
steak with black beans and hot
chiles, 102
custard in banana leaves, 212
fillets
clear soup with spinach and, 32
in wine sauce, 69
-flavored shredded pork, 94
flounder, cucumbers stuffed with,
steamed, 188
hot and sour poached, 100
and hot willow sauce, 101
ma la, 100
salmon-cabbage pillows, 211
spicy halibut steaks on rice, 180
and spinach won tons, 163
soupy noodles with, 162
squirrel, 147
steaks, red-braised, 82
tea-smoked, 224
trout salad, smoked, 226
tuna salad, grilled, 225
vegetarian mock, 150
Fish sauce *(nuoc nam)*, about, 5
Five fragrant spice pork with
asparagus, 57
Flounder, cucumbers stuffed with,
steamed, 188
Flower shrimp, 187
Fresh ginger dressing, 24
Fresh vegetable Buddha's delight, 108
Fried rice
with Chinese sausage, 170
with eggs and scallions, 175
with peas and ham, 171
with roast pork, 172
shrimp, 172
Yang Chow, 170
Fried squid with spicy salt, 99
Fried won tons, 195
Frog legs, garlic, 151
Fruit
ginger sauce, pineapple duck in, 56
salad, tropical, roast duck with, 218
Fukien rice sticks, 168

Garlic
chile, and black bean oil, 23
frog legs, 151
long beans and peanuts with, 113
meat sauce, spicy, eggplant in, 106
oil-wilted spinach, 116
shrimp, red, 63
stewed lamb with ginger, vegetables,
and, 83
Garlic chive(s)
chive dumplings, 201
chive rolls, 205
liver with, 55

Ginger(ed)
about, 5
beef, 51
-braised carrots, 112
custard cream, 232
dressing, fresh, 24
duck roll-ups, 207
fruit sauce, pineapple duck in, 56
lobster with scallions and, 68
mousse, 228
oil, 24
oranges, 229
sautéed sweet potatoes with soy
sauce and, 117
stewed lamb with garlic, vegetables,
and, 83
Glass noodles. *See* Bean threads
Glutinous rice, about, 5
Green beans
with black bean sauce, 110
blistered spicy, 105
in pork sauce, 104
sliced pork with, 60
Grilled lamb salad, 221
Grilled tuna salad, 225
Ground beef and peas, 54
Gummy cake, 236

Halibut steaks on rice, spicy, 180
Ham
chicken with snow peas and, 45
fried rice with peas and, 171
soupy noodles with chicken and, 166
steak
honeyed, 61
Har Kow (shrimp) dumplings, 202
Herbed tofu dip, 22
Hoisin (sauce)
about, 5
beef cubes, 54
beef salad, 220
chicken strips with cilantro, 183
diced chicken, 43
dressing, chicken salad with, 215
-flavored roast filet of beef, 220
-glazed roast chicken with sweet rice
stuffing, 139
peanut dip, 21
Honeydew melon
balls, spicy shrimp and, 98
soup, cold, 33
Honey(ed)
bananas, 230
ham steak, 61
sesame puffs with, 232
Hot and cold northern noodles, 167
Hot and sour cabbage, 104
Hot and sour poached fish, 100
Hot and sour seafood soup, 34
Hot and sour soup, 35
Hot and spicy dishes, 85–106
about, 85
bean curd with ground pork, spicy, 94

black bean beef with asparagus, spicy, 90
blistered spicy green beans, 105
cauliflower and broccoli tossed in hot and sour sauce, 105
chicken cubes with cashews and chiles, 88
chicken drumsticks, hot and spicy, 85
chicken with peanuts and bamboo shoots, spicy, 87
chicken with tangerine peel, spicy, 88
clams, spicy, 99
cod steak with black beans and hot chiles, 102
cold bean curd and bean sprouts with chile oil and cilantro, 106
crunchy very spicy bean curd squares, 103
double-cooked Szechuan pork, 91
eggplant in spicy garlic meat sauce, 106
fish and hot willow sauce, 101
fish-flavored shredded pork, 94
fried squid with spicy salt, 99
green beans in pork sauce, 104
hot and sour cabbage, 104
hot and sour poached fish, 100
Hunan braised beef on a bed of spinach, 89
Kung Pao shrimp, 98
ma la chicken, 86
ma la fish, 100
pork cubes in hot sweet sauce, 92
quick hot bean sprouts, 103
shredded beef, hot and spicy, 90
shredded cold chicken with hot peanut dressing, 86
shrimp and fragrant melon balls, spicy, 98
shrimp in spicy black bean sauce, 96
slivered lamb with turnips and carrots, 96
stewed pork, hot and spicy, 92
super spicy spareribs, 93
Szechuan spicy lamb, 95
velvet pork slices in chile sauce, 93
velvet scallops, chiles, and peas, 102
velvet shrimp with cucumber and peas, spicy, 97
Hunan braised beef on a bed of spinach, 89

Individual steamed rice with poached egg, 174
Indonesian-style rice with chicken and shrimp, 175
Ingredients, 3–8

Jellyfish
about, 5
salad, 135

Jicama
long beans, and cherry tomato salad, 112
pork with, 59

Kung Pao chicken, 46
Kung Pao shrimp, 98

Lamb
chops, soy, with onion on rice, 180
salad, grilled, 221
with scallions, 62
slivered, with turnips and carrots, 96
stewed, with garlic, ginger, and vegetables, 83
strips, red-poached, with noodles and cabbage broth, 185
Szechuan spicy, 95
Leeks, braised duck with, 76
Lemon
chicken, 73
-flavored chicken and bean sprout salad, 214
Lemongrass
about, 5
broth, shrimp in, 34
Lettuce
cups, confetti beef in, 196
leaves, minced Cornish game hens in, 194
Lichee
chicken balls, 46
sorbet, 231
Lime, soupy seafood rice stick noodles with fresh basil and, 168
Liver(s)
calves', with garlic chives, 55
chicken, with oyster sauce, 11
Lobster with scallions and ginger, 68
Lo hon chai **(Buddha's delight), 152**
Lo mein
chicken, 156
pork, 157
shrimp, 158
vegetable, 158
Long beans
jicama, and cherry tomato salad, 112
and peanuts with garlic, 113
Long life noodles in egg sauce, 136
Long-simmered beef, 78
Lotus (leaf, leaves)
duck in, 208
package, eight jewel rice in, 209
pungent pork in, 212
rice packages with peanuts and scallions, 203
sorbet, 235
Lotus root
pickle, 20
simmered pork with, 80

Main-course salads. *See* Salad(s), main-course

Ma la chicken, 86
Ma la fish, 100
Marinated bay scallops with cilantro, 222
Marinated cold tofu, 21
Marinated pressed bean curd, 124
Mashed potato dough, 114
Meat
  sauce
    noodles, 155
    spicy garlic, eggplant in, 106
  stock, rich, 28
Meatballs, pearl, 184
Melon. See also Winter melon
  balls, spicy shrimp and, 98
  winter
    pond, 132
    soup, 36
Minced Cornish game hens in lettuce leaves, 194
Mousse, ginger, 228
Mushroom(s)
  bean curd sticks with, 125
  Chinese, dried
    about, 5
    bean curd, and bok choy on soupy noodles, 164
    braised, 118
    red-braised bean curd with bamboo shoots and, 123
    savory stuffed, 11
  duck braised with bamboo shoots, chestnuts, and, 75
  -filled potato balls, 114
  shredded chicken with tree ears and, 45
Mu shu
  pancakes, 210
  pork packages, 210
  vegetable, 119
Mustard sesame vinaigrette, 25

Noodle(s)
  about, 153
  buckwheat, pork cutlet with, 164
  glass. See Bean threads
  red-poached lamb strips with cabbage broth and, 185
  rice, fresh (ho fun)
    hot and cold northern, 167
    wide, dry-fried spicy beef and, 166
  rice flour, about, 6
  rice stick (mei fun)
    Fukien, 168
    with shrimp and chicken, Thai-style, 171
    with Singapore-style shrimp, 169
    soupy, bean curd, mushrooms, and bok choy on, 164
    soupy seafood, with fresh basil and lime, 168
  sesame, cold, 10
  smoked chicken-, salad, 217

thin fresh (lu mein), in egg sauce, long life, 136
wheat flour. See also Chow mein; Lo mein
  braised, with chicken, 154
  cold, with peanut sauce and cucumbers, 154
  meat sauce, 155
  simple tossed spicy, 156
  soupy, with fish and spinach won tons, 162
  soupy, with ham and chicken, 166
  soupy, with pork won tons and Chinese roast pork, 165
  tempura shrimp, 162
Nuts. See also Almond; Cashews; Peanut(s)
  pine nuts, confetti rice with, 173
  walnuts, sugared, 16

Oil
  chile, 23
    black bean, and garlic, 23
    cold bean curd and bean sprouts with cilantro and, 106
  ginger, 24
  scallion, 24
    white poached chicken with, 182
  -wilted garlicky spinach, 116
Old and new eggs, 136
Omelet
  crabmeat, 67
  shrimp, with Chinese brown sauce, 65
Onion(s)
  pork, and tomato on rice, 179
  sliced beef with tomato and, 50
  soy lamb chops with, on rice, 180
Orange(s)
  beef, 53
  gingered, 229
Oxtail stew, 81
Oyster(s)
  -flavored bean curd, 190
  steamed dried, 148
Oyster sauce
  abalone in, 146
  about, 6
  beef balls with, 184
  beef with, 49
  broccoli, 111
  chicken, broccoli, and water chestnuts in, 42
  chicken gizzards in, braised, 140
  chicken livers with, 11
  -flavored drumsticks, 74
  smoked bean curd with vegetables and, 127

Pancakes, mu shu, 210
Peaches, red, 235
Peanut oil, about, 5–6

Peanut(s)
dressing, hot, shredded cold chicken with, 86
hoisin dip, 21
long beans and, with garlic, 113
lotus leaf rice packages with scallions and, 203
sauce, cold noodles with cucumbers and, 154
sesame cookies, 234
spicy chicken with bamboo shoots and, 87
Pear rolls, vegetable, 17
Pearl meatballs, 184
Peas
fried rice with ham and, 171
ground beef and, 54
shrimp and scallops with, 66
spicy velvet shrimp with cucumber and, 97
velvet scallops, chiles, and, 102
Pea sprouts, shredded chicken with, 48
Peking duck, 142
Peppercorns, Szechuan
about, 7
in wild pepper mix, 25
Pepper(s), sweet bell
green
and beef chow mein, 160
beef with, 49
shredded pork, bamboo shoots, and, in black bean sauce, 60
squid rings with strips of, 70
Pickles
cucumber, 19
daikon and carrot, 20
lotus root, 20
Pineapple
duck in ginger fruit sauce, 56
skewered pork cubes with fresh, 15
Pine nuts, confetti rice with, 173
Pinwheels, cinnamon, 233
Plum-flavored pork tenderloin, 16
Plum sauce, about, 6
Poached brown chicken, 182
Poached cod fillets in sour sauce, 188
Pork. *See also* Ham; Sausage
bean curd with ground, 58
braised bean threads, vegetables, and, 81
cake, steamed, 185
chops, baked, in vegetable rice casserole, 178
chow mein with bok choy stems, 161
cubes
with fresh pineapple, skewered, 15
in hot sweet sauce, 92
in sweet sauce, 57
cutlet with buckwheat noodles, 164
double-cooked Szechuan, 91
and eggplant with black bean sauce, 59

five fragrant spice, with asparagus, 57
with green beans, sliced, 60
ground, spicy bean curd with, 94
with jicama, 59
lo mein, 157
meatballs, pearl, 184
mu shu, packages, 210
onion, and tomato on rice, 179
pungent, in lotus leaf, 212
red bean curd, taro, and, 80
roast
fried rice with, 172
red (*char sui*), 146
rice, Cantonese, 177
soupy noodles with pork won tons and, 165
sweet aromatic, 145
sauce, green beans in, 104
shredded
bamboo shoots, and green pepper in black bean sauce, 60
fish-flavored, 94
and shrimp dumplings, 197
simmered, with lotus root, 80
slices in chile sauce, velvet, 93
spareribs. *See* Spareribs
stewed, hot and spicy, 92
sweet and sour, 58
tenderloin, plum-flavored, 16
won tons, soupy noodles with Chinese roast pork and, 165
Yang Chow lion's head, 79
Potato(es)
balls, mushroom-filled, 114
dough, mashed, 114
Potsticker dough, 199
Potsticker dumplings, 198
Pressed anise beef, 134
Pressed bean curd, 125
marinated, 124
Pudding, rice, star anise, 230
Pungent pork in lotus leaf, 212

Quail, red-braised, 77
Quick hot bean sprouts, 103
Quick tossed bean sprouts with chives, 109

Rainbow vegetables, 118
Raspberries, almond float with, 228
Red bean curd, pork, and taro, 80
Red bean soup, sweet, 234
Red-braised bean curd with mushrooms and bamboo shoots, 123
Red-braised beef, 78
Red-braised duck, 76
Red-braised fish steaks, 82
Red-braised quail, 77
Red garlic shrimp, 63
Red peaches, 235
Red-poached lamb strips with noodles and cabbage broth, 185

Red roast pork (*char sui*)**, 146**
Relish, sweet-spicy cabbage, 19
Rice
 about, 153
 aromatic, 208
 beef, sunnyside egg, 178
 with chicken and shrimp,
  Indonesian-style, 175
 chicken casserole, 177
 confetti, with pine nuts, 173
 eight jewel, in lotus package,
  209
 fried
  with Chinese sausage, 170
  with eggs and scallions, 175
  with peas and ham, 171
  with roast pork, 172
  shrimp, 172
  Yang Chow, 170
 glutinous, about, 5
 lotus leaf packages with peanuts and
  scallions, 203
 with poached egg, individual
  steamed, 174
 pork, onion, and tomato on, 179
 pudding, star anise, 230
 roast pork, Cantonese, 177
 sampan, 173
 scrambled eggs and bacon, 176
 sizzling, 131
  shrimp in broth with, 131
 soup, sizzling, 130
 soy lamb chops with onion on,
  180
 spicy halibut steaks on, 180
 sticky, bundles, chicken in, 207
 stuffing, sweet, hoisin-glazed roast
  chicken with, 139
 vegetable casserole, baked pork
  chops in, 178
 and vegetables, simple, 174
 yellow, with cherry tomatoes,
  176
Rice flour noodles. *See also* Noodle(s)
 about, 6
 wide, dry-fried spicy beef and, 166
Rice paper, about, 6
Rice stick noodles (*mei fun*)
 Fukien, 168
 with shrimp and chicken, Thai-style,
  171
 with Singapore-style shrimp, 169
 soupy seafood, with fresh basil and
  lime, 168
Rich meat stock, 28
Roast duck with tropical fruit salad,
 218
Rolls
 egg crepe, 206
 garlic chive, 205
 spring, 18
 vegetable pear, 17
Roll-ups, ginger duck, 207

Salad(s)
 agar-agar and daikon, 21
 bean sprout, 108
 bean thread and cucumber, 121
 eggplant, Chinese, 10
 jellyfish, 135
 jicama, long beans, and cherry
  tomato, 112
 main-course
  about, 213
  angel hair pasta, tomato, and
   shrimp, 222
  chicken, with hoisin dressing, 215
  crabmeat and cucumber, 224
  grilled lamb, 221
  grilled tuna salad, 225
  hoisin beef, 220
  lemon-flavored chicken and bean
   sprout, 214
  sesame chicken, 214
  smoked chicken-noodle, 217
  smoked trout, 226
  Thai-style beef, 219
  tropical fruit, roast duck with,
   218
 shredded vegetable, 121
 silver and gold, 120
Salad dressing
 ginger, fresh, 24
 vinaigrette
  mustard sesame, 25
  sesame, 25
Salmon-cabbage pillows, 211
Salt-baked chicken, 138
Sampan rice, 173
Satay, chicken, 13
Sauce(s). *See also* Black bean sauce;
  Hoisin (sauce); Oyster sauce; Soy
  (sauce); Yellow bean sauce
 brown, Chinese, 65
  shrimp omelet with, 65
 chile, velvet pork slices in, 93
 congee, 141
 cream, white, 189
 dipping. *See also* Dip
  spicy, 199
 egg, long life noodles in, 136
 firepot, 145
 ginger fruit, pineapple duck in, 56
 hot and sour, cauliflower and broccoli
  tossed in, 105
 hot sweet, pork cubes in, 92
 hot willow, fish and, 101
 meat
  noodles, 155
  spicy garlic, eggplant in, 106
 peanut, cold noodles with cucumbers
  and, 154
 pork, green beans in, 104
 sour, poached cod fillets in, 188
 sweet, pork cubes in, 57
 sweet and sour, easy, 195
 wine, fish fillets in, 69

Sausage(s), Chinese (*lop cheung*)
about, 4
chicken with, 183
fried rice with, 170
Sautéed sea scallops, 68
Sautéed sweet potatoes with soy sauce and ginger, 117
Savory egg custard, 190
Savory pressed bean curd slivers, 138
Savory stuffed mushrooms, 11
Scallion(s)
about, 6
fried rice with eggs and, 175
lamb with, 62
lobster with ginger and, 68
lotus leaf rice packages with peanuts and, 203
oil, 24
white poached chicken with, 182
Scallop(s)
bay, marinated, with cilantro, 222
chiles, and peas, velvet, 102
sea
sautéed, 68
steamed, 187
and shrimp with peas, 66
Scrambled eggs and bacon rice, 176
Sea bass, black, steamed, 186
Seafood. *See also* Fish; Shellfish
rice stick noodles with fresh basil and lime, soupy, 168
soup, hot and sour, 34
Sesame
asparagus spears, 110
chicken salad, 214
mustard vinaigrette, 25
noodles, cold, 10
peanut cookies, 234
puffs with honey, 232
vinaigrette, 25
Sesame oil, Asian, about, 3
Sesame paste, Asian, about, 6
Shark fin
about, 6
soup, 133
Shellfish. *See also* Clams; Crab(meat); Lobster; Scallop(s); Shrimp; Squid
in firepot Hong Kong style, 144
Sherried shrimp with snow peas and water chestnuts, 64
Sherry, dry, about, 5
Shredded chicken with pea sprouts, 48
Shredded chicken with tree ears and mushrooms, 45
Shredded cold chicken with hot peanut dressing, 86
Shredded cucumber and bean threads with drunken shrimp, 223
Shredded pork, bamboo shoots, and green pepper in black bean sauce, 60
Shredded vegetable salad, 121

Shrimp
balls, 12
with black bean sauce, 62
in broth with sizzling rice, 131
deep-fried, in shells, 63
drunken, 223
shredded cucumber and bean threads with, 223
dumplings (*har kow*), 202
flower, 187
fried rice, 172
Indonesian-style rice with chicken and, 175
Kung Pao, 98
in lemongrass broth, 34
lo mein, 158
omelet with Chinese brown sauce, 65
paste, about, 6
and pork dumplings, 197
red garlic, 63
rice noodles with chicken and, Thai-style, 171
salad, angel hair pasta, tomato, and, 222
and scallops with peas, 66
sherried, with snow peas and water chestnuts, 64
Singapore-style, rice sticks with, 169
soup
spicy sour, 37
watercress and, 35
spicy
and fragrant melon balls, 98
velvet, with cucumber and peas, 97
in spicy black bean sauce, 96
tea leaf, 148
tempura, noodles, 162
toasts, 12
velvet, with cashews, 64
Silk squash
soup, 37
stir-fried, 116
Silver and gold salad, 120
Simmered pork with lotus root, 80'
Simple rice and vegetables, 174
Simple tossed spicy noodles, 156
Siu mei flower dumplings, 200
Sizzling rice, 131
shrimp in broth with, 131
soup, 130
Skewered pork cubes with fresh pineapple, 15
Sliced beef with tomato and onion, 50
Sliced chicken with asparagus, 44
Sliced pork with green beans, 60
Slivered lamb with turnips and carrots, 96
Slow-cooked Chinese cabbage, 113
Smoked bean curd with oyster sauce and vegetables, 127
Smoked chicken-noodle salad, 217
Smoked trout salad, 226

Snow peas
  chicken with ham and, 45
  sherried shrimp with water chestnuts
    and, 64
  with water chestnuts, 115
Sorbet
  lichee, 231
  lotus leaf, 235
Soup. *See also* Soupy noodles
  bean curd, 29
  beef ball, 29
  chicken corn, 31
  chicken in coconut broth, 30
  Chinese cabbage, 30
  crab corn chowder, 32
  duck, 134
  egg flower, 33
  with fish fillets and spinach, clear, 32
  hot and sour, 35
  melon, cold, 33
  rice, sizzling, 130
  seafood, hot and sour, 34
  shark fin, 133
  shrimp
    in lemongrass broth, 34
    spicy sour, 37
    and watercress, 35
  silk squash, 37
  sweet red bean, 234
  velvet corn, 31
  watercress
    with bean curd, 38
    Chinese style, 36
  winter melon, 36
  won ton, 39
  zucchini glass noodle, 38
Soupy noodles
  bean curd, mushrooms, and bok choy
    on, 164
  with fish and spinach won tons, 162
  with ham and chicken, 166
  with pork won tons and Chinese
    roast pork, 165
Soupy seafood rice stick noodles with
  fresh basil and lime, 168
Soy (sauce)
  about, 6–7
  chicken wings braised in, 15
  lamb chops with onion on rice, 180
  sautéed sweet potatoes with ginger
    and, 117
  vinegar dip, 18
Spareribs
  barbecued, 14
  steamed, 14
  super spicy, 93
Spicy bean curd with ground pork, 94
Spicy black bean beef with asparagus,
  90
Spicy chicken with peanuts and
  bamboo shoots, 87
Spicy chicken with tangerine peel, 88
Spicy clams, 99

Spicy dipping sauce, 199
Spicy halibut steaks on rice, 180
Spicy shrimp and fragrant melon
  balls, 98
Spicy sour shrimp soup, 37
Spicy velvet shrimp with cucumber
  and peas, 97
Spinach
  with bean curd cheese, 115
  and bean curd dumplings, 198
  clear soup with fish fillets and, 32
  in firepot Hong Kong style, 144
  and fish won tons, 163
    soupy noodles with, 162
  greens, bamboo shoots with, 109
  Hunan braised beef on a bed of, 89
  oil-wilted garlicky, 116
Spring rolls, 18
Squab, crispy, 143
Squash, silk
  soup, 37
  stir-fried, 116
Squid
  chrysanthemum, 149
  fried, with spicy salt, 99
  rings with pepper strips, 70
Squirrel fish, 147
Star anise
  about, 7
  rice pudding, 230
Steak kew, 52
Steamed dishes
  about, 181
  bean curd pockets, 191
  beef balls with oyster sauce, 184
  black sea bass, 186
  catfish, whole, with black beans, 186
  chicken with Chinese sausage, 183
  cucumbers stuffed with flounder, 188
  fish balls on a bed of watercress, 189
  flower shrimp, 187
  hoisin chicken strips with cilantro,
    183
  oyster-flavored bean curd, 190
  pearl meatballs, 184
  pork cake, 185
  savory egg custard, 190
  sea scallops, 187
Steamed dried oysters, 148
Steamed spareribs, 14
Steamer baskets, bamboo, 181
Stews and braises, 71–83
  about, 71
  bean curd casserole, 82
  braised bean threads, pork, and
    vegetables, 81
  braised duck with leeks, 76
  chicken curry, 72
  distilled chicken, 74
  duck braised with bamboo shoots,
    chestnuts, and mushrooms, 75
  empress chicken, 72
  lemon chicken, 73

long-simmered beef, 78
oxtail stew, 81
oyster-flavored drumsticks, 74
red bean curd, pork, and taro, 80
red-braised beef, 78
red-braised duck, 76
red-braised fish steaks, 82
red-braised quail, 77
simmered pork with lotus root, 80
stewed lamb with garlic, ginger, and
    vegetables, 83
Yang Chow lion's head, 79
Stir-fried bean curd, 122
Stir-fried beef, 55
Stir-fried dishes. See Fast and easy
    dishes
Stir-fried silk squash, 116
Stock
chicken, Chinese, 27
rich meat, 28
vegetable, 28
Stuffing, sweet rice, hoisin-glazed
    roast chicken with, 139
Sugared walnuts, 16
Sunnyside egg beef rice, 178
Super spicy spareribs, 93
Sweet and sour cabbage, 111
Sweet and sour pork, 58
Sweet and sour sauce, easy, 195
Sweet aromatic roast pork, 145
Sweet crescents, 229
Sweet potatoes, sautéed, with soy
    sauce and ginger, 117
Sweet red bean soup, 234
Sweets and desserts, 227–36
about, 227
almond cookies, 233
almond float with raspberries, 228
cinnamon pinwheels, 233
ginger custard cream, 232
gingered oranges, 229
ginger mousse, 228
gummy cake, 236
honeyed bananas, 230
lichee sorbet, 231
lotus leaf sorbet, 235
red peaches, 235
sesame peanut cookies, 234
sesame puffs with honey, 232
star anise rice pudding, 230
sweet crescents, 229
sweet red bean soup, 234
toffee apples, 231
Sweet sauce, pork cubes in, 57
Sweet-spicy cabbage relish, 19
Szechuan pepper (or peppercorns)
about, 7
in wild pepper mix, 25
Szechuan spicy lamb, 95

Tangerine peel
about, 7
spicy chicken with, 88

Tapioca flour, about, 7
Taro root
braised, 117
red bean curd, pork, and, 80
Tea eggs, 17
Tea leaf shrimp, 148
Tea-smoked bean curd, 127
Tea-smoked chicken, 216
Tea-smoked fish, 224
Tempura shrimp noodles, 162
Thai-style beef salad, 219
Thai-style rice noodles with shrimp
    and chicken, 171
Toffee apples, 231
Tofu. See also Bean curd
marinated cold, 21
Tomato(es)
angel hair pasta, and shrimp salad,
    222
cherry
    jicama, and long beans salad, 112
    yellow rice with, 176
pork, and onion on rice, 179
sliced beef with onion and, 50
Tree ears (tree fungus)
about, 7
shredded chicken with mushrooms
    and, 45
Trout salad, smoked, 226
Tuna salad, grilled, 225
Turnips, slivered lamb with carrots
    and, 96

Vegetable(s)
braised bean threads, pork, and, 81
kebabs, bean curd and, 124
lo mein, 158
medley, braised, 120
mu shu, 119
pear rolls, 17
rainbow, 118
rice and, simple, 174
rice casserole, baked pork chops in,
    178
salad, shredded, 121
smoked bean curd with oyster sauce
    and, 127
stewed lamb with garlic, ginger, and,
    83
stock, 28
Vegetarian dishes, 107–27
about, 107
baked vegetarian bean curd pockets,
    126
bamboo shoots with spinach greens,
    109
bean curd and vegetable kebabs, 124
bean curd sticks with mushrooms,
    125
bean curd with scrambled eggs, 123
bean thread and cucumber salad, 121
braised Chinese mushrooms, 118
braised taro root, 117

Vegetarian dishes *(cont.)*
braised vegetable medley, 120
crusty bean curd squares in black
  bean sauce, 122
fresh vegetable Buddha's delight,
  108
ginger-braised carrots, 112
green beans with black bean sauce,
  110
jicama, long beans, and cherry
  tomato salad, 112
long beans and peanuts with garlic,
  113
marinated pressed bean curd, 124
mushroom-filled potato balls, 114
oil-wilted garlicky spinach, 116
oyster sauce broccoli, 111
pressed bean curd, 125
quick tossed bean sprouts with
  chives, 109
rainbow vegetables, 118
red-braised bean curd with
  mushrooms and bamboo shoots,
  123
sautéed sweet potatoes with soy
  sauce and ginger, 117
sesame asparagus spears, 110
shredded vegetable salad, 121
silver and gold salad, 120
slow-cooked Chinese cabbage, 113
smoked bean curd with oyster sauce
  and vegetables, 127
snow peas with water chestnuts,
  115
spinach with bean curd cheese, 115
stir-fried bean curd, 122
stir-fried silk squash, 116
sweet and sour cabbage, 111
tea-smoked bean curd, 127
vegetable mu shu, 119
vegetarian mock fish, 150
Velvet corn soup, 31
Velvet pork slices in chile sauce, 93
Velvet scallops, chiles, and peas,
  102
Velvet shrimp with cashews, 64
Vinaigrette
mustard sesame, 25
sesame, 25

Vinegar
about, 7
soy dip, 18

Walnuts, sugared, 16
Wasabi dressing, 225
Water chestnuts
about, 7
chicken, and broccoli in oyster sauce,
  42
sherried shrimp with snow peas and,
  64
snow peas with, 115
Watercress
soup
  with bean curd, 38
  Chinese style, 36
  shrimp and, 35
steamed fish balls on a bed of, 189
Wheat flour noodles *(mein)*. *See also*
  Noodle(s), wheat flour
about, 7
Wheat starch
about, 7
dough, 202
White cream sauce, 189
**White poached chicken with scallion
  oil,** 182
Wild pepper mix, 25
Wine sauce, fish fillets in, 69
Winter melon
pond, 132
soup, 36
Won ton(s)
fish and spinach, 163
  soupy noodles with, 162
fried, 195
pork, soupy noodles with Chinese
  roast pork and, 165
soup, 39
Won ton skins, about, 7–8

Yang Chow fried rice, 170
Yang Chow lion's head, 79
Yellow bean sauce, chicken cubes in,
  42
Yellow rice with cherry tomatoes, 176

Zucchini glass noodle soup, 38

About the Author

Rosa Lo San Ross, born and raised in Hong Kong, has been a Chinese caterer (Wok on Wheels) and cooking teacher in New York City for fifteen years. She is a Certified Culinary Professional with the International Association of Culinary Professionals and has lectured on Chinese food and culture at New York University.

Acknowledgments

This book is for Ron, Sarah, and Samantha, for their love and support for my first effort; for my mother, Edris de Carvalho, a few of whose recipes I have shared with you; and my sisters, brothers, and their spouses for their enthusiasm. I thank all my friends and students for their help and input, but especially thank my friend, Whitney Clay, and my daughter, Sarah, for their patience and time in testing and tasting all the recipes. I particularly wish to thank Susan Wyler for giving me this project and being the perfect editor by providing all the advice and guidance I needed, but allowing me to forge ahead on my own after that.

To order any of the
365 Ways Cookbooks
visit your local bookseller or call 1-800-321-6890

Our bestselling **365 Ways Cookbooks** are wire-bound to lie flat and have colorful, wipe-clean covers.

Each **365 Ways Cookbook** is $17.95 plus $3.50 per copy shipping and handling. Applicable sales tax will be billed to your account. No CODs. Please allow 4–6 weeks for delivery.

> **Please have your VISA, MASTERCARD, or AMERICAN EXPRESS card at hand when calling.**

• 365 •

Easy Italian Recipes 0-06-016310-0
Easy Low-Calorie Recipes 0-06-016309-7
Easy Mexican Recipes 0-06-016963-X
Easy One-Dish Meals 0-06-016311-9
Great Barbecue & Grilling Recipes 0-06-016224-4
Great Chocolate Desserts 0-06-016537-5
Great Cookies and Brownies 0-06-016840-4
One-Minute Golf Lessons 0-06-017087-5
Quick & Easy Microwave Recipes 0-06-016026-8
Snacks, Hors D'Oeuvres & Appetizers 0-06-016536-7
Ways to Cook Chicken 0-06-015539-6
Ways to Cook Fish and Shellfish 0-06-016841-2
Ways to Cook Hamburger & Other Ground Meats
0-06-016535-9
Ways to Cook Chinese 0-06-016961-3
Ways to Cook Pasta 0-06-015865-4
Ways to Cook Vegetarian 0-06-016958-3
Ways to Prepare for Christmas 0-06-017048-4
Ways to Wok 0-06-016643-6

FORTHCOMING TITLES

Days of Gardening 0-06-017032-8
Great Cakes and Pies 0-06-016959-1
20-Minute Menus 0-06-016962-1
Soups and Stews 0-06-016960-5
Low-Fat Recipes 0-06-017137-5
Household Hints 0-06-017136-7
Ways to Cook Eggs 0-06-017138-3
More Ways to Cook Chicken 0-06-017139-1

X02011